Globalization and Sport

GLOBALIZATION AND SPORT

Edited by

Richard Giulianotti and Roland Robertson

BLACKWELL PUBLISHING
350 Main Street, Malden, MA 02148-5020, USA
9600 Garsington Road, Oxford OX4 2DQ, UK
550 Swanston Street, Carlton, Victoria 3053, Australia

First published 2007 by Blackwell Publishing Ltd

Library of Congress Cataloging-in-Publication Data has been applied for

ISBN-13: 978-1-4051-6269-2

A catalogue record for this title is available from the British Library.

Set in 10pt Times
by Oxford Publishing Services

The publisher's policy is to use permanent paper from mills that operate a sustainable forestry policy, and which has been manufactured from pulp processed using acid-free and elementary chlorine-free practices. Furthermore, the publisher ensures that the text paper and cover board used have met acceptable environmental accreditation standards.

For further information on
Blackwell Publishing, visit our website:
www.blackwellpublishing.com

Contents

Notes on contributors   vii

1. Sport and globalization: transnational dimensions   1
   RICHARD GIULIANOTTI AND ROLAND ROBERTSON

2. Not playing around: global capitalism, modern sport and consumer culture   6
   BARRY SMART

3. The grobal in the sporting glocal   28
   DAVID L. ANDREWS AND GEORGE RITZER

4. Steps to an ecology of transnational sports   46
   THOMAS HYLLAND ERIKSEN

5. Recovering the social: globalization, football and transnationalism   58
   RICHARD GIULIANOTTI AND ROLAND ROBERTSON

6. Is baseball a global sport? America's 'national pastime'
   as global field and international sport   79
   WILLIAM W. KELLY

7. More than a game: globalization and the post-Westernization of world cricket   94
   CHRIS RUMFORD

8. Imagined communities in the global game:
   soccer and the development of Dutch national identity   107
   FRANK J. LECHNER

9. The global footballer and the local war-zone:
   George Weah and transnational networks in Liberia, West Africa   122
   GARY ARMSTRONG

Index   141

Notes on Contributors

David L. Andrews is Professor of Physical Cultural Studies in the Department of Kinesiology at the University of Maryland, and an affiliate faculty member of the Departments of American Studies and Sociology. He is author of *Sport-Commerce-Culture: Essays on Sport in Late Capitalist America* (Peter Lang, 2006); and he has recently edited (with S. Wagg) *East Meets West: Essays on Sport and the Cold War* (Routledge, 2007), (with S. J. Jackson) *Sport, Culture and Advertising* (Routledge, 2005), (with M. L. Silk & C. L. Cole) *Sport and Corporate Nationalisms* (Berg, 2005), and *Manchester United: A Thematic Study* (Routledge, 2004).

Gary Armstrong is Reader in the Sociology of Sport in the School of Sport and Education, Brunel University, London. He is the author of *Football Hooligans: Knowing the Score* (Berg, 1998) and *Blade Runners: Lives in Football* (Hallamshire, 1998); and co-author (with Clive Norris) of *The Maximum Surveillance Society* (Berg, 1999) and (with John Garrett) *Sheffield United FC: The Biography* (Hallamshire, 2006). He has co-edited several books with Richard Giulianotti, including *Football in Africa* (Palgrave, 2004) and *Fear and Loathing in World Football* (Berg, 2001).

Thomas Hylland Eriksen is Professor of Social Anthropology at the University of Oslo and Research Director of 'Cultural Complexity in the New Norway' at the same institution. He has written extensively about globalization, identity politics and other topics in anthropology, mostly in English, as well as a number of other books in Norwegian. His most recent books in English are *Engaging Anthropology* (Berg, 2006) and *Globalization: The Key Concepts* (Berg, 2007).

Richard Giulianotti is Professor of Sociology at Durham University. He is author of *Football: A Sociology of the Global Game* (Polity, 1999), and *Sport: A Critical Sociology* (Polity, 2005); and has recently co-authored, with Adrian Walsh, *Ethics, Money & Sport* (Routledge, 2006). He is editor or co-editor of nine books on sport, including (with Gary Armstrong), *Football in Africa* (Palgrave, 2004), *Sport and Modern Social Theorists* (Palgrave, 2005) and (with David McArdle) *Sport, Civil Liberties and Human Rights* (Taylor & Francis, 2006).

William W. Kelly is Professor and Chair of the Department of Anthropology and Sumitomo Professor of Japanese Studies at Yale University. Among his recent publications in sports studies are 'The Hanshin Tigers and Professional Baseball in Japan', in (G. Gmelch, ed.) *Baseball without Borders: The International Pastime* (Bison, 2006). He is the editor of *This Sporting Life: Sports and Body Culture in Modern Japan* (Yale University Council on East Asian Studies Occasional Publications Volume 1, 2007).

Frank Lechner teaches sociology at Emory University in Atlanta. His recent publications include *World Culture: Origins and Consequences* (Blackwell 2005) and an edited volume, *The Globalization Reader* (Blackwell, several editions), both with John Boli, as well as *The Netherlands: Globalization and National Identity* (Routledge 2007). He is working on a general globalization text, *Globalization: The Making of World Society*.

George Ritzer is Distinguished University Professor in the Department of Sociology at the University of Maryland. He has written many books, including *Sociology: A Multiple Paradigm Science* (Allyn & Bacon, 1975), *Metatheorzing in Sociology* (Lexington, 1991), *The McDonaldization of Society* (Pine Forge, 1993), *Enchanting a Disenchanted World* (Pine Forge, 1999), and *The Globalization of Nothing* (Pine Forge, 2003). He has recently edited the *Encyclopedia of Sociology* (Blackwell, 2006) and the *Encyclopedia of Social Theory* (Sage, 2005). His books have been published in over twenty languages.

Roland Robertson is Professor of Sociology and Global Society at the University of Aberdeen. He is also Distinguished Professor of Sociology Emeritus at the University of Pittsburgh, USA, and Honorary Professor of Cultural Studies at Tsinghua University (Beijing). He is the author of many books, articles, and chapters in the fields of globalization and glocalization; religion and culture; social theory; and transdisciplinarity. His work has been translated into nearly twenty languages. Among other projects, he is currently producing a new edition of *Globalization: Social Theory and Global Culture* (Sage, 1992).

Chris Rumford is Senior Lecturer in Political Sociology in the Department of Politics and International Relations, Royal Holloway, University of London. His books include, *The European Union: A Political Sociology* (Blackwell, 2002), *Rethinking Europe: Social Theory and the Implications of Europeanization* (with Gerard Delanty) (Routledge, 2005), and *Cosmopolitanism and Europe* (ed.) (Liverpool University Press, 2007). He is currently editing the *Sage Handbook of European Studies* (forthcoming), and completing a book entitled *Cosmopolitan Spaces: Europe, Globalization, Theory* (Routledge).

Barry Smart has held posts in universities in Australia, England, Japan and New Zealand and he is currently Professor of Sociology in the School of Social, Historical, & Literary Studies, University of Portsmouth, UK. He is the author of a number of influential books and articles in the field of social theory, including *Economy, Culture & Society: A Sociological Critique of Neo-Liberalism* (Open University Press, 2003) and *The Sport Star: Modern Sport and the Cultural Economy of Sporting Celebrity* (Sage, 2005). Current research includes a project on the social, economic, and environmental consequences of consumption.

1

Sport and globalization: transnational dimensions

RICHARD GIULIANOTTI AND ROLAND ROBERTSON

In putting together this special issue, we have been concerned to meet two closely connected objectives. First, we have sought to raise the social scientific status of sport, primarily by seeking contributions from leading mainstream scholars. Second, we have been concerned to advance understanding of transnational processes by examining the highly important role of sport in global change.

Sport has been a hitherto under-explored field of enquiry for mainstream social scientists and global studies specialists. Sport figures occasionally rather than consistently in mainstream social scientific journals and, far less frequently, in the work of leading international scholars. In part, this may be explained by the emergence of 'sport studies' as a thriving, differentiated zone of multi-disciplinary scholarship, wherein globalization has been integral to research and debates since the mid-1990s. In turn, dialogue between mainstream social scientists and sport specialists has been rather circumscribed. We hope that this special issue of *Global Networks* provides an ideal venue for traversing that artificial divide, to ignite that conversation.

In a broad social scientific sense, it is eminently reasonable to have this debate speak to global issues and processes. Globalization is the axial theme of contemporary times, and the broad field of 'global studies' has mushroomed enormously since the mid-1980s, engendering diverse transdisciplinary and transnational networks of scholars. More particularly, like other transdisciplinary substantive fields, global studies have tended to lack a significant sport focus compared to investigations of other cultural forms, such as religion. Yet, we would argue strongly that sport is an increasingly significant subject for global studies, in its dual role as a long-term motor and metric of transnational change.

Sport historians have indicated the extensive interconnections of sport and global processes. The globalization of sport 'took off' from the 1870s onwards, as the 'games revolution' colonized British imperial outposts (e.g. cricket in Asia and Australasia), the 'global game' of football underwent mass diffusion along British

1

trading and educational routes (e.g. in Europe, South America), and distinctive indigenous sports were forged as part of the invention of national traditions in emerging modern societies (e.g. baseball, American football in the United States) (Guttmann 1995; Mangan 1987).

In recent times, sport's transnational status is most perspicuously revealed through the raw data and political conflicts generated by sporting 'mega-events' and their controlling bodies. Consider, for example, the global dimensions of the Olympic Games. According to research commissioned by the governing International Olympic Committee (IOC), the 2004 Olympics in Athens were watched, at least in part, by 3.9 billion of the world's population, producing a cumulative global audience of around 40 billion for the 17 day event (*USA Today*, 12 October 2004). Financially, the Olympics are a major transnational industry, with projected revenues for the Beijing 2008 event standing at $3 billion (*Forbes*, 31 January 2007). Olympism has a global political reach, with 203 National Olympic Committees affiliated to the IOC, giving 11 more national members than the United Nations. The Olympic movement has been a strong catalyst in advancing sport's public status as a human right, and as a medium for development and humanitarian work among NGOs. Yet in turn, Olympism has been critiqued by new social movements and investigative journalists for alleged corruption, and the implicit toleration of athlete harm and infringement of civil liberties (Lenskyj 2000). Whatever one thinks of Olympism and other sporting realms as cultural forms, it is clear that their transnational importance and salience to social science cannot be ignored.

In moving to locate sport's place within mainstream social science, and with reference to the global context, we have assembled a collection of articles by some of the world's most influential scholars, notably those with major standing in globalization studies. Roland Robertson (1970, 1992; Nettl and Robertson 1968; Robertson and Scholte 2007) has been an international authority on world society, social theory and religion since the mid-1960s, and is arguably the founding figure of globalization studies in social science. George Ritzer (1997, 2004) is a highly versatile and world-renowned social theorist who has recently amended his influential McDonaldization thesis to encompass global processes. In sociology, Barry Smart (1999, 2005) is a globally recognized theorist who has made telling contributions on McDonaldization, postmodernism and post-structuralism; Frank Lechner (1991; Boli and Lechner 2005) has emerged as a global figure in the distinct yet interconnected sociologies of globalization and religion; and Chris Rumford (2002; Rumford and Delanty 2005) has emerged as a leading theorist of European political cultures. In anthropology, William Kelly (1985, 2004) is long established as one of the world's leading scholars on Japanese society and East Asia, while the prolific Thomas Hylland Eriksen (2003, 2007) has been pivotal in shifting world anthropology's focus to the global dimensions of local processes.

Our three contributors from sport studies have diverse disciplinary, theoretical and substantive backgrounds: David Andrews (2006) in blending cultural studies and contemporary social theory to explore national and global sport cultures; Gary Armstrong (1998, 2001) through anthropological ethnographies of local and transnational football cultures; and the sociologist Richard Giulianotti (1999, 2005) through analytical and qualitative studies of world football, sport and globalization. All three, most notably Armstrong and Giulianotti (e.g. 1998, 2004), have enjoyed extensive prior collaborations, on transnational sporting themes that bring together international fields of scholars.

Certainly, this special issue does not have a standing start. Some of our mainstream social scientific contributors have examined sport in other work, notably Smart (2005) on sport stars; Kelly's (1997, 1998, for example) various studies of Japanese baseball; Lechner (2007) on Dutch football; Ritzer (and Stillman 2001) on baseball stadiums; and Robertson on global football (Giulianotti and Robertson 2004, 2006, 2007). However, this special issue does provide the first extensive and self-contained examination of sport by leading mainstream social scientists.

Contents

We have arranged the articles to allow the reader to move from reflecting on the general to the more particular aspects of globalization and sport. Thus, we move from analyses of broader globalizing and multi-sport issues towards consideration of how transnational processes impact upon individual sports, and regional and national dimensions.

The first three articles explore the complex interrelations of the local and the global in relation to a variety of sports. Our opening article, by Barry Smart, investigates the historical and political economic aspects of sport's globalization. Crucial historical transformations identified by Smart include sport's global insti-tutionalization, its heightened mediatization, and the growth of consumerism along with the proliferation of sporting merchandise. The next contribution brings together David Andrews and George Ritzer to explore the inextricable interpenetrations of local and global processes within a variety of modern sports. The analysis elaborates Ritzer's (2004) earlier dichotomy of the 'grobal' and the 'glocal' to argue that all sporting institutions, practices and identities contain variable and highly complex mixtures of creativity and dependency, in cultural and commercial terms. Our third paper, by the leading global anthropologist Thomas Hylland Eriksen, assesses the uneven globalization of sports, and so challenges the presumption of a constant local-global dialogue. Deploying metaphors of evolution and survival, Eriksen observes that many sports have neither sought nor experienced their worldwide popularization, in part by their failure or reluctance to undergo translation into new terrain.

Our next three articles discuss globalization issues in regard to different individual sports; notably, each discussion accords particular consideration to Asia. First, interweaving the theories of glocalization, transnationalism, connectivity (and consciousness) and cosmopolitanism, the article by Giulianotti and Robertson explores the much-neglected social dimensions of globalization with reference to football. Illustrative case-studies are drawn from supporter formations, sport journalism, and the specific realm of Japanese football. Next, in a rich analysis, William Kelly explores and explains the limited global reach of baseball. While the quintessential American sport underwent substantial glocalization in Japan, to become 'samurai baseball', Kelly demonstrates that its global diffusion has been hampered rather ironically by the centrist power and self-protectionism of North America's major commercial power in baseball, MLB. Analysis of the transnational aspects of cricket allows Chris Rumford, in his article, to challenge contemporary theories of globalization and postcolonialism. Rumford argues that cricket's recent history illustrates processes of 'postwesternization', which point in part to the rising global influence of the East. In cricket, postwesternization is signalled by the huge commercial value and popular appeal of one-day international fixtures in Asia, and the emerging hegemony of that region within the sport's governance.

We conclude with two articles that situate national sporting cultures firmly within 'the global'. To most international football followers, the Netherlands have been a metonym for beautiful, free-flowing 'total football' since the early 1970s. Yet, as the article by Frank Lechner explains, this 'invented tradition' is demythologized by many Dutch football fans themselves, and has contributed significantly to the constant reformulation of the Netherlands' national identity within the global context. The final article explores football in Liberia, where a maelstrom of individual, local, national and transnational forces, are struggling to dominate and simply to survive within sport and society. Drawing upon extensive field-work in the war-torn state, Gary Armstrong examines the particular case of George Weah, a retired world football star, failed national presidential candidate, local folk hero, and vehicle for various transnational companies and NGOs. Weah's remarkable and inconclusive story embodies many of the conflicts, complexities and ambiguities that this special issue seeks to capture in regard to the uneven relationships between local, national and transnational forces, as illuminated through sport.

References

Andrews, D. L. (ed.) (2004) *Manchester United: a thematic study*, London: Routledge.

Andrews, D. L. (2006) *Sport, commerce, culture*, London: Peter Lang.

Armstrong, G. (1998) *Football hooligans: knowing the score*, Oxford: Berg.

Armstrong, G. (2004) 'Players, patrons and politicians: oppositional cultures in Maltese football', in G. Armstrong and R. Giulianotti (eds) *Fear and loathing in world football*, Oxford: Berg.

Armstrong, G. and R. Giulianotti (eds) (1998) *Football, cultures and modernity*, Basingstoke: Macmillan.

Armstrong, G. and R. Giulianotti (eds) (2004) *Football in Africa*, Basingstoke: Macmillan.

Boli, J. and F. Lechner (2005) *World culture*, Oxford: Blackwell.

Cohen, R. and P. Kennedy (2007) *Global sociology*, Second Edition, Basingstoke: Palgrave.

Delanty, G. and C. Rumford (2005) *Rethinking Europe: social theory and the implications of Europeanization*, London: Routledge.

Eriksen, T. H. (ed.) (2003) *Globalisation: studies in anthropology*, London: Pluto.

Eriksen, T. H. (2007) *Globalization*, Oxford: Berg.

Giulianotti, R. (1999) *Football: a sociology of the global game*, Cambridge: Polity.

Giulianotti, R. (2005) *Sport: A Critical Sociology*, Cambridge: Polity.

Giulianotti, R. and R. Robertson (2004) 'The globalization of football: a study in the glocalization of the "serious life"', *British Journal of Sociology*, 55, 545–68.

Giulianotti, R. and R. Robertson (2006) 'Glocalization, globalization and migration: the case of Scottish football supporters in North America', *International Sociology*, 21, 171–98.

Giulianotti, R. and R. Robertson (2007) 'Forms of glocalization: globalization and the migration strategies of Scottish football fans in North America', *Sociology*, 41, 133–52.

Guttmann, A. (1995) *Games and empires*, New York: Columbia University Press.

Kelly, W. W. (1985) *Defence and defiance in 19th century Japan*, Princeton: Princeton University Press.

Kelly, W. W. (1997) 'How to cheer a Japanese baseball team: an anthropologist in the bleachers', *Japan Quarterly*, October–December, 66–79.

Kelly, W. W. (1998) 'Blood and guts in Japanese professional baseball', in S. Linhart and S. Frühstück (eds) *The culture of Japan as seen through its leisure*, Albany, NY: SUNY Press, 95–112.

Kelly, W. W. (ed.) (2004) *Fanning the flames: fandom and consumer culture in contemporary Japan*, Albany, NY: SUNY Press.

Lechner, F. (1991) 'The case against secularization: a rebuttal', *Social Forces*, 69, 1103–19.

Lechner, F. (2007) *The Netherlands: national identity and globalization*, London: Routledge.

Lenskyj, H. (2000) *Inside the Olympic industry*, New York: SUNY Press.

Mangan, J. A. (1987) *The games ethic and imperialism*, London: Viking.

Nettl, J. P. and R. Robertson (1968) *International systems and the modernization of societies*, New York: Basic Books.

Ritzer, G. and T. Stillman (2001) 'The postmodern ballpark as a leisure setting: enchantment and simulated de-McDonaldization', *Leisure Sciences*, 23, 99–113.

Ritzer, G. (1997) *The McDonaldization thesis: explorations and extension*, London: Sage.

Ritzer, G. (2004) *The globalization of nothing*, Pine Forge Press.

Robertson, R. (1970) *The sociological interpretation of religion*, Oxford: Blackwell.

Robertson, R. (1992) *Globalization: social theory and global culture*, London: Sage.

Robertson, R. and J. A. Scholte (eds) (2007) *Encyclopaedia of globalization*, London: Routledge.

Rumford, C. (2002) *The European Union: a political sociology*, Oxford: Blackwell.

Smart, B. (1999) *Facing modernity: ambivalence, reflexivity and morality*, London: Sage.

Smart, B. (2005) *The sport star*, London: Sage/TCS.

2

Not playing around: global capitalism, modern sport and consumer culture

Throughout the twentieth century leading sporting figures, chairmen of economic corporations with direct and indirect interests in sport, think tanks, and social analysts preoccupied with making sense of the contemporary world recognized the unique local appeal and global significance of sport. At the beginning of the present century, in the context of a wide-ranging analysis of the consequences associated with the global implementation of neo-liberal free-market economic policies, sport was described as 'the most important thing in the world' (Beck 2000: 62).

Early in the last century Walter Camp, a formative figure in the development of American football, reportedly referred to sport as '"the broad folk highway" of the nation' (Pope 1997: 3). In 1939 Mass Observation confirmed the status of sport as a key social institution by pointing out that sport-related economic activity represented 'the biggest English industry' (Kuper 2003: 147–8). In 1985 the Henley Centre estimated that sport constituted the sixth largest employment sector in the UK (Mason 1989: 10). In the closing decade of the century the founder and chairman of *Nike* commented that sport was at the heart of contemporary culture and increasingly defined 'the culture of the world' (cited in Katz 1994: 199).

Sport is an economically significant, highly popular, globally networked cultural form. It occupies a prominent place in a 'deep area of the collective sensibility' (Eco 1987: 160) and is able, as Nelson Mandela reportedly suggested, to mobilize the sentiments of people in all countries in an unrivalled manner (Carlin 2003). The Secretary General of the United Nations subsequently endorsed this view when he remarked of one sport, football, that it is 'more universal' than the UN and that the FIFA World Cup brings the 'family of nations and peoples' together 'celebrating our common humanity' in a way that few other cultural events can equal (Annan 2006).

As the century progressed, the commercial world drew increasingly on sport's cultural capital value to raise the global profile and appeal of corporate brands and to expand the global market for their products. Taking stock towards the close of the twentieth century, one analyst remarked that professional sport, the media and corporate sponsorship constituted a seemingly indivisible trinity, 'a golden triangle' from which each of the parties was able to derive substantial profit (Aris 1990: 9). Subsequently, professional sport became more closely articulated with the media, in particular television, commerce and the world of corporate sponsorship (Smart 2005). This state of affairs received a ringing endorsement from FIFA President Sepp Blatter who, speaking in defence of the growth in World Cup sponsorship money in the run-up to the 2006 tournament, remarked that '[w]hat is important is a partnership between soccer, the economy and television which benefits all sides' (Anonymous 2006). Without doubt, the growth of a global sport network has been very closely articulated with the pursuit of economic interests and the promotion of consumer culture (Jarvie 2006: 94).

The popular appeal of sport increased significantly during the course of the twentieth century, becoming truly worldwide in scope and intensity with the growth of international sporting bodies, competitions, tournaments, migratory flows of competitors and associated globally extensive forms of media representation, especially in the form of terrestrial (later satellite) television and the internet (Maguire 1999). Its closer links with the corporate world over this period transformed the institution of sport. It was not just a case of business values intruding into sport, of sport being turned into a business, and sport events and participants becoming commodities. It was also a matter of recognizing that the distinctive qualities sport and its participants possessed, notably its popular cultural appeal and unrivalled aura of authenticity, were of potential value in the increasingly competitive process of capital accumulation in a fully-fledged consumer society. It was about its unique value in enhancing corporate brands, global marketing, and the promotion and sale of products associated with popular sport events and iconic celebrity sporting figures (Hickey 2000; Klein 2001; Smart 2005).

The formative roots of the close contemporary relationship between professional sport, corporate sponsorship, the media, and consumer culture, which has contributed to the growth of a globally extensive popular culture of sporting celebrity, lie in the 'take-off' phase of the globalization of sport. The discussion is directed to an analysis of key interconnected aspects of the formation of a global sport network. This includes turn-of-the-century manifestations of sport's globalization exemplified by developments in tennis and the Olympics, the establishment of sports goods companies in Europe and the USA, early signs of an emerging culture of sporting celebrity, as well as the growth in media interest and associated developments in sport sponsorship.

Institutional manifestations of sport's globalization

From the late nineteenth century, the global diffusion of modern sport gathered momentum. The period from the 1870s to the 1920s represented a 'take-off' phase, an important period in which international competitions, tournaments and tours began to occur with increasing frequency. Spectatorship grew and numerous international sports governing bodies were established (Maguire 1999). A number of inaugural international sport events took place in this period that served to reduce local variations in sporting activities and promote forms of global standardization (Van Bottenburg 2001). These included the first international rugby and football matches between Scotland and England held in Edinburgh (1871) and Glasgow (1872) respectively, the first cricket test match between Australia and England (1877), the first England international football team tour to continental Europe (1908) and the first Wallabies tour of the UK and USA (1908/9). In addition, a number of international sports organizations, including the International Football Association Board (1886), the International Rugby Football Board (1886), the Fédération Internationale de Football Association (1904) and the International Amateur Athletic Association (1912) were established. There were a number of other manifestations of a steadily accelerating process of sport globalization during this period and it is to particular developments in respect of both tennis and the Olympic Games that we now turn.

Tennis: the first global sport?

One of the first modern sports to go international and begin to develop a global profile was tennis. An early semi-official international tennis tournament, including players from America, Canada and England, was staged in 1878 in Newport USA by Dr James Dwight. The tournament was a forerunner to the first international team tennis competition established in 1900, officially called the International Lawn Tennis Challenge Trophy, donated by American doubles champion Dwight Davis, and subsequently known as the Davis Cup. The competition was open to all nations that had established official tennis associations to govern the organization and development of the sport. At the time, only a few nations were eligible to compete for the trophy, namely Australia (including New Zealand), the British Isles, South Africa (under British rule), Canada, India and the United States. Of these, only the British Isles took up the first challenge, losing 3–0 to the USA team. In 1904 France became the third nation to participate in the Davis Cup and in the same year the Lawn Tennis Association of Australasia (including New Zealand) was established. For many years Great Britain, Australia, France and the USA were the only countries to compete for the Davis Cup. Only with the opening up of tennis at the end of the 1960s as professionalism was finally accepted did the Davis Cup become truly global in scope as teams from more than 50 nations began to compete for the trophy (Gillmeister 1998).[1]

In addition to formally designated international tournaments such as the Davis Cup in which players competed against one another in national teams, towards the close of the nineteenth century other tennis tournaments were becoming more international. American players were competing at Wimbledon and English players were taking part in the Newport, Rhode Island tournament, which in time was to become the American Open. In 1913 the International Lawn Tennis Federation was established and when America joined in 1923 the championships of the four leading member states, England, France, Australia and the USA, were raised to the status of 'official championships', later to become known colloquially as the Grand Slam tournaments (Gillmeister 1998).

The growing worldwide appeal of tennis in the 1920s is partly attributable to the emergence of two outstanding players. They were Suzanne Lenglen in France and Bill Tilden in America and their dominance over women's and men's tennis respectively during this period is regarded as marking 'the beginning of an age in which tennis players became public celebrities' (Rader 1983: 220). Lenglen and Tilden were highly controversial figures who drew spectators to tournaments and attracted the attention of international journalists. Lenglen, a very successful and powerful player who was considered to hit the ball 'like a man', was said to be 'hot tempered' and to have a 'racy private life', and for good measure she flouted the tennis dress code convention for women, electing to wear more 'colourful and sensual' clothing (Bouchier and Findling 1983). Tilden was a no less controversial figure who, while winning seven US national singles championships and three Wimbledon singles championships, continually came into conflict with the USLTA for not complying with the rule forbidding players from profiting directly from tennis by endorsing equipment, teaching, or writing about the sport (Walker 1989).

What ultimately contributed most to the global transformation of the status and image of the sport was the acceptance of professionalism and the establishment of 'Open' tennis from the late 1960s. In addition, increased public access was made possible by an extensive worldwide tournament calendar, developments in broadcasting technology, especially television, and the availability of jet travel allowing players to move relatively easily from one country to another to participate in events. As one former Grand Slam winner remarked, 'With tournaments in every continent and with the players often moving to a different country each week, tennis is a sport dependent on jet travel. ... Flying certainly allowed our tour to become more global and it's opened up new horizons for tennis' (Courier 2004).

In tennis and a number of other sports, including association football and athletics, a global network of tournaments has grown in tandem with developments in air travel and television coverage. Corporate commercial interest in acquiring a cosmopolitan image for products and brands through sport event sponsorship and endorsement contracts offered to players in the wake of playing success and the achievement of a popular cultural profile has also helped (Smart 2005).

The Olympic Games and globalization

At the annual conference of the Union des Sociétés Françaises des Sports Athlétiques in 1892, the secretary general of the organization, Baron de Coubertin, who considered international sporting events to have the potential to promote peace and understanding between nations, proposed a revival of the Olympic Games of Ancient Greece. An international sport congress in Paris in 1894 led to the foundation of an International Olympic Committee, which proposed that the first Olympics of the modern era be staged in Athens in 1896 (Coubertin 1896; Gillmeister 1998).

De Coubertin campaigned around the world to gather support for the idea of nations joining together to engage in a global competitive sport event. He noted that an international network of sporting events was developing, that Switzerland had 'invited rifle marksmen from abroad for its federal competitions', that cyclists were racing against one another 'on all the cycle tracks of Europe', that French and Italian fencers were meeting in international events, and that Britain and the USA had already 'challenged each other upon water [sailing] and grass [tennis]' (Coubertin 1896: 1). Evidence of increasing international competition in a growing number of sports convinced de Coubertin that a successful revival of the Olympic Games was a real possibility. It duly came to pass, as he had hoped, although the IOC's eager embrace of private enterprise, sponsorship and commercial marketing techniques to fund the games in the latter part of the twentieth century ultimately thwarted his wish to see the Olympics 'purify' sport of the 'commercial spirit' that he recognized was developing (Coubertin 1896: 2; Preuss 2006).

In Athens, in 1896, more than 200 male athletes drawn from 13 nations participated in 43 events in track and field, weightlifting, rifle and pistol shooting, tennis, cycling, swimming, gymnastics and wrestling. The Summer Games has been held every four years since then, with the notable exception of the war years of 1916, 1940 and 1944. The number of countries participating has increased steadily, reaching 203 by 2006, a figure just below FIFA's 207 member associations, but in excess of the 191 state membership of the United Nations.[2]

The first Winter Olympic Games was held in 1924 at Chamonix, France, although some 'winter events', such as figure skating and ice hockey, had already featured at the 1920 Summer Games at Antwerp, Belgium. Subsequently, the Winter Games has been held every four years, with the exception of the Second World War years and 1994, when following the IOC's policy decision in 1986 the game's schedule was changed to improve the financial prospects and reduce the organizational load on National Olympic Committees. The year 1992 was the last time the Winter Games (Albertville, France) and Summer Games (Barcelona, Spain) were held in the same year. The 1994 games in Lillehammer, Norway, marked the beginning of a separate, four-year cycle for the Winter Games, which, with fewer countries participating, has remained less popular than the Summer Games.

The Summer Olympics ranks alongside the FIFA World Cup as one of the world's most popular sporting festivals. Both are truly global sporting events that attract substantial interest from the public, broadcasting organizations and commercial corporations alike. The 2004 Athens Olympics exceeded all broadcasting expectations with 3.9 billion people accessing television coverage of events. Given the scale and reach of global television coverage it is not surprising to find that the Olympic Games is now regarded as one of the most important events for commercial corporations seeking to promote their brands, particularly as consumers tend to associate Olympic sponsors with leadership in their respective product fields (McCall 2004).

Paralleling developments in this take-off phase of international sporting events, matches and tournaments were increases in the number of spectators paying to attend events, the formation of international governing bodies exercising jurisdiction over international competitions, and far more media interest exemplified by the emergence of sports magazines, press coverage and radio broadcasting. A significant commercial market for sports goods also began to emerge as 'falling real prices and rising wages brought an increase in prosperity' and innovations in sporting equipment and specialized sports clothing attracted growing consumer interest (Flanders 2006: 435).

The establishment of sport goods companies in Europe and USA

In the globalization take-off phase a largely unregulated, free-market capitalist economic system sought to shift emphasis away from catering for elite forms of conspicuous consumption. To realize the potential of mass-production techniques it was necessary to promote forms of mass consumption, including activities and commodities associated with sport, which was growing rapidly in popularity and already beginning to display the potential to become 'a great and profitable industry' (Polanyi 1968; Vamplew 1988: 55). A reduction in working hours and recognition that the prospect of continued capitalist economic development was less bound up with saving than spending led to the nurturing of mass consumerism, the development of commercial recreation, and increases in associated forms of consumer expenditure (Goldman 1983–4).

It was in this context, stimulated by the growth of professional forms of sport, that evidence of the existence of a growing audience for sports events around the world became apparent. With the rising demand for sports goods and equipment, among amateurs as well as professionals, a number of sports goods companies began to emerge in Europe and America. They included Spalding, Slazenger, Dunlop, J. W. Foster & Sons (subsequently to become Reebok), Converse, Wilson, and Gebruder Dassler (later to split into Adidas and Puma). All these companies subsequently went on to achieve a significant economic and cultural profile as global sports brands (Flanders 2006).

The world's first major sports goods company was established in the USA in 1876 by Albert G Spalding, a major league baseball pitcher and self-confessed 'father of American baseball' (Levine 1985: xi). The company initially concentrated on manufacturing baseballs but soon diversified into manufacturing golf clubs, tennis rackets, basketballs and other products connected with sport. By 1909 it had retail stores in thirty American cities plus another six overseas (Levine 1985). In England in 1881 the Slazenger brothers moved to London from Manchester to manufacture rackets and balls for a new game, 'Sphairistike', developed a few years earlier in 1874 by Major Walter Clopton Wingfield. In due course, the game would become better known as lawn tennis. Slazenger has been official supplier of tennis balls to the Wimbledon Championships since 1902 and this represents possibly the oldest sporting sponsorship in the world. The Slazenger brand is now prominent not only in the world of tennis but also in squash, cricket and golf.

In 1888 John Boyd Dunlop, a Scottish vet living in Belfast, developed the pneumatic tyre that would 'revolutionize cycling and harness racing in the next decade' (Betts 1953: 248). In 1900 the Dunlop Rubber Company Ltd was established and began to produce car tyres and then, in 1910, aeroplane tyres and the first Dunlop golf ball (Jones 1984). In due course Dunlop produced a range of other sports goods, including tennis and squash rackets, balls, golf clubs, sports clothing and footwear. To date, Dunlop has 'won' more Grand Slam tennis tournaments than any other brand and like Slazenger it is an integral part of British sporting history.

The Wilson Sporting Goods Company provides a comparable American example. In 1914 the Ashland Manufacturing Company began to produce sports goods and, following the appointment of Thomas Wilson as president of the company, it was renamed the Thomas E. Wilson Company. In 1931 it became the Wilson Sporting Goods Company. The company began by making golf equipment and in 1922 appointed golf star Gene Sarazen to its advisory staff. The company diversified into manufacturing balls and racquets for tennis and squash, as well as footwear and other sporting goods, including jerseys and uniforms. Wilson has a reputation for innovative manufacturing and marketing strategies and was among the first of the American manufacturers to use sporting celebrities – Knute Rockne (football), Gene Sarazen and Sam Snead (golf), 'Lefty' Gomez and Ted Williams (baseball) and Jack Kramer (tennis) – to endorse its products (Sullivan 2005). Wilson now makes sports equipment and clothing for golf, racquet sports (badminton, racquetball, squash and tennis), and team sports (baseball, basketball, football, soccer and volleyball).

The market for specialized sports clothing was growing rapidly as the century drew to a close and a number of new companies sought to make their mark by introducing innovative sporting footwear. For example, in 1893 Joseph Foster, an English athlete, customized some running shoes by adding spikes and, on receiving considerable interest from other runners, he set up a shoe company. By 1895 his company, J. W. Foster & Sons, had acquired an international reputation and clientele and was regularly supplying distinguished athletes with handmade shoes. The company was moderately successful, providing the running shoes worn at the 1924 Summer Olympics, but its profile remained relatively low. In 1958 Foster's grandsons created a companion company, named Reebok, that later took over J. W. Foster & Sons to create a unified brand. In 1979 Paul Fireman secured the North American distribution licence and started the company known as Reebok USA taking their global sales from $300,000 in 1980 to $1.4 billion in 1987 (Smit 2006). In 2006 Adidas, the German sports goods company, acquired Reebok, giving the combination a market share that closed the gap on the market-leader, Nike (Figure 1).

In 1908 the Converse shoe company was established at Malden, Massachusetts. By 1910 some 4000 shoes were being produced each day and in the period 1915–18 the canvas tennis shoe business doubled in size. The first sneaker to be mass produced in North America, subsequently known as the 'All Star', appeared in 1917 and after 'Chuck' Taylor, a basketball player for the Akron Firestones, started wearing them in 1918 the shoes rapidly grew in popularity. Taylor joined the Converse sales team in 1921 and travelled across the country promoting the game of basketball, allegedly selling his favourite sports footwear from the boot of his Cadillac. In 1923, in acknowledgement of his role in promoting the All Star shoe, modifying its design, and increasing its popularity with consumers, his name was added to the ankle patch.[3]

Figure 1: Branded athletic footwear market share for 2004

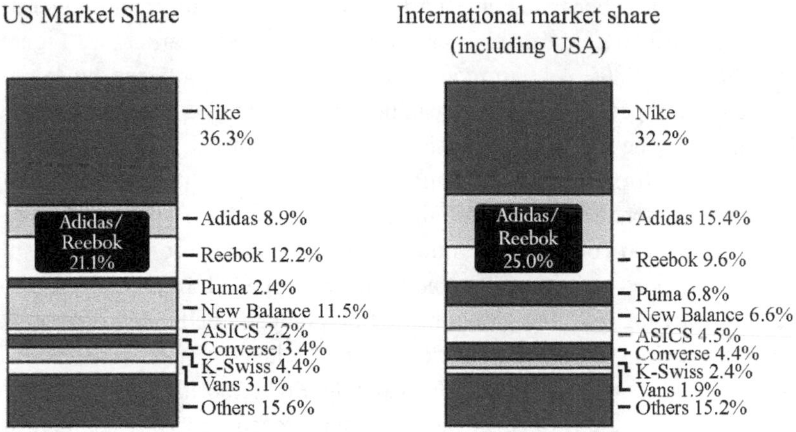

US Market Share

International market share
(including USA)

Source: Sporting Goods Intelligence cited in Associated Press (2006).

A later generation of basketball stars, including Larry Bird, Magic Johnson and Isiah Thomas, endorsed leather versions of the company's All Star sneakers and the brand retained its popularity as market leader until the mid-1980s. That was when Nike launched its high performance sports shoes, employing Michael Jordan, the figure whose endorsements would in due course transform the company's profile, the game of basketball and the nature of sports representation, as their 'signature athlete' (Smart 2005). Converse could not keep pace with its new corporate competitor and, in 2001, after being declared bankrupt, Footwear Acquisitions Inc bought it out and shifted production to Asia. Demand for Converse's 'retro' shoes subsequently grew and in 2003 the company was acquired by Nike, by which time it was estimated that over 580 million pairs of All Star 'Chuck Taylor' sneakers had been sold.

In 1920 in Herzogenaurach, Germany, Adolf 'Adi' Dassler made his first sports shoe for runners and, four years later, he set up Gebruder Dassler with his brother Rudolph. While production was initially directed to track and field footwear, from 1925 onwards they produced football boots and then in 1931 the company manufactured its first tennis shoe. Dassler was one of the first companies to use sports stars and sports events to promote innovative sports footwear. The mere fact that stars competing in a prestigious event were seen to be wearing a particular design of footwear effectively served to advertise and endorse the product.[4] At the Amsterdam Olympic Games in 1928 many of the participating athletes wore Dassler footwear and, by the mid-1930s, 100 employees were making 30 different styles of footwear for a total of 11 sports. The track successes in the 1936 Berlin Olympics of the African-American athlete Jesse Owens, who won four gold medals wearing Dassler spikes, convinced athletes and trainers around the world of the quality and value of the company's footwear and enhanced its reputation.

After the Second World War growing tensions led to a feud between the two brothers and in due course the business was split with Adi Dassler setting up a company with the name Adidas in 1948 and in the following year registering the three stripes trademark. His brother Rudolph established Puma Aktiengesellschaft Rudolf Sport, which quickly became Puma (Adidas n.d.; Smit 2006). Subsequently, both companies established a significant share of the sports goods market (see Figure 1).

Until the mid-1980s Adidas monopolized the sports footwear business and a measure of the company's dominance can be gauged from the fact that 80 per cent of medal winners at the Summer Olympic Games in Montreal in 1976 were wearing Adidas products. Horst Dassler, the only son of Adi and Kathe Dassler, recognized the commercial potential of sport and the prospect of building partnerships between sports federations and commercial corporations keen to promote their brands through sponsorship of sports events. To exploit this he founded International Sport and Leisure (ISL) in 1982, the first global marketing company dedicated to sports events, which soon acquired the global marketing and television rights to the Olympic Games, the World athletics championships and the FIFA World Cup (Smit 2006).

In the course of the 1980s, however, Adidas faced growing competition and, needing investment to counter a deteriorating debt to capital ratio, became a limited partnership in 1989. This change followed the rapid growth in market share of Reebok and, more significantly, Nike, an American sports goods company established in 1962 as Blue Ribbon Sports, but renamed in 1968 after the Greek goddess of victory, securing its trademark logo, the Swoosh, in 1971. By 1990 Nike had overtaken Adidas in global sales of sports footwear, securing 33 per cent of the American market compared with the 3 per cent held by Adidas. The purchase of Converse in 2003 increased Nike's share of the global sports shoe market and strengthened the product and brand range. Adidas's subsequent acquisition of Reebok in 2006 was part of its global strategy to make up ground on Nike.

The signs of commerce are now a prominent feature of global sports events. The logos of sponsors promoting their brands through sports events and sports star endorsement are a routine part of the landscape of sport, adorning the walls of stadiums, the perimeter of playing areas and arenas, the clothing worn by players and the equipment that is used, as well as influencing the titles of television sports programmes. As competition between corporations for a bigger share of the global market for sportswear, sports goods and equipment became increasingly intense in the late twentieth century, so recognition of the value of association with sports events and sporting figures grew. Companies like Nike and Adidas increased their investment and elevated sports stars to the status of celebrity figures and global icons by virtue of the enhancement their public profiles received from involvement in commercial endorsement and advertising campaigns targeted at a growing consumer market.

In some respects contemporary sports events have come increasingly to resemble a contest between competing corporate brands – the 'swoosh' versus 'the stripes', or Nike versus Adidas. When the USA played Brazil in the 1994 FIFA World Cup Finals in the USA, Phil Knight, the American chief executive of Nike, demonstrated that corporate loyalty took precedence over national identity by declaring: 'I rooted for Brazil because it was a Nike Team. America was Adidas' (cited in Coakley 2003: 399). In a comparable manner, in the build up to the 2006 FIFA World Cup held in

Germany, Herbert Hainer, the chief executive officer of Adidas, unlike Nike one of the official event sponsors, remarked that 'the two companies are "fighting like sports teams"' (Islam 2006).

Consumer culture and the emergence of sporting celebrity

During the take-off period in the globalization of sport, which lasted from the late nineteenth century to the 1920s, the prestige of economic liberalism was at its height. Society was being run 'as an adjunct to the market' (Polanyi 1968: 57) and America and Europe were experiencing an economic boom. As the development of the capitalist market economy accelerated, 'society [became] preoccupied with consumption, with comfort and bodily well-being, with … spending and acquisition' (Leach 1994: xiii; see also Flanders 2006) and, in turn, the signs of an emerging global sporting network could be clearly discerned (Van Bottenburg 2001).

Between 1909 and 1929 there was a rapid increase in the provision of commercial recreation and the development of the business of sport. One can witness the growth in professional sport (and also in US collegiate sport) and associated increases in spectatorship, the construction of stadiums and arenas, the dedication of more and more space to sports reporting in the press, and the expansion of the sports goods industry (Goldman 1983–4; see also Flanders 2006). In this period, there was a growing recognition that the cultural capital that high-profile sporting figures had accumulated through their sporting prowess might be profitably invested in product promotion. Initially, it was the sports goods companies that sought to imply that the success of the players in their advertisements was, in part at least, attributable to the use of a particular product – a golf club or ball, a sports shoe or boot, a racquet and so on. The implication here is that an ordinary consumer's performance would also be enhanced by using the product (Goldman 1983–4). Increasingly, companies and organizations beyond the world of sport come to recognize that the marketing and sale of their products could benefit from association with successful athletes and performers, in short that endorsement by and/or association with sports stars would accord products an invaluable aura of authenticity (Smart 2005).

The 1920s has been described as the 'Golden Age of American Sport', a period in which, in a range of popular sports, outstanding individuals emerged to be greeted by journalists and radio broadcasters eager to transform them into larger than life celebrity figures. 'Babe' Ruth (baseball), Jack Dempsey (boxing), 'Red' Grange (grid-iron football), Bobby Jones (golf) and Bill Tilden (tennis) each became publicly feted figures, the recipients of promotional and marketing skills that served to 'sell' them to the public (Danzig and Brandewein 1948). In turn, the popular profile such sporting figures enjoyed drew the interest of companies eager to convey the impression of some form of association between their products or services and the authentic achievements and attractive accompanying qualities of outstanding athletes and players. For example, Ruth's playing successes led him to be offered lucrative commercial opportunities, including ghost-written articles in newspapers and magazines, vaudeville tours, fees for appearing at banquets, openings and celebrity golf tournaments, and endorsement contracts for a wide range of goods – hunting and fishing equipment, men's clothing, baseball gear and cars (Rader 1983). To handle his commercial affairs Ruth appointed a business adviser. In a comparable manner 'Red' Grange appointed an Illinois promoter C. C. Pyle, often regarded as the first 'sports agent', who later would establish the first professional tennis tour.[5] Pyle negotiated a $3000 per game contract for Grange to play for the Chicago Bears who drew record crowds to professional football (Shropshire and Davis 2003). Grange's playing success led to a range of commercial opportunities, including endorsement contracts for sweaters, shoes, caps and soft drinks, a film contract, and the manufacture of a 'Red' Grange football doll and 'Red' Grange chocolates (Rader 1983).

The adoption in the USA of managers and/or agents to handle the commercial activities of leading sporting figures exemplified the growing consumer ethos and developing celebrity culture that was becoming a more prominent part of social life in general and sports in particular. By the 1940s it was becoming clear that as the development of consumer culture was gathering momentum, the idols of the masses were increasingly celebrity figures, 'idols of consumption' from the worlds of entertainment and sport (Lowenthal 1961). In the course of the twentieth century corporate interest in the global commercial potential of sport increased significantly and from the 1960s as leading sporting figures became more and more aware of the lucrative opportunities open to them they increasingly appointed agents to handle their affairs (Smart 2005).

In 1960 Mark McCormack established the International Management Group (IMG) and it relatively quickly became the leading organization as far as the representation of sports celebrities was concerned. The rapid growth in the influence of agents in sport is generally attributed to McCormack, described in 1990 by *Sports Illustrated* as 'the most powerful man in sport' and in a BBC obituary in 2003 as the 'king of sports marketing'.[6] McCormack was confident that the global popularity and economic marketing potential of successful sport performers would render national borders and differences of language, custom, and culture commercially irrelevant, and that leading sporting figures would be known and held in high regard around the world even by those with little or no interest in sport. The establishment of IMG is considered to have 'changed the face of professional sport', but it is the media, and terrestrial and satellite television in particular that have significantly raised the global profile of commercially sponsored sport, enhancing its popularity by presenting it to the world with an increasingly spectacular 'face' (Kelso 2003).

Growing media interest in sport

Since the late nineteenth century, the development of modern professional sport has been bound up with a succession of communications media that have reported on sporting events and the deeds of sports participants. The growth in global television coverage and the increasing commercialization of sports has provided the corporate sponsors of sports events with a compellingly persuasive platform to achieve a global profile for their brands. Press, radio and television have not only communicated information and images about sport to the fans, they have also served to promote sport to a wider public. They have increased its popularity and made the names and, in the case of the visual media, the faces of sporting figures known even to those with little real interest in sport (Smart 2005). Developments in television technology, particularly the emergence of satellite television broadcasting, have contributed significantly to the globalization of sport. Worldwide live coverage of events, and digitalization and pay-per-view, along with the emergence of new media delivery platforms, including the Internet and mobile phone, have contributed further to the global diffusion of sports information and images.

From the mid-twentieth century television broadcasting media have created a cultural-commercial force field that has radically transformed sport. The FIFA World Cup tournament was televised for the first time in 1954 and the Summer Olympic Games in 1960. Television coverage has significantly increased the global popularity of both events and competitive bidding for broadcasting rights has radically transformed the political economy of these and other sporting events (Smart 2005). The IOC has been a major beneficiary of the bidding war for broadcasting rights and since 1980 has concluded agreements worth more than US$ 10 billion (Figure 2).

Figure 2: Olympic Broadcast Revenue Charts

Olympic Games

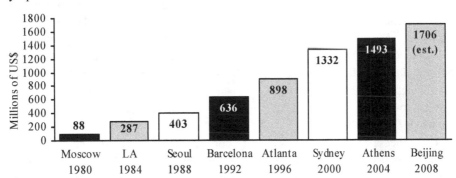

Olympic Winter Games

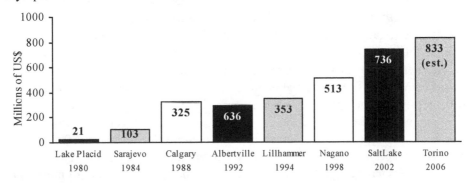

Source: IOC http://www.olympic.org/uk/organisation/facts/revenue/broadcast_uk.asp retrieved 10 June 2006; Lee (2005).

Global research conducted by Sports Marketing Surveys on behalf of the IOC revealed that television broadcasting of the Athens 2004 Summer Games achieved new levels of global popularity with 3.9 billion people having access to coverage compared with 3.6 billion for the 2000 Sydney Games. There were 35,000 hours of coverage of the Athens Games compared with 29,600 for Sydney, 25,000 for Atlanta (1996) and 20,000 for Barcelona (1992). It has been estimated that in 2004 'globally, every individual viewer watched over 12 hours of Olympic Games coverage'. The 2004 games were also notable for the fact that for the first time streaming video and highlight clips were available in a number of countries through mobile phone handsets and over the Internet.[7]

The data on broadcasting coverage of the World Cup, the tournament described by FIFA as 'the world's no. 1 sports event', reveal a comparable pattern of increases in broadcasting rights revenue secured, number of global television viewers, and hours of coverage watched. Revenue secured from the sale of World Cup television broadcasting rights increased steadily from 95 million Swiss Francs in 1990 to 135 million in 1998, rising rapidly to 1.3 billion in 2002 and reaching 1.5 billion in 2006.[8] Over the period from 1990 to 2002, cumulative global television viewing audiences reported by FIFA indicated a steady increase from 26.7 billion for the tournament held in Italy in 1990 to 28.8 billion in 2002 when the finals were held in Japan/Korea. Described by FIFA as 'the most extensively covered and viewed event in television history', the 2002 tournament is represented as having set a new record for a sports event for the total number of hours of television coverage watched by viewers worldwide.[9] While the range of data utilized by FIFA may risk overstating the degree of public interest, independent audience research conducted on behalf of potential sponsors and advertisers has confirmed the tournament's unrivalled global appeal by revealing that the World Cup Final between Italy and France was television's most viewed sports event in 2006, attracting 'more than twice as many viewers as any other program' (Cone 2006).

The process of the globalization of sport accelerated with the development of television technology, especially after the establishment in 1979 of the Entertainment Sports Programming Network (ESPN), which first exploited the television trans- mission potential of channel space on communication satellites (Halberstam 2001). By the mid-1980s, when ABC purchased ESPN, a technological revolution in sport television coverage was well underway and subsequently the quantity, quality and diversity of televised sport have increased significantly (Smart 2005). Alongside such developments in television technology there was in this period an increasing concentration of broadcasting rights ownership by multinational media corporations with interests in the sport field. News Corp, the global media corporation Rupert Murdoch established in the closing decades of the twentieth century, provides one significant example. For him, securing television-broadcasting rights for globally popular sports has served as a '"battering ram" to enter new markets', a means of gaining access through sports-driven viewer subscriptions to the homes of millions of people around the world (cited in Marqusee 2005). Increasingly, a few powerful multinational corporations dominate the sport-media complex. In 2004, the 17 leading sport-media companies were based in either Europe or America and, it is argued, this has led to a 'tendency towards a cultural convergence and homogenisation of ... sports television coverage across the globe' that contributes to the impression that there is indeed one world of sport (Jarvie 2006: 134; see also Sugden and Tomlinson 1998: 76).

In the closing decades of the twentieth century, television coverage became an increasingly vital part of the cultural economy of modern sports. With the increasing global exposure and promotion it provided, it simultaneously enhanced the attractiveness of sport and sporting figures to commercial organizations willing to spend increasingly large capital sums on various forms of sports advertising and sponsorship (Smart 2005). For example, FIFA's sponsorship revenue has risen significantly as corporations have come to appreciate that 'embedding advertising' in such a globally popular cultural event as the World Cup, an event that through television coverage reaches more people worldwide than any other, constitutes an 'advertiser's dream and ... an unparalleled opportunity' (Maidment 2006).

Global sport sponsorship: the World Cup and the Olympics

Between 1993 and 2003 the global sponsorship market grew from $10 million to $27 billion and, in 2003, more than two-thirds of that market, $18 billion, was attributable to sports related business activity (Smart 2005). Leading global corporations seek to associate their brands with the unique aura of authenticity that is a corollary of the exceptional performances and attributes of sport stars, individuals who through media representation acquire 'image' and the potential to become cultural icons. Well-established, globally popular sporting events are ideal vehicles for corporate sponsors seeking to raise the global profile of their brands. Such events transcend cultural differences and, being universal in appeal, open up access to consumer markets around the world in a way that few other social and cultural practices can equal.

With the increasing choice in communications media and the fragmentation of audiences, reaching consumers through advertising and marketing via broadcasting, billboards and magazines has become a more precarious business. In an over-saturated communications media context, popular sporting events constitute one of the few cultural forms that retain a capacity to attract a global audience to broadcasting programme schedules and thereby they offer businesses a unique global promotional platform, the potential to expose consumers around the world to associated corporate advertising, marketing and branding campaigns (Marqusee 2006). It is not surprising that by 2006 the sports sponsorship market was reported to have increased significantly in value and to be worth $43 billion (Viscusi 2006).

Sponsorships and endorsements have been a factor in professional sport for well over a century. In 1898 Nottingham Forest, champions of the English football league, had a commercial contract with the beverage company *Bovril*. In 1903 the *News of the World* sponsored the Professional Golf Association Match Play championship. In 1910 *Gillette* hired an American baseball star Honus Wagner to sell razor blades, and in 1926 *Coca-Cola* was accorded product sampling rights for the 1928 Amsterdam Olympic Games (Pope 2003; Smart 2005; http://www.geocities.com/jawo66/ olympic.html retrieved 17 July 2006). In the 1920s 'Red' Grange, an American football player, held a number of endorsement contracts with companies manufacturing clothing and soft drinks, as did American golfer Walter Hagen with manufacturers of golf equipment. In the aftermath of the Second World War, leading English sportsmen, notably Dennis Compton, Tom Finney, Billy Wright and Stanley Matthews, had endorsement contracts with companies producing hair products, breakfast cereals and football boots respectively (Smart 2005).

Although one might argue that the first sign of commercial sponsorship in sports was the inclusion of advertisements in the official programme for the first modern Olympics in Athens, only in the last quarter of the twentieth century, in association with developments in sports television broadcasting, did corporate sponsorship begin to have a marked impact on sports (Lasch 1979; Sandler and Shani 1993; Smart 2005). From the mid-1970s corporate sponsorship of sport events with a global popular appeal and commercial potential, for example the FIFA World Cup and the Olympic Games, has grown significantly.[10]

FIFA was the first global sports organization for which corporate sponsorship became a major source of revenue generation, with the World Cup becoming the main tournament for securing lucrative global commercial sponsorship agreements and for auctioning the sale of global television broadcasting rights. Following the election of João Havelange as president in 1974, FIFA's future development was considered to be bound up with the deployment of appropriate marketing strategies targeted at potential global corporate sponsors. In his campaign for the FIFA presidency, Havelange had promised to increase the number of countries participating in the World Cup Finals, to introduce a World Youth tournament, and to enhance the global appeal of football by establishing a programme to help develop the game in Africa and Asia. Such commitments necessitated significant increases in funding. With the assistance of Horst Dassler and Patrick Nally, who from 1977 to 1982 shared a sports marketing partnership SMPI (Société Monégasque de Promotion Internationale), FIFA and President Havelange set out to establish exclusive marketing rights agreements with major global corporations. They began with the 1978 World Cup tournament in Argentina, for which contracts were negotiated with six major corporate sponsors, including Coca-Cola, Gillette, and Seiko (Sugden and Tomlinson 1998; Smit 2006; Yallop 1999). This established a template that would be followed in subsequent tournaments (Table 1).

From 2007 FIFA's global commercial strategy became even more exclusive as prospective marketing partners were grouped into three categories: 'six FIFA Partners, six to eight FIFA World Cup sponsors and four to six National Supporters'. Appropriately the first to sign up as a FIFA Partner for the period 2007–14 was Adidas, which paid $350 million, followed by Hyundai, sum undisclosed, Sony $305 million, Coca-Cola $500 million (through to 2020), and Emirates Airline $195 million (Viscusi 2006). The 1982 World Cup tournament held in Spain was the first to have an organized corporate sponsorship programme, with a reported $19 million being raised in total from nine 'partner' sponsors. For the 2006 tournament in Germany the 15 partner companies paid on average $35 million each to be a part of the FIFA sponsorship programme (Maidment 2006).

Table 1: Official Partners of FIFA World Cup 1982–2006

FIFA World Cup™	2006	2002	1998	1994	1990	1986	1982
Adidas	X	X	X				
Avaya	X	X					
Anheuser-Busch	X	X	X		X	X	
Coca-Cola	X	X	X	X	X	X	X
Continental	X						
Deutsche Telekom	X						
Emirates	X						
Fujifilm	X	X	X	X	X	X	X
Fuji Xerox		X					
Gillette	X	X	X	X	X	X	X
Hyundai	X	X					
JVC		X	X	X	X	X	X
Korea Telekom/NTT		X					
MasterCard	X	X	X	X			
McDonald's	X	X	X	X			
Philips	X	X	X	X	X	X	
Toshiba	X	X					
Yahoo!	X	X					
Canon			X	X	X	X	X
Snickers*			X	X	X		
Opel**			X	X		X	
Energizer				X			
Alfa Romeo					X		
Vini d'Italia					X		
Bata						X	
Cinzano						X	
R. J. Reynolds***						X	X
Seiko						X	X
Iveco							X
Metaxa							X

*   1990 Mars/M&M's
**   1994 General Motors
***   1986 Camel/ 1982 Winston

Source: FIFA *InfoPlus* http://eur.i1.yimg.com/eur.yimg.com/i/eu/fifa/do/paren.pdf retrieved 18 July 2006.

At the 1976 Olympic Games there were 628 sponsors and suppliers but only US$ 7 million in revenue was generated. For the 1984 games sponsorship was organized into three categories: 'Official Sponsors' (34), companies with 'supplier' rights (64) and 'licensees' (65). The IOC describes the 1984 Games as inaugurating the most successful era of corporate sponsorship in Olympic history.

In 1985 International Sport and Leisure (ISL), the most influential sports marketing agency throughout the 1980s and 1990s, drew on experience gained with FIFA when assisting the IOC to establish a lucrative marketing rights plan, The Olympic Partner (TOP) programme (Smit 2006; Sugden and Tomlinson 1998). The programme offers exclusive global marketing rights to a select group of corporate sponsors who pay a higher premium in exchange for the greater value flowing from an exclusive relationship with one of the world's leading sporting events. The attractiveness of the TOP programme to global corporations can be gauged from the fact that, as the IOC reports, 'the program enjoys one of the highest sponsorship renewal rates of any sports property'.[11] Over the 20-year period that the programme has been in existence the revenue generated from sponsorship agreements with a limited number of global corporate partners has grown significantly (Table 2).

Table 2: TOP global sponsorship programmes 1985–2008

	Olympiad	Partners	NOCs	USD million
TOP I	1985–1988	9	159	95
TOP II	1989–1992	12	169	175
TOP III	1993–1996	10	197	279
TOP IV	1997–2000	11	199	579
TOP V	2001–2004	11	202	603
TOP VI	2005–2008	11	202	866

Source: IOC Factsheet – Revenue Generation and Distribution December 2005 – http://www.olympic.org/uk/organisation/facts/introduction/100years_uk.asp# retrieved 17 July 2006.

Global sports events now take the form of recurring spectacular commercial media festivals. Consumer cultural events take place in which sports stars, and those elevated to an iconic global celebrity status, represent local and/or national communities. The celebrities serve as role models, as objects of adulation and identification, but also increasingly as exemplars of consumer life-styles to which spectators and television viewers alike are enticed to aspire. This is achieved through the marketing campaigns of sponsoring corporations seeking to promote their brands through association with the positive qualities displayed in popular sports competitions and expressed by sporting figures granted lucrative product endorsement contracts.

Concluding remarks: the serious business of global sport

Since the late nineteenth century, proceeding from England, the birthplace of modern sport, there has been a complex process of diffusion of sports around the world (Elias 1986; Mandell 1984). While in the course of the twentieth century a number of American sports, including grid-iron football, baseball, ice hockey and basketball, began to achieve a degree of popularity in some parts of the world, the difficulties and disappointments encountered to date in attempting to build a significant international following suggest that 'the outcome of globalization is less likely to be the hegemony of American sports' (Whitson 1998: 70; Leifer 1995). However, if global television ratings and levels of match attendance for American sports events held overseas have tended to be relatively disappointing, the extensive commercialization of sport that first became evident in America, exemplified by the cultivation of sport as an entertainment spectacle, developments in television sports broadcasting, and the extension of a culture of celebrity to include sports stars, seems destined to continue to exercise a powerful influence over any sport seeking to maintain its 'place in a mediated global culture' (Whitson 1998: 71; Leifer 1995).

Global sport is now a serious and increasingly financially rewarding business. In the mid-twentieth century concern was being expressed about the detrimental impact of increasing professionalism, seriousness and commercialism on sport's 'pure play-quality' or 'play-spirit' (Huizinga 1949). By the late 1970s, the 'intrusion of the market into every corner of the sporting scene' was considered to be promoting the degradation of sport (Lasch 1979: 117). At the close of the century, concern was being expressed about the challenges being posed to the institutions of sporting governance and sport's credibility by the global sport business (Katwala 2000).

Sport is now an established part of a globally extensive entertainment industry and sportsmen and sportswomen have eagerly embraced the notion that they have a responsibility not only to be successful in competition but also to entertain spectators and viewers by participating in the promotion of sport as spectacle. In turn, sportsmen and sportswomen have come to recognize that the global popularity and media profile that sporting success brings can deliver lucrative opportunities to them. This is done with the assistance of agents, advisers and media consultants who market their images to commercial corporations seeking to raise global awareness of their brands, increase their share of world markets, and gain an edge on the competition through association with prestigious sports events and celebrity sports stars. Global sports events and iconic global sporting celebrity figures have become increasingly important to the promotion of commodity consumption. This is achieved through displaying corporate logos and marketing campaigns at sports events, deploying sporting imagery and prestigious global sporting event trademarks in corporate advertising in the media, and involving the high-profile products of sports celebrities like Tiger Woods, David Beckham, Venus and Serena Williams and Maria Sharapova in product and brand promotion (Smart 2005).

More than 100 years ago it was noted that to expand global trade successfully and to exploit fully the market for goods and services around the world, it was necessary to give a 'cosmopolitan character to production and consumption in every country' (Marx and Engels 1968: 83). As the twentieth century unfolded, commercial corporations increasingly recognized that few if any cultural forms have as much potential to be cosmopolitan as modern sports. Sports are universal signifiers, they 'travel across borders', rise above differences of politics, culture and religion, and promote a positive feeling of shared experience and a sense of common meaning. They achieve this through the rituals of competitive play, themselves rendered universal by the formation of a global sporting network, to which the growth of media coverage and corporate sponsorship has made such a decisive contribution (Aris 1990).[12] The association of corporate logos, products and services with global sports events and iconic globally popular sporting figures increasingly accords a cosmopolitan character to production and consumption in every country.

At the beginning of the twentieth century it was remarked that the pursuit of business and wealth generation had acquired 'the character of sport' (Weber 1976: 182). By the end of the century the character of sport had been radically transformed, in substantial part by the corporate world, by transnational business activity and the global pursuit of wealth, and by the development of communications media and the growth of consumer culture (Sennett 2006). As modern sport has become global in scope it has largely lost its playful character and its professional practice has become both a global media spectacle and a serious and financially significant global business.

Notes

1. See also http://people.mills.edu/nscott/TennisHistory.html and http://www.all-about-tennis.com/history-of-tennis.html retrieved 13 June 2006.
2. See http://www.olympic.org/uk/organisation/noc/index_uk.asp and http://www.un.org/Overview/unmember.html retrieved 14 June 2006.
3. See http://www.sneakerhead.com/manufacture-converse.html retrieved 11 June 2006.
4. The tennis player Fred Perry employed a comparable approach to promote his brand of tennis clothing. The Fred Perry brand emerged at the end of the 1940s when Perry, an English tennis player who won the Wimbledon Singles title in 1934, 1935 and 1936, and was the first player to win all four Grand Slam titles, was persuaded to market a sweatband bearing his name. The Fred Perry sweatbands were marketed by giving them away to top players who wore them at tournaments. In 1952 the Fred Perry shirt with laurel logo was launched and successfully marketed in exactly the same way. Perry was not the only tennis player of his era to move into the production of sport and recreational clothing. René Lacoste, who won two Wimbledon, three French Open and two US Open singles titles before retiring in 1929, founded Lacoste to mass produce a shirt embroidered with a logo created for his personal use on the tennis courts (Smart 2005).
5. Late in 1926 C. C. 'Cash and Carry' Pyle offered the French tennis player Suzanne Lenglen $50,000 to tour the USA playing a series of matches against Mary K. Browne, the first American woman to play professional tennis. The tour was so successful that Lenglen was awarded a $25,000 bonus (Smart 2005).
6. See http://news.bbc.co.uk/sport1/hi/front_page/3035005.stm retrieved 10 June 2006.
7. See http://en.beijing-2008.org/87/55/article211635587.shtml retrieved 11 July 2006.
8. See http://eur.i1.yimg.com/eur.yimg.com/i/eu/fifa/do/tven.pdf retrieved 11 July 2006.

9. See http://eur.il.yimg.com/eur.yimg.com/i/eu/fifa/do/tven.pdf retrieved 11 July 2006 and http://www.fifa.com/en/marketing/newmedia/index/0,3509,10,00.html retrieved 2 January 2007.
10. As one of the chief executives of a commercial partner to both the IOC and FIFA, Scott McCune, director for worldwide sports at Coca-Cola, has stated, 'The Olympics and the World Cup are the only two [commercially significant sport] properties that are global and that people really care about' (Viscusi 2006).
11. See http://www.olympic.org/uk/organisation/facts/programme/sponsors_uk.asp retrieved 10 June 2006.
12. In his capacity as ISL's deputy managing director with responsibility for marketing the 1988 Olympic Games, Jurgen Lenz remarked that 'There are only four things that travel across borders: sport, music, violence and sex. And it's difficult to find sponsors for violence and sex' (cited in Aris 1990: 169).

References

Adidas (n.d.) 'Group history' at http://www.adidas-group.com/en/overview/history/default.asp retrieved 30 March 2006.

Annan, K. (2006) 'Football envy at the UN', *Guardian*, 12 June, p. 30.

Anonymous (2006) 'With one week to go, FIFA deny World Cup spoiled by money-making', *Espnstar.com*, http://www.espnstar.com/fworldcup/fworldcup_newsdetail_1691010.html retrieved 13 June 2006.

Aris, S. (1990) *Sportsbiz: inside the sports business*, London: Hutchinson.

Associated Press (2006) 'Adidas: Reebok deal poses challenge to Nike', 26 January, http://msnbc.msn.com/id/11026473/ retrieved 8 June 2006

Beck, U. (2000) *The brave new world of work*, Cambridge: Polity Press.

Betts, J. R. (1953) 'The technological revolution and the rise of sport, 1850–1900', *The Mississippi Valley Historical Review*, 40 (2) September, 231–56.

Bouchier, N. B. and J. E. Findling (1983) 'Little Miss Poker Face', in R. B. Browne and M. W. Fishwick (eds) *The hero in transition*, Bowling Green, OH: Bowling Green University Popular Press, 229–40.

Carlin, J. (2003) 'Rwanda's magic moment', *Guardian Unlimited*, Sunday 13 July, http://observer.guardian.co.uk/sport/story/0,6903,997414,00.html retrieved 30 November 2005.

Coakley, J. (2003) *Sport in society: issues and controversies*, New York. McGraw Hill.

Cone, J. (2006) 'Soccer World Cup final had sport's largest TV audience of 2006', http://bloomberg.com/apps/news?pid=20601077&sid=aOYdMOmxoV4c&refer=intsports retrieved 2 January 2007.

Coubertin, P. D. (1896) 'The Olympic Games: Athens 1896', *Olympic-Legacy.Com*, http://www.mediaconcerto.com/olympic/athens1896/coubertin_96.php retrieved 14 June 2006

Courier, J. (2004) 'Tennis is dependent on jet travel', *CNN.Com*, 6 December http://www.cnn.com/2004/TECH/12/02/explorers.jimcourier/index.html retrieved 21 June 2006.

Danzig, A. and P. Brandewein (eds) (1948) *Sport's golden age: a close-up of the fabulous twenties*, New York: Harper & Bros.

Eco, U. (1987) *Travels in hyper-reality*, London: Picador.

Elias, N. (1986) 'The genesis of sport as a sociological problem', in N Elias and E. Dunning (eds) *Quest for excitement: sport and leisure in the civilizing process*, Oxford: Blackwell, 126–49.

Flanders, J. (2006) *Consuming passions: leisure and pleasure in Victorian Britain*, London: Harper Press.

Gillmeister, H. (1998) *Tennis: a cultural history*, London: Leicester University Press.

Goldman R. (1983–4) '"We make weekends": leisure and the commodity form', *Social Text*, 8, 84–103.

Halberstam, D. (2001) *Playing for keeps: Michael Jordan and the world he made*, London: Yellow Jersey Press.

Hickey, G. (2000) 'Corporations love sports', *Insight on the News*, 13 November, http://www.findarticles.com/p/articles/mi_m1571/is_42_15/ai_72328785 retrieved 8 June 2006.

Huizinga, J. (1949) *Homo ludens: a study of the play element in culture*, London: Routledge & Kegan Paul.

Islam, F. (2006) 'Stripes versus swoosh in the marketing World Cup', *Observer*, 28 May, http://observer.guardian.co.uk/business/story/0,,1784544,00.html retrieved 26 June 2006.

Jarvie, G. (2006) *Sport, culture and society: an introduction*, London: Routledge.

Jones, G. (1984) 'The growth and performance of British multinational firms before 1939: the case of Dunlop', *The Economic History Review*, NS37, 35–53.

Katwala, S. (2000) *Democratising global sport*, London: The Foreign Policy Centre.

Katz, D. (1994) *Just do it: the Nike spirit in the corporate world*, Holbrook, MA: Adams Publishing.

Kelso, P. (2003) 'Sport's promoter McCormack dies', *Guardian*, 17 May, http://sport.guardian.co.uk/print/0,3858,4671001-108678,00.html retrieved 31 May 2006.

Klein, N. (2001) *No logo*, London: Flamingo.

Kuper, S. (2003) *Ajax, the Dutch, the war: football in Europe during the Second World War*, London: Orion.

Lasch, C. (1979) *The culture of narcissism: American life in an age of diminishing expectations*, London: WW Norton & Company.

Leach, W. (1994) *Land of desire: merchants, power, and the rise of a new American culture*, New York: Vintage Books.

Lee, J. K. (2005) 'Marketing and promotion of Olympic Games', *The Sport Journal*, 8, 3.

Leifer, E. M. (1995) *Making the majors: the transformation of team sports in America*, London: Harvard University Press.

Levine, P. (1985) *A. G. Spalding and the rise of baseball*, New York: Oxford University Press.

Lowenthal, L. (1961) *Literature, popular culture and society*, Englewood Cliffs, NJ: Prentice Hall.

McCall, J. (2004) 'Marketing opportunities for 2004 Olympics proved solid', *PR Week*, 30 August, http://www.prweek.com/us/login/required/220714 retrieved 23 June 2006.

Maguire, J. (1999) *Global sport: identities, societies, civilizations*, Cambridge: Polity.

Marx, K. and F. Engels (1968) *The Communist manifesto*, Harmondsworth: Penguin.

Maidment, P. (2006) 'For the sponsors, huge global exposure', *Forbes.com*, http://money.uk.msn.com/MyMoney/Insight/Special_Features/Pennywise/article.aspx?cp-documentid=553081 retrieved 13 June 2006.

Mandell, R. (1984) *Sport: a cultural history*, New York: Columbia University Press.

Marqusee, M. (2005) 'Cricket stamped with Murdoch footprint', *The Hindu*, 13 November, http://www.mikemarqusee.com/index.php?p=157 retrieved 13 March 2006.

Marqusee, M. (2006) 'New World Cup order', *Guardian*, 30 May 2006, 26.

Mason, T. (1989) 'Introduction', in T. Mason (ed.) *Sport in Britain: a social history*, Cambridge: Cambridge University Press, 1–11.

Polanyi, K. (1968) *The great transformation: the social and economic origins of our time*, Boston, MA: Beacon Press.

Pope, J. (2003) 'Gillette, NASCAR ink sponsorship pact', *USA Today*, 14 November.

Pope, S. W. (1997) *Patriotic games: sporting traditions in the American imagination*, New York: Oxford University Press.

Preuss, H. (2006) *The economics of staging the Olympics: a comparison of the Games 1972–2008*, Cheltenham: Edward Elgar.

Rader, B. (1983) *American sports: from the age of folk games to the age of spectators*, London: Prentice Hall.

Sandler, D. M. and D. Shani (1993) 'Sponsorship and the Olympic Games: the consumer perspective', *Sport Marketing Quarterly*, 2 (3) 38–43.

Sennett, R. (2006) *The culture of the new capitalism*, London: Yale University Press.

Shropshire, K. L. and T. Davis (2003) *The business of sports agents*, Philadelphia: University of Pennsylvania Press.

Smart, B. (2005) *The sport star: modern sport and the cultural economy of sporting celebrity*, London: Sage.

Smit, B. (2006) *Pitch invasion: Adidas and the making of modern sport*, London: Allen Lane.

Sugden, J. and A. Tomlinson (1998) *FIFA and the contest for world football*, Cambridge: Polity Press.

Sullivan, T. E. (2005) 'Sporting goods manufacturing', *Encyclopedia of Chicago* http://www.encyclopedia.chicagohistory.org/pages/1183.html retrieved 31 May 2006.

Vamplew, W. (1988) *Pay up and play the game: professional sport in Britain 1875–1914*, Cambridge: Cambridge University Press.

Van Bottenburg, M. (2001) *Global games*, Urbana: University of Illinois Press.

Viscusi, G. (2006) 'The high price of World Cup exposure', *Business Report and Independent Online*, 20 June, http://www.busrep.co.za/index.php?fArticleId=3299772&fSectionId=2515&fSetId=662 retrieved 19 July 2006.

Walker, H. (1989) 'Lawn tennis', in T. Mason (ed.) *Sport in Britain: a social history*, Cambridge: Cambridge University Press, 245–75.

Weber, M. (1976) *The Protestant ethic and the spirit of capitalism*, London: George Allen & Unwin.

Whitson, D. (1998) 'Circuits of promotion: media, marketing and the globalization of sport', in L. A. Wenner (ed.) *MediaSport*, London: Routledge, 57–72.

Yallop, D. (1999) *How they stole the game*, London: Poetic Publishing.

3

The grobal in the sporting glocal

DAVID L. ANDREWS AND GEORGE RITZER

It is the responsibility of any true intellectual leader to challenge, provoke, and stimulate debate, which is something David Rowe (2003) unquestionably achieved in his article 'Sport and the repudiation of the global'. Looking to re-animate the stagnating globalization of sport debate, Rowe called into question widely acknowledged assumptions pertaining to the constitutive interdependence of the (sporting) global and the (sporting) local. This he achieved by contesting sport's ability to 'resonate at the global level' and argued that sport may, in fact, 'be unsuited to carriage of the project of globalization in its fullest sense' (Rowe 2003: 281). His position was prefigured on sport's importance as an enduring emotive marker of local (communal, regional, national) belonging and identification. Specifically, sport's 'constant evocation of the nation as its anchor point and rallying cry' evidences its 'affective power', making it impossible for sport to be 'reconfigured as postnational and subsequently stripped of its "productive" capacity to promote forms of identity' (Rowe 2003). Accordingly, sport's symbiotic relationship with 'localized, nationally inflected forms of identity' make it antithetical to the process of globalization; the emergence of supra-national social systems and institutions that transcend the local in establishing a post-particular global order (Rowe 2003).

Suitably roused, within this discussion we provide a counterpoint to Rowe's provocations; not least because critical engagement is the sincerest form of intellectual flattery, but also since his repudiation of the very possibility of the sporting global falsely polarizes globalization and localization in a manner that implicitly privileges, perhaps even romanticizes, the local. Thus, our aim is to challenge this tendency observable within the sociology of sport, and more broadly in the literature on globalization in general, including that within cultural studies. For, as Grossberg noted:

> Current thinking about globalization is too often structured by an assumed opposition between the local and the global, where the local is offered as the intellectual and political corrective of the global. This is captured in the popular demand to "think globally and act locally" ... Such celebrations of the

local are often under-theorised, based on either a particular definition of knowledge as facts and a model of inductive empiricism, or an assumed identification of the local with the site of agency and resistance.

(Grossberg 1997: 8)

Rather than articulating the global and the local as polarities upon the globalization continuum (an approach which virtually necessitates the privileging of one pole over the other), it is important to view the 'complementary and interpenetrative' relations linking homogenization and heterogenization, universalism and particularism, sameness and difference, and the global and the local; the global being complicit in the 'creation and incorporation' of the local, and *vice versa* (Robertson 1995). There are, of course, a number of examples of sport-related research that have explored the constitutive interdependence of the (sporting) global and the (sporting) local. For instance: Houlihan (1994: 357) highlighted the differential exposure to, and reception of, globalizing sport forms within contrasting local cultural contexts; Donnelly (1996) stressed the need to reassert the 'articulation between the local and the global'; Miller et al. (2001) provided countless examples of the interconnective, yet productive, tensions between global corporate capital and local sport cultures; and, Maguire (1999, 2000) exhaustively explicated the multidirectional and multicausal aspects of global–local sporting interdependencies.

While the aforementioned represent important contributions to understanding the global–local nexus as it pertains to sport, this strand of inquiry has yet to be exhausted. Returning to Grossberg, there is a general recognition that 'the local and the global are mutually constitutive, although the exact nature of this "mutual constitution" remains to be specified, and has yet to be adequately theorized' (Grossberg 1997: 9). Given the applicability of such an observation to the sociology of sport, this project accents the need for globalization theorists to fully engage the complexities and variations issuing from the constitutive inter-relationship between the global and the local. In looking to further the understanding of the contemporary sporting landscape, we offer an alternative approach that counters the tendency to fetishize the local by reinscribing the influence of the *global* in shaping structures, practices, and experiences of the local. In doing so, we illustrate some (if by no means all) of the variants through which global–local forces and tensions become manifest within the sporting realm.

The dominant perspective on this issue, most associated with the work of Roland Robertson, is the idea of the glocal (and the process of glocalization) involving the integration of the local and the global (similar terms in the literature are 'hybridization' and 'creolization'). However, this ignores a second key idea – the grobal (and grobalization) – that highlights the fact that there are global processes that overwhelm the local rather than neatly integrating the two. Given these two terms, the key dynamic in the process of globalization shifts from the tension between the local and the global to that between the glocal and the grobal: whereas glocalization theorists view cultural forms as practices as operating in a constant tension between the global and the local, we view the terms grobal and glocal more instructive in this regard.

This is based on the assumption that virtually no 'areas and phenomena throughout the world are unaffected by globalization' (Ritzer 2004: xiii). This implies the declining, or even disappearing, relevance of the local and the need to reconceptualize virtually everything we think of as local as glocal. Rather than viewing the core tension as existing being between the global and the local, and certainly as evidenced within the sporting realm, our contention is that the *local* has been so effected by the *global*, that it has become, at all intents and purposes, *glocal* (Ritzer 2004: xiii, xi). Thus, the processual and empirical continuum through which we conceptualize globalization is bounded by *grobalization* ('the imperialistic ambitions of nations, corporations, organizations, and the like and their desire, indeed need, to impose themselves on various geographic areas') and *glocalization* ('the interpenetration of the global and the local, resulting in unique outcomes in different geographic areas'): the *grobal* and the *glocal* (Ritzer 2006: 338, 337).

However, the local persists in the glocal and grobalizing forces can never be totally triumphant over the glocal; they are not, and could never be, universal in scale and scope. However, simply because of the impossibility of a grobal monoculture in sport, or any other cultural realm for that matter, it would be injudicious to summarily repudiate, à la Rowe (2003), any meaningful influence of the grobal in favour of a privileging of the glocal, let alone the local. Hence, within the following sections, we briefly discuss four suggestive sporting scenarios, and illustrate the manner in which they exhibit – in varying inflections and to varying intensities – the necessary, but never guaranteed, interpenetrative relationship between the grobal and the glocal.

Indigenous incorporation

Contemporary sport represents a particularly complex, and at times contradictory, domain. In one sense, there is a compelling case to be made for sport being the 'most universal aspect of popular culture' (Miller et al. 2001: 1); virtually all contemporary societies incorporate, and in many cases strongly identify with, some form of competitively-based, popular physical culture. While sport's very ubiquity suggests its grobal scope, its uneven social resonance points to the importance of glocal particularities in shaping the contours of the sporting landscape. Hence, the appeal of the glocalization thesis is apparent. However, adherence to it limits the ability to explain the complexities underpinning the development of the modern sport order. Put another way, sport's evolution is simply more complex than that which involves the interpenetration of the global and the local.

Pre-modern sport forms could certainly be considered local; they were focused around substantively distinct, place bound, and organically conceived, controlled, and experienced physical cultural practices. As such, the pre-modern sporting landscape was comprised of a patchwork of localized game forms that, although displaying significant common elements, were sufficiently distinct (localized) according to local rules and customs so as to prohibit them acquiring wider resonance and mobility. The initial stages of the transformation from pre-modern particularity to today's post-particular, universalized (grobalized) sport system can be traced to eighteenth and nineteenth century Britain (Bottenburg 2001; Elias and Dunning 1986; Guttmann 1978; Holt 1989a). The nation's position at the forefront of the socially, politically, economically, and culturally transformative processes of urbanization and industrialization, led to the standardization, codification, and bureaucratization of many traditional sport forms first occurring within the British context. Britain's imperial reach and aspirations (and such 'imperialism' lies at the heart of grobalization) at this time subsequently led to its popular sport forms (particularly association football, cricket, field hockey, and rugby, but also, boxing, golf, horse racing, rowing, track and field athletics, and tennis) becoming globally diffused along complex chains of global interdependency (Maguire 1999) which derived from, and indeed helped facilitate, intensifying colonial and/or commercial relationships forged between Britain and the rest of the world. Britain – particularly during what Hobsbawm (1989) described as the Age of Empire, 1875–1914 – acted as a forceful agent of grobalization in seeking to impose itself, and its interests, economically, militarily, politically, and culturally, around the globe.

The modern sport forms developed within a British context were subsequently spread and legitimated through what were expansive imperial and commercial networks; sport thus becoming a vehicle and expression of British-led grobalizing forces. These sports were differentially popularized according to the nature, and thereby the social constitution and sporting habitus, of the British incursion (Bottenburg 2001: 176). Cricket's elite social habitus made it an important vehicle for the advancement of the British imperial project. Since '"Playing the game" was a combined physical and moral activity, and exercise in the art of being "British"' (Holt 1989b: 236), it was used as a vehicle for embodying and imposing the physical and cultural superiority of the colonizer over the colonized. Conversely, the working-class demeanour of association football (by the late nineteenth century it had outgrown its patrician beginnings), meant commercial and trade links were the 'most propitious outlets' in the export of the game to the rest of the world. Thus, the sizeable British working-class diaspora of manual labourers, combined with the influence of expatriate artisans, teachers, and cosmopolitans, helped establish the game wherever their roving employment took them (Giulianotti 1999).

Regardless of the particular forces responsible for the grobal diffusion of 'British' sporting practices, their rapid intrusion into foreign climes created grobal–local sporting tensions. The spread of this incipient universal sport order resulted in the displacement of many localized traditional pastimes, and their replacement by, what were, alien sport forms. However, local sporting cultures did not disappear, they became glocal. In other words, within many national cultural contexts, newly transplanted sport forms were rapidly popularized and incorporated into local (communal, regional, but primarily national) sporting cultures and soon became perceived and experienced as authentic or natural expressions of cultural collectivity. The indigenous incorporation of alien sport forms into the local resulted in the British provenance of many modern sport forms being rapidly obscured, if sometimes never wholly forgotten. For instance, C. L. R. James' (1963) classic account of cricket in the West Indies vividly illustrated the transformation of an imposed or transplanted sporting practice into a local context. Initially an embodied symbol of British colonialism, James illustrated how cricket's enthusiastic and creative appropriation by the West Indies' populace rendered it an emotive and embodied expression of self-identification and – ironically but not surprisingly – cultural resistance over the colonial power from whence the game originated (see also Beckles 1998). A similar scenario was also enacted in India, where the gradual indigenous appropriation and incorporation of the game into the Indian sense of self, ultimately resulted in cricket's position and influence as a central part of the 'colonial ecumene' becoming so eroded that the very 'idea of the [*independent*] Indian nation emerged as a salient cricketing entity' (Appadurai 1996: 91, 97, italics added). Given its more widespread diffusion, there are even more examples of organic glocalization within the football world, where the acknowledged 'global game' (Giulianotti 1999) simultaneously exists and operates as a source of collective identity and pride for the national populaces, in numerous locations, at one and the same time.

The grobalization of sport was further instituted during the late nineteenth and early twentieth centuries with the emergence of the international sporting organizations and competitions, national governing bodies and leagues, that structured, regulated, and administered sport at regional, national, and international levels. The establishment of the International Rugby Board (originally the International Rugby Football Board) in 1886, the International Olympic Committee in 1896, the *Fédération Internationale de Football Association* in 1904, the International Cricket Council (originally the Imperial Cricket Council) in 1909, the International Association of Athletics Federations in 1912, and the *Fédération Internationale de Basketball* in 1932, created the universal institutional architecture to which national sporting bodies were compelled to adhere if they desired to be included within the international community of sporting nations. Hence, with regard to participation and spectatorship, sport mirrored, and helped literally embody, broader grobalizing trends pertaining to the hegemony of the nation-state as the organizing structure of modern society (Hobsbawm 1990). It also proved to be the regulated embodiment, and affirming expression, of the distinctly Western (specifically North Atlantic) values of competition, progress, and achievement; modern values which, unsurprisingly, simultaneously underpin the liberal democratic, urban industrialist, and market capitalist societies from whence the modern sport order emerged.

Corporate re-constitution

The first phase of sporting grobalization created a universal structure for sport within which glocal (national) sporting traditions flourished: 'distinctive corporeal techniques, playing styles, aesthetic codes, administrative structures and interpretive vocabularies' (Giulianotti and Robertson 2004: 549). This 'universalization of particularism' (Robertson 1992: 100) has become a core feature of the second phase of sport's grobalization; that in which, from the mid-twentieth century onwards, imperial capitalism has increasingly been replaced by 'late', or cultural, capitalism as the motor of grobal change (Jameson 1991, 1998). According to the precepts of late capitalism, 'culture is integral to the economy; it provides the economy with a new dynamic, a new source of growth, a new world of possibilities for profit and for control' (McRobbie 2005: 155). So, in the second half of the twentieth century, sport (initially in the United States and Canada, subsequently in Western Europe, Japan, Australasia and beyond) became commandeered by the advancing late capitalist order (a key grobalizing force), and became evermore aggressively structured in a manner which placed economic (profit maximization) ahead of sporting (utility maximization) motives. Not that sport was previously devoid of any commercial association; however, the magnitude of sport's post-war commercial reformation was certainly unprecedented, as it became irreversibly incorporated into the workings of global capitalism.

Today, virtually all aspects of the global sport institutions (governing bodies, leagues, teams, events, and individual athletes) are now un-selfconsciously driven and defined by the inter-related processes of: corporatization (the management and marketing of sporting entities according to profit motives); spectacularization (the primacy of producing of entertainment-driven [mediated] experiences); and, com-modification (the generation of multiple sport-related revenue streams). Moreover, since sport cultures around the world have become evermore subject to revision by this late capitalist strain of grobalization, sport's institutional infrastructure is beginning to reflect a high degree of global uniformity. Geographically disparate examples of the corporate sport modality (Andrews 1999, 2006; McKay and Miller 1991) now openly embrace a profit-driven managerial structure and marketing orientation. That contemporary sport (leagues, teams/ franchises, tournaments/events) should display high levels of organizational commonality can be attributed to the commercially-driven corporation becoming the primary organizing institution of late capitalist society. The commercial corporation is, effectively, the institutional vehicle through which late capitalism has become grobal; corporatized elements such as sport (education, religion, and health domains being equally applicable in this regard) becoming both a product, and an important process facilitating the grobalization of late capitalism.

Despite corporate sport's grobalized/grobalizing countenance, in many senses it remains inveterately glocal. Whereas earlier phases in the instantiation of global economic relations attempted (with limited success) to engage the global marketplace as a unitary, un-differentiated entity, the cultural orientation of late capitalism has led to a recognition and embracement, however superficial, of the particularities of the micro (city, region, or indeed, nation-based) marketplace. Presently, transnational strategizing involves the mobilization of the cultural differences earlier forms of global strategizing had sought to overcome (Dirlik 1996: 29; Morley and Robins 1995). Many sport organizations may be grobal in their scale (through their very corporate structure) and scope (constantly looking to extend market geographies through team and/or broadcast expansion); nevertheless, much of their commercial strategizing focuses on sport's enduring capacity for stimulating popular (consumer) consciousness and behaviour at the glocal level. This is especially true of sport teams/ franchises (be they in the National Football League, English Premier League, or

Super 14 competitions), which collectively comprise a glocal sport economy of particular versions (the individual teams/franchises) of a 'very general phenomenon' (Robertson 1995: 40); the particularity of which is routinely constituted through contrived and formulaic appeals to some form of indigenous sporting and cultural authenticity, be that linked to their 'home' constituencies or the external markets they seek to penetrate through various international initiatives (Giulianotti and Robertson 2004).

More generally acknowledged transnational corporations (for that is what major sport teams/franchises have become) are perhaps even more adept at shaping and using glocal sport practices, symbols, and celebrities as conduits for realizing their grobal ambitions; ensuring their corporate footprints transcend the boundaries of nation-states, by operating 'simultaneously in different countries around the world, on a global scale' (Morley and Robins 1995: 223). Rather than seeking to neuter cultural difference through a strategic global uniformity, these transnational corporations have acknowledged that securing a profitable global presence necessitates operating in the languages of the local. This frequently involves the appropriation, within marketing campaigns, of evocative aspects of the local culture – such as glocalized sport practices, teams, and celebrities – as a means of ingratiating the transnational brand within the glocal context, and thereby interpellating glocal consumers. Interestingly, both sport-related (i.e. Adidas, Nike, Reebok) and non-sport (i.e. Coca-Cola, McDonalds, Vodafone) corporations, have mobilized sport's unparalleled position as a vehicle of glocal identification and resonance, during the process of becoming transnational (Amis and Cornwell 2005; Jackson and Hokowhitu 2002; Silk and Andrews 2005; Silk et al. 2005). Nike is a particularly interesting case in this regard because, within certain contexts, the corporation is positioned as being unequivocally grobal. As Nike's co-founder, and then CEO, Phil Knight stated:

> We want the brand to stand for the same thing all over the world. We don't want the brand to be different in Europe or Asia, but we know that is not easy … I accept our Americanism with an asterisk. Our goal is to be a global company. We will never duck our American heritage, and that's not a bad place to be. As a friend of mine once said to me, America and sports is like France and cooking.

> (Quoted in Hatfield 2003)

This sentiment can be contrasted with the glocalized nature of much of Nike's advertising, which either through universal, or more geographically focused campaigns, offers a multi-accented vision of the Nike brand (Silk and Andrews 2001). Evident within Nike's engagement with its major national markets, this transnational sporting glocalization is perhaps best exemplified within a recent campaign for Nike Japan. The campaign developed by Wieden and Kennedy-Tokyo is focused on encouraging Bukatsu, the Japanese school sports club system, and thereby youth sport participation in general (in a manner not dissimilar from Nike's global 'Just Do It' or 'I Can' campaigns). However, the means by which this is communicated are unambiguously domestic. The entire campaign is centred around the birth and exploits of an anthropomorphized breaded pork cutlet, created in the kitchen of the archetypal Japanese grandmother. Within a series of television commercials this, doubtless, staple part of Japanese home cooking: jostles while training with Japanese soccer star Junichi Inamoto; plays one-on-one basketball while its shedded breading covers the court floor; and, creates similar problems while running in a high school track race. The peculiar juxtaposition between the traditional food item and youth sport participation is explained by the fact that the Japanese for breaded pork cutlet is *Katsu-kun*, and *Katsu* also means to win. Hence, the *double entendre* proves meaning-ful for the local initiate.

As with transnational campaigns in general, Nike's *Katsu-kun* campaign asserts the 'new dynamics of *re*-localization' (Morley and Robins 1995: 115) wherein indigenous cultures become imagined through the commercially inspired inflections of the local. Thus, grobal entities such as Nike are responsible for instantiating multiple glocals, in a manner which 'does not mean any serious recognition of the autonomy of the local' but is intended to recognize and advance superficial and largely caricatured 'features of the local so as to incorporate localities into the imperatives of the global' (Dirlik 1996: 34). All of which points to the fundamental grobal–glocal problematic, that cultures, both national and sporting, are increasingly being constituted by an external and commercially propelled locus of control; the glocal thus being imagined and authenticated 'from above or outside' since much 'of what is often declared to be local is in fact the local expressed in terms of generalized recipes of locality' (Robertson 1995).

Universal differentiation

Williams (1994: 377) has charged sport (specifically what he termed 'sporting "muzak"') as being a major contributor to the 'flattening out of difference in post-organized capitalism' through the indiscriminate global dissemination of sports 'taken from localized cultural contexts'. Countering this explicitly grobal position, there is an argument to be made that, rather than producing a sporting monoculture, high profile 'global sport spectacles' (Tomlinson 2005: 59) have been co-opted into the apparatus of grobal-glocal capitalism, such that they actually contribute toward the 'constant reinvention of particularity' associated with the process of glocality (Giulianotti 2005: 204). There are a number of sporting spectacles that superficially unite the world's populace in acclamation for sport in general (namely the Olympic Games or the Commonwealth Games), or for a particular sport (namely the FIFA Men's World Cup or the IAAF World Championships), or for a particular nation (the NFL Super Bowl). However, such institutionalized and spectacularized paeans to sporting universalism are misleading and inaccurate (c.f. Martin and Reeves 2001), since these globally disseminated events actually contribute, in a glocal sense, to the instantiation of what Maguire (1999, 2006) characterized as being a condition of diminishing contrasts and increasing varieties, and that which Robertson (1992: 102) referred to as the 'particularization of universalism'.

The grobal penetration of Olympic Games television coverage is remarkable, with worldwide audience figures for the 2004 Athens Olympics approaching 3.5 billion individual viewers; meaning approximately 60 per cent of the world's population watched an Olympic broadcast at least once (Wilson 2004). However, the grobal commonality nurtured by these sporting 'mega-events' (Roche 2000) is more a spectacular unity-in-difference, than a serious contribution to global homogenization. Rather than transcending them as was the original, if naïve intent (Guttmann 2002), today's staged presentations, and mediated representations, of the Olympic Games have consistently been forums for the accommodation and advancement of highly nationalized interests and concerns. As Tomlinson noted, illustrating the implicit strategic glocalization of the modern Olympic phenomenon in its late capitalist incarnation, 'the allegedly pure Olympic ideal has always been moulded into the image of the time and place of the particular Olympiad or Games' (Tomlinson 1996: 599).

Grobal in reach and philosophy, the Olympic Games are inveterately glocal in performance. Nowhere is this glocality better exhibited than in the highly chor-eographed spectacle of the game's opening ceremonies (Hogan 2003; Tomlinson 1996, 2005). Although making perfunctory reference to the modern Olympics' internationalist origins through a 'quota of Olympic-style spirit–youth, universalism, peace, and the like' (Tomlinson 2005: 11), the interpretive programmes within opening ceremonies, and indeed the structure and delivery of the games as a whole, speak to the 'staging of the nation' for internal and external audiences (Hogan 2003). The former is motivated by a need to advance historical, contemporaneous, and aspirational senses of self for an expectant, and potentially politically malleable, home audience (Silk 2002). The latter is prompted by the need to spectacularize, through 'place marketing' strategies, urban/national space as a mechanism for stimulating tourism and other forms of global capital investment (Whitson and Macintosh 1993, 1996; Wilson 1996), within what is a 'period of intense inter-urban competition and urban entrepreneurialism' (Waitt 1999: 1061).

Despite being at the forefront of a 'worldwide sport culture given an unpre-cedented profile in the mediated global culture' (Tomlinson 2005: 36), even in terms of regular Olympic television broadcasts, glocal cultural proclivities often impinge upon the mediated grobal spectacle. Most of the television coverage of such events is selected from the international feeds of the host broadcaster. Those nations with sufficient economic and technological resources are able to locally embellish the generic coverage – much of which is bound up with the host's 'presentation of self' to the global (tourist and commercial) marketplace (Silk 2001: 297) – through preferred event and athlete selection, customized commentary, expert analysis, and feature segments. The largest client broadcasters also utilize their own 'unilateral' cameras in order to better address the Olympic preferences of their national viewership (MacNeill 1996; Silk 2001; Silk and Amis 2000). In MacNeill's (1996) terms, this demonstrates how realizing a spectacle of accumulation (based on revenues tied to viewership) is significantly related to it also being a spectacle of legitimation (corroborates normalized discourses pertaining to sport, the nation, and their relation). Hence, global coverage of the Olympic Games results in myriad different glocal representations of the Olympic spectacle, linked to a concomitant multiplicity in terms of the different ways the Olympics are lived at the glocal level (Bernstein 2000; Knight et al. 2005; Spa et al. 2003). Depending on the venue, partner broadcasters also frequently look to incorporate and mobilize difference within their coverage through recourse to the Otherness (social, cultural, historical, political, and/or geographic) of the host location. Such broadcasts of sport spectacles thus adopt both interiorized and exteriorized forms of strategic glocalization, in that they simultaneously seek to customize coverage to internal indigenous markets, while embellishing it through recourse to aspects of external (pertaining to the host context) local differences (Silk 2001).

Corporate sport's glocal underpinnings are equally evident in the strategies of the transnational broadcasters, and corporate entities, for whom sport is a highly resonant and effective means of incorporating 'localities into the imperatives of the global' (Dirlik 1996: 34). Among the grobally-oriented media oligarchies (McChesney 1997), Rupert Murdoch's News Corporation is arguably the most informed and aggressive mobilizer of the sporting glocal. Paraphrasing Chyi and Sylvie (2001), while News Corporation's television network is grobal, its sporting content is deliberately not. News Corporation has consistently used sport to facilitate what are effectively glocal growth strategies, (Andrews 2003; Herman and McChesney 1997). As an archetypal transnational corporation, News Corporation recognized the importance of incorporating elements of localized difference and particularity within their grobal strategizing (Morley and Robins 1995; Robertson 1995). As Murdoch himself outlined:

> You would be very wrong to forget that what people want to watch in their own country is basically local programming, local language, local culture … I learned that many, many years ago in Australia, when I was loading up … with good American programs and we'd get beat with second-rate Australian ones.
>
> (Quoted in Schmidt 2001: 79)

Sport was identified as commanding 'unparalleled viewer loyalty in all markets' and could therefore be used as a 'battering ram' to enter media markets more effectively, and indeed rapidly, than any other entertainment genre (Murdoch 1996). Nationally inflected sport coverage (i.e. EPL in the United Kingdom, NFL in the USA) thus provided a mechanism for inserting what were new and unfamiliar television broadcast platforms (BSkyB and Fox respectively), into indigenous cultures. Within these and other national broadcast contexts, News Corporation exemplifies the very essence of corporate transnationality; its sport-oriented 'environmental scanning' (Gershon 2000: 83) underpinning strategies through which it is able to seamlessly operate within the language of the sporting glocal, simultaneously, in multiple locations (Dirlik 1996: Silk and Andrews 2001).

Dichotomous agency

It should not be overlooked that individuals, and indeed groups, do have the opportunity to 'adapt, innovate, and maneuver' within the sporting world we have outlined (Ritzer 2006: 337). In other words, and paraphrasing Marx's maxim, people do make their own grobal–glocal sporting lives, but not in the conditions of their own choosing. One's ability to act with some degree of autonomy is contingent on the contemporaneous nature of grobal–glocal relations, and the individual/group's particular social, political, and/or economic location. Nevertheless, there are numerous examples where popular resistance to corporate sport has become mobilized and expressed through locally inspired antagonisms toward the forces and expressions of sporting grobalism (as well as glocalism).

Returning to News Corporation's prototypical glocal sport strategizing, the market uncertainties implicit within the sport media economy – particularly the imponderables surrounding bidding wars for television broadcasting rights – galvanized News Corporation's vertical integration agenda (Schmidt 2001), and led to investments in sport leagues, teams, and stadia ownership. These provided News Corporation with a position of ascendancy within the television rights fees scramble, since the purchasing or establishment of sport leagues relinquishes the need to bid for television rights, while the ownership of sport teams puts media corporations in the advantageous position of negotiating with themselves. In addition, the control afforded by sport property ownership also provides networks with the ability to generate significant revenue from the migration of game coverage to lucrative pay-per-view television platforms: something central to News Corporation's long-term transnational strategizing (Herman and McChesney 1997; Murdoch 1996). News Corporation's initial phase of vertically integrating its sport media empire came within the sport of rugby league in both Australia and the United Kingdom. While the transformation of the economically floundering but highly traditional British Rugby Football League (RFL) into the fully-corporatized Super League under the stewardship of BSkyB (News Corporation's subsidiary in the British television market) represents an interesting case study of grobal–glocal sporting tensions (Denham 2000; Falcous 1998), concomitant developments within Australian rugby league provide a better illustration of the glocal response to grobalizing forces, or perceptions thereof (Grainger and Andrews 2005; Phillips and Hutchins 2003).

In April 1995, and aware of the need to generate popular programming content for its new Foxtel pay television platform, News Corporation invested AUS$500 million in a Super League, made up of six teams comprised of elite players prized away from the rival Australian Rugby League (ARL) owned by Kerry Packer. Two rival leagues proved unsustainable in the Australian market leading, in December 1997, to the ARL-Super League merger to form the National Rugby League (NRL). Owned in equal partnership between the Murdoch and Packer camps, like its British counterpart, the Australian Super League initiative paid due deference to contemporary sport's grobalizing proclivity, through seeking to rationalize and modernize the game along strictly commercial lines (Crowe 1999; McGaughey and Liesch 2002; McKay and

Rowe 1997). The most significant consequence of the ARL-Super League union was a 'program of club rationalization', the most prominent casualty of which appeared to be the storied South Sydney Rabbitohs club (nicknamed the Souths), which was slated to be closed due to its lack of profitability (Phillips and Hutchins 2003: 225). Thus News Corporation wielded the axe on one of the original, and most celebrated and successful, teams in Australian rugby league history (Grainger and Andrews 2005). Fortunately for the Souths, there was a widespread backlash against the decision to deny the club entry into the new NRL. Since the club had a long established relationship with the working-class, Redfern, community from whence it originated, the Souths' travails came to be seen as something of a metaphor for working-class communities in Australia in general. According to Rabbitohs' legend, George Piggins, an 80,000 strong protest march on 12 November 2000 in support of the club's reinstatement, included many people 'who had no interest in rugby league. They were there because what had happened to us was a symbol of what was happening elsewhere in Australia ... as giant corporations cut and closed, downsized and played havoc with the lives of ordinary people' (Piggins 2002: 290).

As well as being emblematic of the demise of the Australian working class, Souths also became a medium for the expression of wider anti-grobalization, pro-'Australian', sentiment. There existed a burgeoning resentment toward the expanding infiltration and influence of grobal corporate values and interests in general. Piggins continued, 'Many ordinary Aussies, football fans or not, saw us as part of a much bigger picture – a society in which economic rationalism and corporatisation and globalization had already had a crushing effect on many' (Piggins 2002: 230). Within the Australian rugby league context, Murdoch came to be seen as the ruthless face of grobal capitalism; Souths the core Australian 'values and attitudes that mean little to the game's new paymasters' (Hadfield 1999: 7).

That there should be an organized popular resistance to such rationalized grobal sporting initiatives is telling in and of itself, regardless of whether it had any influence on the club's eventual success in the Australian Federal Court which led to its forced reinstatement in the NRL in March 2002. Nevertheless, it is less clear whether the Souths reinstatement was indeed a telling example of resistance to grobalization. What on the surface appears to be a 'glocal alternative' may in fact have become an example of the grobalization of cultural processes and practices that exudes the *nothingness* associated with grobality, meaning, as Ritzer (2004: 3) puts it 'a social form that is generally centrally conceived, controlled, and comparatively devoid of distinctive substantive content'. For example, there is a very real possibility that the Souths' (re)incorporation into the league could ultimately lead to the club's traditional working-class, community-based identity becoming diminished in the face of the NRL's aggressive corporatization, spectacularization, and commodification. For, 'revivals of anything local, especially those that are successful, are likely to be grobalized and thereby lose their local character' (Ritzer 2004: 170).

Grobal sport processes, practices, and artefacts can frequently be subject to forms of defensive resistance by glocal constituencies. Conversely, there are also instances where grobal artefacts and practices are mobilized as *de facto* expressions of opposition to the sporting glocal; the importation and mobilization of externally derived expressions of sporting difference can act as expressions of resistance within, and indeed toward, a glocal context. For those sport consumers looking to express their alterity from the cultural mainstream, the aim is to provide the opportunity to consume the sporting Other. Within many settings, this revolves around the engagement with expressions of American popular culture, or Americana (Jones 1988; Lealand 1988). Far from seeking to realize a sporting monoculture, the exportation of American sport forms – even more than the American film and music genres that have become the cultural vernacular of the global popular (Kellner 2003) – represent a potential source of identity rooted in difference and opposition for, predominantly, youth and young adults located in disparate national settings (Andrews et al. 1996). The complicating factor being, the sense of sporting and aesthetic American Otherness communicated in, and through, these exports is by no means uniform in its cultural significance, nor in the manner in which it is consumed at the local level. As Van Elteren (1996) noted, there are 'multifarious, and often complex ways in which US popular culture forms [*and indeed the very idea of America itself*] are mediated and received abroad among various audiences and in diverse local contexts'. Nevertheless, the complexity of the relationship between the grobal and the glocal is once again underscored, for as the sporting grobal (in the guise of a New York Yankees cap or a Manchester United shirt) is performed as part of a culturally alternative youth identity, so the perceived traditional elements of the sporting glocal are normatively reasserted.

Conclusion

Through this discussion we have examined sporting scenarios that exhibit – in varying ways and to varying intensities – the necessary, but never guaranteed, interpenetrative nature of the relationship between the sporting grobal and the sporting glocal. Such relationships are never easy to discern. Witness Manchester United's supporters', at times, violent and vitriolic response to the club's purchase by the American businessman, Malcolm Glazer. Although intuitively tempting to view this as a clash between grobal and local interests, the Manchester United–Glazer conflict actually encompasses a tertiary phase of sporting grobalization being confronted by an already glocalized sport culture, which has convinced itself of its own organic local-ness:

> You get the impression [*from the vociferous anti-Glazer response*] that Manchester United has been run as some sort of worker's cooperative or hippie commune for the benefit of mankind. And it hasn't. The fact that one rich man owns it now, and a different rich man owned it last week will make no difference at all to these fans, no difference whatsoever. They've had no say in the running of the club, they've still got no say in the running of the club.
> (Mick Dennis, *Daily Express* journalist, on Simon Mayo Show, BBC Radio 5, 20 May 2005)

Manchester United fans are by no means the only constituency to have fallen foul of fetishizing the sporting glocal, by not acknowledging the grobal relations complicit in the structure and experience of contemporary sport forms. This affliction is also in evidence within the sociology of sport community. Under the influence of what has become a persuasive glocal hegemony within the sport literature – and itself prompted by the celebratory populism that pervades much cultural analysis (McGuigan 1997) – many researchers are transfixed with identifying, and subsequently seeking to rescue, the residues of the sporting local. The inference of such projects would appear to be that the organically local, sporting or otherwise, is somehow actively resistant to the forces of globalization. Within a late capitalist world dominated and driven by expressions of *nothingness*, sporting *somethings*, described by Ritzer (2004:7) as 'a social form that is generally indigenously conceived, controlled, and comparatively rich in distinctive substantive content', are a virtual impossibility. Therefore, the rescuing and resuscitating of the sporting local represents a highly questionable form of oppositional intellectual practice. Blinded by the political potentialities of the sporting local, many researchers cannot extricate themselves (even if they wanted to), from the binary logic of the global–local relation. It is in this sense that Grossberg referred to theory as letting researchers 'off the hook', by providing interpretive logics, and indeed frameworks, through which researcher's *a priori* assumptions are confirmed through their filtered engagement with the empirical (Grossberg 1992: 113). Rather than replicating such tautologous theorizing, within this discussion we have sought to disrupt the global–local hegemony by both problematizing the very possibility of the local within conditions of intensive and extensive globalization (leading to the concept of the glocal), and simultaneously reinscribing the importance of the global (through the concept of the grobal). The complexity and variability within the grobal-glocal schema encourages one to excavate the 'continuities and differences' (Giulianotti and Robertson 2004: 562) which mark the multitudinous expressions of sporting globalization. As such, it represents a more useful and insightful model for examining the contemporary sporting popular.

The issues addressed here in the study of sport are repeated in work on many other areas of the social world, especially as they relate to globalization. There is a widespread tendency to glorify the power of the actor, the local and more recently the glocal. As a result, the importance of the global, or more specifically what is called here the grobal, tends to denigrated. There is no question that the actors, local and glocal are important, but it would seem unquestionable that the grobal is also of great importance. A more fully adequate analysis of globalization needs to examine the interrelationship among all four (if not more) of these elements – the actor, the local, the glocal and the grobal.

Yet, a wide range of social scientists are inclined to exaggerate the importance of the first three and to downplay, if not totally deny, the importance of the last element – the grobal. One does not have to, indeed one should not, give primacy to grobalization in order to include it as part of a wide-ranging analysis of globalization.

Why the widespread tendency to privilege the actor, the local, and the glocal? In part, we think, it is linked to the political sympathies, the populism, of most social scientists. They are generally on the side, explicitly or implicitly, of 'the underdog' and in most grand narratives on, or totalizations about, globalization, the actor, local, even the glocal are seen as at risk in the face of grobalization. There is a tendency to look for, and as a result to find, 'heroism' at all of these levels in the face of grobaliz-ation. While there are certainly instances of such heroic stands at all three levels, the tendency to look for and therefore to find them leads to what Veseth (2005) has called 'globaloney'. More specifically, the tendency to identify such heroism in the world of sport at the level of the actor, the local or the glocal would also qualify for the label of globaloney. Veseth argues that any attempt to simplify complex issues leads to globaloney. More specifically, globaloney is characterized by the elevation of one image – say, the heroic local sport fan or club – to represent globalization in its totality. Thus, the message here is that the study of the globalization of sport requires that researchers and analysts look at all of the key elements, without *a priori* elevating the significance of one or more and denigrating the importance of others.

Another cause of this imbalance in the study of globalization is remnants of the impact of postmodernism. While few of those who adopt the positions being criticized here can be seen as postmodernists, they seem to have been affected, explicitly and implicitly, by many of its tenets and critiques of modernism. This leads, for example, away from a focus on such totalizations as globalization (and perhaps grobalization) and toward a concern for narrower and more specific elements such as the actor, the local and even the glocal. Similarly, it is related to the postmodern tendency to 'decentre' analyses away from the centre (the global or grobal) and in the direction of what are seemingly more peripheral elements in the globalization process (actor, local, glocal). But this move clearly goes too far when all we focus on is the periphery and in the process totally ignore, or greatly reduce in significance, processes at the centre of globalization.

As pointed out above, the study of sport is not alone in this tendency. One also sees this, to take another example, in the study of consumption. Here, there is a decided tendency to accord power to the consumer (the consumer as 'hero' rather than 'dupe') and the process of consumption (including 'shopping') and simultaneously to greatly minimize, if not eliminate, the power of advertising, marketing, and a wide array of consumption settings like Wal-Mart and Disney World.

That the study of sport is not alone in this tendency is *not* anywhere near a suf-ficient excuse for it to continue to churn out endless slices of 'globaloney' in its analyses of the globalization of sport.

References

Amis, J. and T. B. Cornwell (eds) (2005) *Global sport sponsorship*, Oxford: Berg.

Andrews, D. L. (1999) 'Dead or alive? Sports history in the late capitalist moment', *Sporting traditions: Journal of the Australian Society for Sports History*, 16, 73–85.

Andrews, D. L. (2003) 'Speaking the "universal language of entertainment": News Corporation, culture and the global sport media economy', in D. Rowe (ed.) *Critical readings: sport, culture and the media*, Maidenhead: Open University Press, 99–128.

Andrews, D. L. (2006) *Sport-commerce-culture: essays on sport in late capitalist America*, New York: Peter Lang.

Andrews, D. L., B. Carrington, S. Jackson and Z. Mazur (1996) 'Jordanscapes: a preliminary analysis of the global popular', *Sociology of Sport Journal*, 13, 428–57.

Appadurai, A. (1996) *Modernity at large: cultural dimensions of globalization*, Minneapolis: University of Minnesota Press.

Beckles, H. (1998) *The development of West Indies cricket – volume 1: the age of globalization*, Jamaica/London: University of the West Indies Press/Pluto Press.

Bernstein, A. (2000) '"Thing you can see from there you can't see from here": globalization, media, and the Olympics', *Journal of Sport & Social Issues*, 24, 351–69.

Bottenburg, M. V. (2001) *Global games* (B. Jackson, Trans.), Urbana, IL: University of Illinois Press.

Chyi, H. I. and G. Sylvie (2001) 'The medium is global, the content is not: the role of geography in online newspaper markets', *Journal of Media Economics*, 14, 231–48.

Crowe, J. (1999) 'He's hanging it up', *Los Angeles Times*, 13 January, p. D1.

Denham, D. (2000) 'Modernism and postmodernism in the professional rugby league in England', *Sociology of Sport Journal*, 17, 275–94.

Dirlik, A. (1996) 'The global in the local', in R. Wilson and W. Dissanayake (eds) *Global local: cultural production and the transnational imaginary*, Durham: Duke University Press, 21–45.

Donnelly, P. (1996) 'The local and the global: globalization in the sociology of sport', *Journal of Sport & Social Issues*, 20, 239–57.

Elias, N. and E. Dunning (1986) *Quest for excitement: sport and leisure in the civilizing process*, Oxford: Basil Blackwell.

Falcous, M. (1998) 'TV made it all a new game: not again! – rugby league and the case of super league in England', *Occasional Papers in Football Studies*, 1(1), 4–21.

Gershon, R. A. (2000) 'The transnational media corporation: environmental scanning and strategy formulation', *Journal of Media Economics*, 13, 81–101.

Giulianotti, R. (1999) *Football: a sociology of the global game*, Cambridge: Polity Press.

Giulianotti, R. (2005) *Sport: a critical sociology*, Cambridge: Polity.

Giulianotti, R. and R. Robertson (2004) 'The globalization of football: a study in the glocalization of the "serious life"', *The British Journal of Sociology*, 55, 545–68.

Grainger, A. and D. L. Andrews (2005) 'Resisting Rupert through sporting rituals? The transnational media corporation and global–local sport cultures', *International Journal of Sport Management and Marketing*, 1, 3–16.

Grossberg, L. (1992) *We gotta get out of this place: popular conservatism and postmodern culture*, London: Routledge.

Grossberg, L. (1997) 'Cultural studies, modern logics, and theories of globalisation', in A. McRobbie (ed.) *Back to reality? Social experience and cultural studies*, Manchester: Manchester University Press, 7–35.

Guttmann, A. (1978) *From ritual to record: the nature of modern sports*, New York: Columbia University Press.

Guttmann, A. (2002) *The Olympics: a history of the modern games*, Urbana, IL: University of Illinois Press.

Hadfield, D. (1999) 'Letter from Sydney: one man's plan to keep the Rabbitohs running', *The Independent*, 15 November, page 7.

Hatfield, S. (2003) 'What makes Nike's advertising tick: Phil Knight is prepared to take risks to give his company a sporting chance', *The Guardian*, 17 June.

Herman, E. and R. W. McChesney (1997) *The global media: the new missionaries of corporate capitalism*, London: Cassell.

Hobsbawm, E. J. (1989) *The age of empire 1875–1914*, New York: Vintage Books.

Hobsbawm, E. J. (1990) *Nations and nationalism since 1870: programme, myth, reality*, Cambridge: Cambridge University Press.

Hogan, J. (2003) 'Staging the nation: gendered and ethnicized discourses of national identity in Olympic opening ceremonies', *Journal of Sport & Social Issues*, 27, 100–23.

Holt, R. J. (1989a) 'Empire and nation', in *Sport and the British: a modern history*, Oxford: Clarendon Press, 203–26.

Holt, R. J. (1989b) *Sport and the British: a modern history*, Oxford: Clarendon Press.

Houlihan, B. (1994) 'Homogenization, Americanization, and creolization of sport: varieties of globalization', *Sociology of Sport Journal*, 11, 356–75.

Jackson, S. J. and B. Hokowhitu (2002) 'Sport, tribes, and technology: the New Zealand All Blacks Haka and the politics of identity', *Journal of Sport & Social Issues*, 26, 125–39.

James, C. L. R. (1963) *Beyond a boundary*, London: Stanley Paul.

Jameson, F. (1991) *Postmodernism, or, the cultural logic of late capitalism*, Durham: Duke University Press.

Jameson, F. (1998) *The cultural turn: selected writings on the postmodern 1983–1998*, London & New York: Verso.

Jones, S. (1988) *Black culture, white youth*, London: Macmillan.

Kellner, D. (2003) *Media spectacle*, London: Routledge.

Knight, G., M. MacNeill and P. Donnelly (2005) 'The disappointment games: narratives of Olympic failure in Canada and New Zealand', *International Review for the Sociology of Sport*, 40, 25–52.

Lealand, G. (1988) *A foreign egg in our nest? American popular culture in New Zealand*, Wellington, New Zealand: Victoria University Press.

MacNeill, M. (1996) 'Networks: producing Olympic ice hockey for a national television audience', *Sociology of Sport Journal*, 13, 103–24.

McChesney, R. W. (1997) *Corporate media and the threat to democracy*, New York: Seven Stories Press.

McGaughey, S. L. and P. W. Liesch (2002) 'The global sports-media nexus: reflections on the "Super League Saga" in Australia', *Journal of Management Studies*, 39, 383–416.

McGuigan, J. (1997) 'Cultural populism revisited', in M. Ferguson and P. Golding (eds) *Cultural studies in question*, London: Sage, 138–54.

McKay, J. and T. Miller (1991) 'From old boys to men and women of the corporation: the Americanization and commodification of Australian sport', *Sociology of Sport Journal*, 8, 86–94.

McKay, J. and D. Rowe (1997) 'Field of soaps: Rupert v. Kerry as masculine melodrama', *Social Text*, 50, 69–86.

McRobbie, A. (2005) *The uses of cultural studies*, London: Routledge.

Maguire, J. A. (1999) *Global sport: identities, societies, civilization*, Cambridge: Polity Press.

Maguire, J. A. (2000) 'Sport and globalization', in J. Coakley and E. Dunning (eds) *Handbook of sports studies*, London: Sage, 356–69.

Maguire, J. (2006) *Power and global sport: zones of prestige, emulation and resistance*, London: Routledge.

Martin, C. R. and J. L. Reeves (2001) 'The whole world isn't watching (but we thought they were): the Super Bowl and United States solipsism', *Culture, Sport, Society*, 4, 213–36.

Miller, T., G. Lawrence, J. McKay, and D. Rowe (2001) *Globalization and sport: playing the world*, London: Sage.

Morley, D. and K. Robins (1995) *Spaces of identity: global media, electronic landscapes and cultural boundaries*, London: Routledge.

Murdoch, R. (1996) *Annual report: Chief Executive's review*, News Corporation.

Phillips, M. G. and B. Hutchins (2003) 'Losing control of the ball: the political economy of football and the media in Australia', *Journal of Sport & Social Issues*, 27, 215–32.

Piggins, G. (2002) *Never say die: the fight to save the Rabbitohs*, Sydney: Macmillan.

Ritzer, G. (2004) *The globalization of nothing*, Thousand Oaks, CA: Pine Forge Press.

Ritzer, G. (2006) 'Globalization and McDonaldization: does it all amount to … nothing?', in G. Ritzer (ed.) *McDonaldization: the reader* (second edn.), Thousand Oaks, CA: Pine Forge Press, 335–48.

Robertson, R. (1992) *Globalization: social theory and global culture*, London: Sage.

Robertson, R. (1995) 'Glocalization: time-space and homogeneity-heterogeneity', in M. Featherstone, S. Lash and R. Robertson (eds) *Global modernities*, London: Sage, 25–44.

Roche, M. (2000) *Mega-events and modernity: Olympics, expos and the growth of global culture*, London: Routledge.

Rowe, D. (2003) 'Sport and the repudiation of the global', *International Review for the Sociology of Sport*, 38, 281–94.

Schmidt, R. (2001) 'Murdoch reaches for the sky', *Brill's Content*, June, 74–9, 126–9.

Silk, M. (2001) 'Together we're one? The "place" of the nation in media representations of the 1998 Kuala Lumpur Commonwealth Games', *Sociology of Sport Journal*, 18, 277–301.

Silk, M. (2002) '"Bangsa Malaysia": global sport, the city and the mediated refurbishment of local identities', *Media, Culture & Society*, 24, 775–94.

Silk, M. and D. L. Andrews (2001) 'Beyond a boundary? Sport, transnational advertising, and the reimagining of national culture', *Journal of Sport & Social Issues*, 25, 180–201.

Silk, M. L. and J. Amis (2000) 'Institutional pressures and the production of televised sport', *Journal of Sport Management*, 14, 267–92.

Silk, M. L. and D. L. Andrews (2005) 'The spatial logics of global sponsorship: corporate capital, cola wars and cricket', in J. Amis and T. B. Cornwell (eds) *Global sport sponsorship*, Oxford: Berg, 67–88.

Silk, M. L., D. L. Andrews and C. L. Cole (2005) *Sport and corporate nationalisms*, Oxford: Berg.

Spa, M. d. M., N. K. Rivenburgh and J. F. Larson (2003) 'Local visions of the global: some perspectives from around the world', in D. Rowe (ed.) *Critical readings: sport, culture and the media*, Maidenhead: Open University Press, 186–209.

Tomlinson, A. (1996) 'Olympic spectacle: opening ceremonies and some paradoxes of globalization', *Media, Culture & Society*, 18, 583–602.

Tomlinson, A. (2005) *Sport and leisure cultures*, Minneapolis: University of Minnesota Press.

Van Elteren, M. (1996) 'Conceptualising the impact of US popular culture globally', *Journal of Popular Culture*, 30, 47–89.

Veseth, M. (2005) *Globaloney: unravelling the myths of globalization*, Lanham, MD: Rowman & Littlefield Publishers.

Waitt, G. (1999) 'Playing games with Sydney: marketing Sydney for the 2000 Olympics', *Urban Studies*, 36, 1055–77.

Whitson, D. and D. Macintosh (1993) 'Becoming a world-class city: hallmark events and sport franchises in the growth strategies of western Canadian cities', *Sociology of Sport Journal*, 10, 221–40.

Whitson, D. and D. Macintosh (1996) 'The global circus: international sport, tourism, and the marketing of cities', *Journal of Sport & Social Issues*, 20, 278–95.

Williams, J. (1994) 'The local and the global in English soccer and the rise of satellite television', *Sociology of Sport Journal*, 11, 376–97.

Wilson, H. (1996) 'What is an Olympic city? Visions of Sydney 2000', *Media, Culture & Society*, 18, 603–18.

Wilson, S. (2004) 'Athens Olympics draws record TV audiences', *USA Today*, 12 October.

4

Steps to an ecology of transnational sports

THOMAS HYLLAND ERIKSEN

Why do some phenomena spread while others do not?

Descriptions of global networks and transnational flows tend to account for themselves by discussing a number of necessary conditions for them to come about, such as the deregulation of capitalism, the development of instantaneous communication technologies and modernization processes that, at least to some extent, standardize consumer preferences. Yet necessary conditions are never the same as sufficient conditions, and I have often wondered why some phenomena travel whereas others do not. Sometimes, the explanation is straightforward – Coca-Cola has a larger marketing budget and more local agents than Irn-Bru; Chinese-made plastic toys are cheaper than Japanese-made plastic toys, and so forth – but such explanations do not always work. Why Microsoft has developed a near-monopoly in the office software market is mysterious, given that competition continued until as late as the 1980s, and nothing about Microsoft's products appeared to be superior to anyone else's. On the other hand, as the evolutionary biologist Stephen Jay Gould (1989) has shown in his detailed analysis of the mass extinctions of the Burgess Shale, evolution involves chance and necessity, and circumstances, which may be dubbed bad timing and bad luck, and may render sophisticated and initially well-adapted species extinct. 'The fittest', which by definition survives under selective pressure, may be the beneficiary of climatic change rather than inherently superior genes. Some 150,000 years ago, humans were in fact so rare that they would easily have made it onto the endangered species list of today (Grinde 2002: 73). Many species survive through occupying marginal niches in ecosystems dominated by stronger species, others by adapting to deserts.

By analogy, when concepts, ideas, activities and commodities spread across the world, they follow courses caused by complex systems of communication, competition and interaction, and by definition, the 'fittest' survive. However, survival need not entail global domination and the annihilation of the competition, but could also refer to the long-term appropriation of a delineated, secure niche.

The *channels* enabling commodities and concepts to travel are well known from the literature of globalization (for example, Held et al. 1999; Scholte 2005), but if we want to understand why some do and others do not, specific explanations are necessary, similar to the way we understand the long-term appearance and disappearance of natural species. As noted above, fortuitous coincidences may account for the sudden proliferation or extinction of particular species in nature; the same can be the case with cultural phenomena. Malcolm Gladwell's thought-provoking book about 'tipping-points' (Gladwell 2000) shows how extraordinary individuals with personal charisma and large networks may, more or less on their own, set snowballs rolling, tipping the scales in favour of one particular product or idea, be it Hush Puppies shoes or swing jazz. Given the right circumstances, that is. Sometimes, it appears that a product or idea spreads largely by virtue of its intrinsic qualities, such as a bank offering (and actually paying out) a considerable reward for a modest investment. If the entrance ticket is too high, only a small audience is prepared to pay it, and therefore Madonna is better known than Boulez, although both have been globally disseminated into very different niches. (Ants are more common than elephants, Boulez fans will be quick to point out, but they have shorter life spans.)

As a writer producing much of my work in a small language (Norwegian), I have a special personal interest in trying to discover the ecology of popularity and translations in the book world. What is it about Dan Brown's novels that makes them so attractive to so many people, who are otherwise very different? The short answer is that *The Da Vinci code* at a certain time reached a tipping point in its sales, following which it became a bestseller everywhere because it had been established as a bestseller in a particular location first, where it appeared at the right time when the appropriate niche was vacant. Why is Jostein Gaarder the only contemporary Norwegian author with a large global readership? Reviewers at home do not regard his books as major achievements; when a jury made a list of the 25 best Norwegian novels of the last 25 years in summer 2006, none of his books were included. Nevertheless, the Norwegian novelists who are routinely described as Nobel Prize material by the domestic press are hardly translated and rarely read outside Scandinavia. Leaving substance and detail aside, it should be clear that the quality of a book, or a record, is not a main criterion for its global dissemination or lack thereof. Nor is there an inverse relationship between quality and dissemination; any idea to the effect that consumers follow the path of least resistance is insufficient, since there exist many easily digestible cultural products that never take off.

Some phenomena are big at home and unknown abroad; some are deeply globalized yet unknown among the masses; and others become well known, popular and familiar worldwide. There is scarcely a general, satisfactory answer to why this is the case, but a few possible factors can be mentioned provisionally: globally popular phenomena (i) require little culturally specific knowledge – they have a short learning curve; (ii) have an emotional, sensory or intellectual appeal which transcends local concerns; and (iii) are effectively marketed transnationally. In other words, low common denominators, a cheap entrance ticket and immediate gratification are factors facilitating global dissemination. The hamburger, the rock song and the thriller, as generic forms, are examples of cultural products that satisfy these requirements.

Sport and natural selection

Let us now turn to sport. There exists an extraordinary number of sports in the world, many of them transnational in the sense that world championships are organized regularly, they have an international governing body and national associations in all six continents. At the same time, what is interesting on the basis of the above discussion is their differences in terms of attention from the media, spectator interest, economic turnover and number of active participants, as well as their transnational distribution. Some sports have large numbers of participants worldwide but few spectators or media coverage; with other sports, it may be the other way around. Some sports are huge, in terms of both popular interest and participation, in limited parts of the world, and virtually non-existent elsewhere. The media in most countries tend to concentrate intensively on a few sports such as tennis, certain track & field disciplines and, of course, football, with a sprinkling of golf, swimming, ice hockey and other sports.

The dominance of football in many parts of the world has led to the relative marginalization of other sports, just as the brown rat has almost entirely displaced the black rat in most of Europe and North America. In the majority of countries in Europe, Latin America and Africa, football dominates the newspapers' sports pages, sport on television and adolescents' sport activity, clearly to the detriment of other, often traditional sports with less transnational appeal, glamour and economic might. The qualities of football, or its 'magic', have been explored by many excellent writers inside and outside of academia (Archetti 1999; Armstrong and Giulianotti 1997; Foer 2006; Giulianotti 1999; Kuper 1994); nevertheless, the attention of audiences tends to be a zero-sum game, and when the floodlights illuminate the football field, everything else is left in the dark.

Football is not the only culprit in the presently skewed ecology of sports, but it has a privileged position in large parts of the contemporary world. The starting point for my exploration of a few non-globalized or recently marginalized sports, is that the kind of competition they face from the more spectacular sports can be likened to a natural selection process, and the question is how and to what extent these sports manage to survive in an era where transnational fame can easily come to overshadow local recognition.

Unevenly spread sports

There is a deep irony, often commented upon, in the fact that the United States, often seen as the main source of global culture, despised by middle classes everywhere else, is almost an island unto itself when it comes to team sports. The largest spectator sports in the USA are baseball, American football, basketball and ice hockey, and none of them can be considered truly global in their reach. Ice hockey is confined to cold countries, and basketball is an unimportant sport in most countries (with Lithuania and Croatia as interesting exceptions in Europe). Baseball and American football, although played in some countries outside the USA, are considered 'American' in the rest of the world. European football (soccer) is popular among adolescents and women in the USA, but it has to date not succeeded commercially. Indeed, successful American soccer players look to Europe for career opportunities. There is a parochialism to the world of sport in the USA which goes against the conventional wisdom about American cultural imperialism (cf. Marling 2006 for other examples).

One partial explanation for the non-spread of typical American sports could be that the niches they might have filled had already been taken by other sports at the outset of 'the American century'. Cricket in Britain and the British Empire, for example, goes far back in history, and would not be ousted by baseball. Cricket is, incidentally, itself an interesting case of an unevenly spread sport. Apart from a few newcomers such as the Netherlands, cricket is seriously played only in the New Commonwealth countries, and all ten test-playing nations have a British imperial history. Its popularity in the Indian subcontinent matches the enthusiasm for football seen in Latin America. Just as football seems to be played wherever there are a few square metres with no traffic in a Brazilian city, cricket is played by children on village dirt roads and in the back-alleys of Indian cities. For subcontinental diasporic groups as far from the source as in Scandinavia, the weekly cricket matches give them a rare opportunity for a noncontroversial recreational activity that simultaneously strengthens their cultural (and male) identity (Walle 2005).

On a trip to India in 1992, I had left Norway with an awareness of the media-produced impression that the Winter Olympics in Albertville were a global sport event. Arriving in Bombay, I immediately discovered that a parallel event of much greater global import was taking place simultaneously, namely the cricket World Cup. These two domains – the world of winter sport and the world of cricket – were both presented as global and were almost entirely oblivious of each other.

Such unevenly spread transnational sports as cricket and winter sports (including bandy, biathlon, Nordic combined etc.) create conditions for a selective cultural geography in the countries involved. West Indians, living in cricket-obsessed countries, are acutely aware of the geographical location of New Zealand and Zimbabwe, but are likely to have vaguer notions of where Mali and Belarus are. Norwegians know a thing or two about Slovenes (home to some of the world's best ski jumpers) but may have less to say about Slovaks. Finns have vivid notions about Canadians (because of ice hockey and bandy), but generally have far less clear ideas about New Zealanders. Baseball, curiously, could have given Cubans and Americans a non-conflictual field of interaction and a pretext for deepening mutual knowledge, had it not been for the American embargo. The transnational networks developed selectively through sports, thus, create structures of relevance that can be exploited for other purposes.

In spite of the incessant media talk about not mixing sports and politics, they are far from being independent entities. As an Iranian colleague comments (Alghasi 2006), before the 2006 football World Cup, television channels worldwide produced brief presentations of the participating countries. As he points out, the short documentary from Mexico on Norwegian state television depicted happy people in colourful costumes waving Mexican flags and cheering on their national team. The documentary from Iran, however, focused largely on the earthquake-ravaged city of Bam. There were no smiles or flags there, and nobody who talked about football. In other words, the pre-World Cup introductions of the countries taking part were far from innocent.

All sports presuppose a great deal of tacit, or recipe, knowledge among their supporters. The lyrical ambiguity in the title of C. L. R. James's classic book on cricket and colonialism, *Beyond a boundary* (James 1963), was lost on almost anyone outside the New Commonwealth. Outside North America, Babe Ruth is either unknown or recognized as some obscure American athlete, and many foreign readers of Stephen Jay Gould's essays in natural history understand everything he says except when he begins to develop parallels between evolution and baseball.

Small fish in big ponds

With football, many boundaries dissolve, and its increasingly transnational character makes the relationship to territory and identity a complex one. Before the 2006 World Cup, I discovered that my son (who was then nine) disapproved of the Swedish striker Zlatan Ibrahimovic. I wondered if he had already developed a scepticism towards Swedish athletes (the friendly rivalry between Sweden and Norway in sport goes back a hundred years), whether the reason might be Zlatan's controversial personality or – heaven forbid – that it had anything to do with Mr Ibrahimovic's Yugoslav origins. Eventually, it turned out that the problem was that Zlatan played for Juventus, a team my son disliked. As a faithful Gunners supporter, he rooted for France in the World Cup, since Arsenal's star player Thierry Henry had a pivotal place in the French squad.

The intensely transnational character of contemporary football, through widespread knowledge about the great leagues of England, Germany, France, Spain and Italy, makes it difficult to continue being a large fish in a small pond. Teams are now compared transnationally, the transfer market is emphatically international (increasingly so after the famous Bosman case in 1996, which loosened the restrictions on foreign players in European teams), and on most elite teams, there are few players with local origins (but see McGovern 2002 for a modification of this view). The Antwerp team Beveren indeed reached the Belgian cup finals in 2004 with a team consisting largely of players from the Ivory Coast. There are about two English players on Arsenal's 2006/2007 first team (in 1990, there was one non-English player), and the French national team that won the 1998 World Cup was famously led by Zinedine Zidane, a player of Algerian origin. The entire team was dominated by players with non-French origins, and was accordingly denounced by the nationalist leader Jean-Marie Le Pen as 'artificial'. During the 2006 World Cup, Le Pen repeated this view by suggesting that 'maybe the coach exaggerated the proportion of players of color and should have been a bit more careful' (Zirin and Cox 2006). Apart from the fact that Le Pen refuses to learn about French demography, this shows that fish about to outgrow the local pond are sought out by the owners of bigger ponds, and thus racial purity becomes an ecological impossibility in football at the highest level.

In the icy waters along the northern coast of Norway, a fertile ground for all kinds of marine life, the smallish local crabs are currently facing stiff competition for food and space from invading Russian giant crabs. The very same process is taking place in football too; the giant crabs of Juventus and Real Madrid are conquering the hearts of small-country football supporters through television, transfers and travel. The small endemic crabs have to devise a survival strategy.

Being a star footballer in a small national league means, to players and spectators alike, that one didn't succeed in securing a contract with a team of real importance – one has by definition remained in the margins of the ecosystem. Our local club, FC Lyn Oslo, depends on Icelanders, Swedes and Nigerians for its (modest) successes. Its sports director frankly admitted that when they brought 17-year old Nigerian talents into the club, they saw it as an investment, hoping that when the players matured, they could be sold with a nice profit to a team in England or Italy. In fact, in 2006, FC Lyn made a profit of about £4 million (a substantial sum for a Norwegian club) when they sold the young Nigerian John Obi Mikel to Chelsea (following an unpleasant legal wrangle involving two agents and Manchester United). In this kind of world, there is little security and stability for anyone. As Bill Buford comments in his book on football hooliganism, *Among the thugs* (Buford 1992), a Man U supporter who had tattooed Bryan Robson's name on his forehead had performed a very daring stunt indeed, because who knew if Robson wouldn't be sold to another club next season?

As the system boundaries expand, the former centre is suddenly relegated to a central location in a minor subsystem. Local clubs have traditionally functioned as farmer teams for national elite clubs like FC Lyn, feeding them with talent and reaping modest profits from the transfers; but the latter now increasingly see themselves as farmer teams for transnationally respected clubs. The Omani national goalkeeper Ali al-Habsi seems to be better off, economically and in terms of prestige, as Bolton's second goalkeeper than he was when, during his years in FC Lyn, he was the best goalkeeper in the Norwegian league. When transfer windows close, local managers express disappointment rather than pleasure if they have been unable to sell some of their most gifted players.

The growth of transnational media (such as Eurosport and Sky Sport) has increased the familiarity of football supporters with players in other countries, and the annual European tournaments make direct comparisons between teams easy. Another important factor is, of course, the differences in economic power between clubs in Europe: most have to settle for the second best when the market is transnational and no primordial club loyalties are expected of players.

Using the analogy from ecological and evolutionary thinking, we may now begin to consider the alternatives, not for the smaller football clubs, but for the other team sports living increasingly in the shadow of football.

Big fish in small ponds

Hunters and gatherers surrounded by agriculturalists who slowly move closer, eventually colonizing and domesticating their traditional hunting grounds, have traditionally been forced to withdraw to ever more barren and marginal territory. Some, however, become assimilated into the farming community. Others devise new ways of surviving. In the world of sport, football and a few other sports are the invaders; football is like the English language or franchised shops, creating a global conversation at the expense of removing diversity. In most of the world today, even children have an acute awareness of where the fame and money is. The scramble for Europe now under way in Africa consists in no small part in attempts by young boys to be discovered by a football scout (Bale 2004). In European societies, people involved in other sports often complain about the disproportionate attention given to football in the media and as a result, by sponsors.

What would be an ecologically sound and sensible reaction to this kind of predicament? Competing in the same field as the dominant ones (with broken English, or with inadequate ploughing tools)? Surprisingly many do, notwithstanding the clear hierarchy between national football cultures. Some withdraw to their shrunken territory, while others posit an alternative sport culture based on values other than global fame and money.

Being a locally valued footballer does have its benefits. The star players in the Norwegian league make the headlines domestically just as often as their British or Spanish counterparts do – just as locally valued authors are solemnly and respectfully interviewed by all the domestic media, their books are praised and awarded prizes. The fact that these media are perused by a fraction as many readers as the large European media, or that the prizes are relatively valueless outside the country, does not necessarily detract from the thrill of being a big fish in, admittedly, a small pond. Some footballers, as well as writers, try their hand at international career-building, and a few succeed reasonably well. The vast majority are nonetheless condemned to remain at home, reaping the not negligible benefits of being world-famous in Norway. Footballers can keep up appearances with a decent showing in domestic matches, unlike tennis players, whose global ranking is everything. Yet, as I have argued, being a big fish in a small pond is increasingly difficult, as that pond is no longer an entity unto itself.

On marginal land

Some sports which were popular and prestigious a few decades ago have dwindled dramatically. In the 1970s, Scandinavian newspapers still regularly covered the national and international championships in orienteering. This sport evolved out of the boy scout movement, and consists of tracing a route and finding posts in a varied, usually forested area, with the help of a map and a compass. Not exactly a spectator sport, orienteering nevertheless had its stars 30 or 40 years ago, whose names and faces would be recognized in the post office. Today, the national and international championships are still organized, and more than 30 countries have national orienteering federations, but one would be hard pressed to find a trace of glamour there. While researching this essay, I came across the names of the leading orienteers, both male and female, of our day – I had heard of none of them before, not even the Scandinavians.

However, orienteering was never huge in any way. With speed skating, the decline has been more dramatic in northern Europe. For 80 years – the first eight decades of the twentieth century – speed skating was an undisputed national sport in Norway and the Netherlands. Swedes, Finns, Russians, Germans and others also competed in a serious way, and their domestic media duly covered the international championships, but it was only in the Netherlands and Norway that the sport had a popularity comparable to that of football. The peculiar links between countries with similar sporting affinities mentioned earlier, flourished in the world of speed skating, and Dutch and Norwegian skaters often learned each others' languages, sometimes even marrying into the other country.

Demanding patience and concentration from the spectators, a classic skating championship would take a weekend. Beginning on Saturday morning with the 500m sprint followed by the 5000m distance in the afternoon, skaters raced in pairs drawn according to a ranking system based on their recent performances. The points at the end of the first day (where 500 metre seconds and 5000 metre seconds were weighted so that one 500m second equalled ten 5000m seconds) decided who would qualify for the final 10,000 metre, that is the 16 best after the first day.

Sunday began with the intermediate 1500m distance, followed by the marathon 10,000 metres – 25 laps on the 400 metre track (skating arenas were often used for track & field in summer). The 10,000 metre race was an endurance test both for skaters and onlookers. Each pair took a quarter of an hour, and frequently, an ice preparation machine had to be run over the rink to even out the surface. In Norway (unlike the Netherlands, with its milder winters and more artificially frozen rinks), competitions invariably took place outdoors. Many of us were frozen to the bone by the time of the finishing ceremony.

In the 1960s and 1970s, on the weekends of a big competition, the Friday newspapers printed forms where audiences, most of them watching television or listening to the radio, could fill in the lap times, finish times, and calculate their own, 'unofficial' points. Everyone seemed to follow ice skating in those days. Even today, many Norwegians remember, or remember having been told about, the Swedish janitor who decided to prepare the ice during the World Championship in 1963, just before the Norwegian favourite, Knut Johannessen ('Kuppern') ran the decisive 10,000 metres. As a result of this decision, many Norwegians have continued to believe to this day, that the Swede Jonny Nilsson won the championship.

Some 30 years on, the television channels broadcast only edited or partial versions of the big championships, which have been forced out of their once comfortable niche. The national championship is hardly covered by the press at all. For a while in the 1980s, it was difficult even to find a shop in Oslo that stocked speed skates. As Norwegians began to win medals and championships again in the 1990s, public interest grew slightly, but the sport as such, a symbol of Norwegian winter sport along with cross-country skiing since independence (1905), has now become a quaint and old-fashioned activity in the eyes of many Norwegians.

There have been attempts to revive speed skating by making it more viewer-friendly. Suggestions have been made to remove the 10,000 metre distance and to replace it with 3000 metres. Championships in single distances are now arranged, as it is believed that the attention spans of spectators have become shorter. Short track skating (much faster, more explosive and more television-friendly than the elegant long-track version) has been introduced with some success in Canada and East Asia. In spite of these attempts, there can be no doubt: like orienteering, speed skating is past its days of glory. Both sports are slower than their competitors and difficult to adapt to the viewing rhythms encouraged by multi-channel television. Among the winter sports, alpine skiing and spectator-friendly novelties such as freestyle skiing have grown much faster than anything else over the last 20 years, finding ecological niches where the older, slower sports had to give in. In order to follow a skating championship with any level of enthusiasm, one has to sit through it from beginning to end, since there are so many figures and possibilities to keep track of. Notwith-standing the climatic difficulties, speed skating has too much complexity – the cultural entrance ticket is too expensive, and it lacks the television-friendly explosiveness of the competition – to retain its position in the new media situation. Speed skating is probably to a great extent a victim of postmodern television, not of football. It has been forced onto the barren wastelands and is, today, unable even to produce a medium-size fish in its shrunken pond.

Defending viable niches

Several team sports involve a grassy field, two goals and a leather ball. Rugby, American football and soccer are the most familiar ones to most of us. However, Australian rules football is hugely popular in Australia (and nowhere else). Originally developed for cricketers to keep in shape during the winter months, in the same way as bandy in the Nordic country was often, in the day of amateurs, played by men who were footballers in summer, the game resembles both rugby and football (soccer) but has its own circuits of competition, prestige and money.

The two national sports in Ireland deserve special attention here. My own interest in the non-globalized sports began on a trip to Ireland when I discovered, glancing through the Irish newspapers, that Gaelic football and hurling were given wider coverage than soccer. This is in spite of the fact that the Irish are no less connected to the world of global communication than anyone else in Western Europe, and have a decent national football team for a country with less than four million inhabitants.

The popularity of the entirely, and stubbornly, national sports of hurling and Gaelic football is initially puzzling. Why would a young aspiring athlete choose a sport that does not get him anywhere? It is said that if you are on the team that wins the Irish championship in either sport, you will never have to pay for a pint at your local for the rest of your life. Yet there are no large sums of money involved in these sports, nor is there an international transfer market. It is as though a young shark chose to stick to his diet of shrimp rather than moving up to tuna.

Hurling and Gaelic football are extremely fast, demanding and very physical sports. Gaelic football could be described as an amalgam of rugby and soccer, although the Gaelic Athletic Association (GAA) emphasizes that it predates both these games. Hands are allowed, there is no offside rule, and the goals resemble rugby goals. In hurling, the same field is used as in Gaelic football, but the game uses a smaller ball (called a *sliotar*) and a stick (the *hurley*). Both are hugely popular sports in Ireland, in terms of both participation and audiences. The GAA has more than 2,500 clubs in Ireland alone.

How can this be, in a world and, certainly, a continent where minor sports have so often been sidelined by the predatory presence of football? The answer seems to be partly political, partly strategic.

On the website of the GAA (www.gaa.ie), we learn that: 'The Gaelic Athletic Association (GAA) was founded on November 1st 1884, by a group of spirited Irishmen who had the foresight to realise the importance of establishing a national organisation to revive and nurture traditional, indigenous pastimes.' The establishment of the GAA was a nationalist response to British imperialism – Ireland remained a colony until 1922 – and the organization promotes Irishness just as much as sport. The GAA's official guide states, as one of its goals, to 'actively support the Irish language, traditional Irish dancing, music, song, and other aspects of Irish culture'. There are even nationwide competitions in some of these cultural activities. The province of Ulster (Northern Ireland), politically a part of the United Kingdom, participates in both hurling and Gaelic football tournaments, but just as Northern Irish Catholics never (or hardly ever) play soccer at a higher level, Protestants do not participate in the Irish sports.

Unlike contemporary soccer clubs, the Gaelic sports recruit players from their home area, although, as the GAA informs, 'in certain cases, e.g. universities, the club will represent an organisation or institution and will draw their players from the members of that organisation' (www.gaa.ie/page/organisation.html).

The political dimension of Gaelic sports explain, at least to some extent, their popularity in the late nineteenth and early twentieth centuries, when Irish nation-building had to be anti-British in order to be viable. Since the British had football and rugby, the Irish had to come up with something else. Interestingly, the Argentines followed the exact opposite strategy in the early twentieth century (Archetti 1999). While not a British colony, Argentina was dominated economically by the British at the time, and instead of positing an alternative, they decided to beat the British at their own game (which they succeeded in doing as early as the 1920s). While the Irish behaved like hunter-gatherers who sharpened their spears and improved their bows when the farming peoples drew near, the Argentines were like hunter-gatherers who rapidly took on the new technology and excelled at it.

Gaelic sports have carved out an entirely local niche that has proven to be locally competitive and internationally insulated in an era where everything seems to militate against that which is merely local. In a strategically wise move, the GAA have fixed the tournaments to the period when football is asleep, that is the summer months, reaching a climax in September. This sounds like good ecological thinking, good Darwinian sense. The motivations of the players who choose a career in Gaelic sports rather than in transnational sports are bound to be complex; partly cultural nationalism, partly big-fish-in-small-pond.

Why has speed skating not succeeded in the same way? For one thing, it was never monopolized by a single nation and could not easily be used in nation-building.

For another, it lacks the visceral qualities, the speed and the violent imagery, of the Gaelic sports, which they in turn share with football. In spite of their emphatically local character, Gaelic sports have retained the magic of football. The latter has become a symbol of a smaller world; the former are used to instil emotions in a self-conscious small nation on the margins of Europe.

Conclusions

The sociologist George Ritzer (2004), in his original and entertaining book *The globalization of nothing*, contrasts 'the grobalization of nothing' with 'the glocalization of something', which he sees as the two main faces of globalization. In many ways, contemporary football fits his description of 'grobalization of nothing', the neologism grobalization being a fusion of growth and globalization. National distinctiveness in football has been reduced because of shared, similar aims – to win international tournaments – and the rationality of industrialism has entered the field (see Dobson and Goddard 2001 on the economics of contemporary football). In the last World Cup, the most entertaining teams were, in the opinion of many, some of the African ones, who were unceremoniously defeated, apparently because of the poor organization of their defence. Commentators around the world complained that the tournament was generally boring, that the best teams were better defenders than attackers, and that the most boring team of all ended up winning.

Such subjective comments are always debatable; the point is that this was a wide-spread sentiment. With Gaelic football and hurling, the situation is very different, but this does not mean that necessarily they conform to Ritzer's notion of 'the glocalization of something', by which he means a product, a service, a place or a person with substantial local content, but which is entwined in global networks. In fact, these sports represent something that cannot, and will not, be globalized because they symbolize a cultural identity that is by default associated with a particular place. Unlike folkloric cultural products elsewhere, including several regionally based sports, Gaelic sports are not marketed overseas (but are played in Irish diasporas). While foreign visitors to matches are welcomed, they are not numerous, and the games are not aggressively marketed as tourist attractions. They are there for internal use. Ritzer's sociology of globalization needs a third term to grasp this kind of phenomenon, which is exclusively local.

In the context of the Darwinian selection and ecological niche-thinking used above to make sense of the uneven globalization of sports, Ritzer's approach, along with other theories of globalization, is limited because it rules out the possibility of anything being merely local. Although the world of transnational flows in sport is arguably less spatially bounded than most of the world's ecosystems, the self-contained, local system continues to exist, by carving out a niche where there is sufficient nourishment and no external competition. In football, however, such niches have become difficult to defend due to the intensification of transnational flows and 'the spectre of comparisons' (Anderson 1998).

References

Alghasi, S. (2006) Personal communication.

Anderson, B. (1998) *The spectre of comparisons: politics, culture and the nation*, London: Verso.

Archetti, E. (1999) *Masculinities: football, polo and the tango in Argentina*, Oxford: Berg.

Armstrong, G. and R. Giulianotti (eds) (1997) *Entering the field: new perspectives on world football*, Oxford: Berg.

Bale, J. (2004) 'Three geographies of African football migration', in G. Armstrong and R. Giulianotti (eds) *Football in Africa: conflict, conciliation and community*, London: Palgrave Macmillan, 229–46.

Buford, B. (1992) *Among the thugs*, New York: W.W. Norton.

Dobson, S. and J. Goddard (2001) *The economics of football*, Cambridge: Cambridge University Press.

Foer, F. (2006) *How football explains the world*, London: Arrow.

Giulianotti, R. (1999) *Football: a sociology of the global game*, Cambridge: Polity.

Giulianotti, R. and R. Robertson (2004) 'The globalization of football: a study in the glocalization of the "serious life"', *The British Journal of Sociology*, 55, 545–68.

Gladwell, M. (2000) *The tipping point: how little things can make a big difference*, London: Abacus.

Gould, S. J. (1989) *Wonderful life: the Burgess Shale and the nature of history*, New York: W.W. Norton.

Grinde, B. (2002) *Darwinian happiness: evolution as a guide for living and understanding human behaviour*, Princeton: Darwin Press.

Held, D., A. McGrew, D. Goldbaltt and J. Perraton (1999) *Global transformations*, Cambridge: Polity.

James, C. L. R. (1963) *Beyond a boundary*, London: Yellow Jersey Press.

Kuper, S. (1994) *Football against the enemy*, London: Orion.

McGovern, P. (2002) 'Globalization or internationalization? Foreign footballers in the English league, 1946–95', *Sociology*, 36, 23–42.

Marling, W. H. (2006) *How 'American' is globalization?*, Baltimore: Johns Hopkins University Press.

Ritzer, G. (2004) *The globalization of nothing*, London: Sage.

Scholte, J. A. (2005) *Globalization: a critical introduction*, 2nd edition, London: Palgrave.

Walle, T. M. (2005) '"Cricket is my passion!" The non-recognition of masculine space in the days of the "Muslim Monster"', Paper presented at CASCA conference, *Translocality: discussing culture and change in the 21st century*, Mérida, 3–8 May.

Zirin, D. and J. Cox (2006) 'French soccer and the future of Europe', *www.edgeofsports.com*, 6 July.

5

Recovering the social:
globalization, football and transnationalism

RICHARD GIULIANOTTI AND ROLAND ROBERTSON

Since the early twentieth century, across Europe, Latin America, Africa, and Asia football has provided perhaps the strongest form of cultural life through which easy sociability has been practised. Particularly among males, the game has long been a crucial subject for breaking the ice between strangers or recreating 'phatic communion' between friends and fellow citizens.

Social relations in association football acquire particular significance in transnational circumstances. Devoid of a common language, individuals have established forms of friendship and interpersonal trust by swapping, in heavily accented terms, the names of favourite football players, especially those belonging to the interlocutors' nations. The 'world memories' of heavily mediatized international fixtures – notably major football tournaments like the World Cup finals – provide a substantive *lingua franca* that sets international peoples talking.

Leading international politicians inside and outside football suggest that this international sociability flows easily into a social universalism. For President Chirac of France, the game poses no threat to cultural or linguistic autonomy: 'Today, football speaks all languages. Everywhere it spreads, it adapts to the local culture, it bonds with national and popular traditions, it transcends social distinctions.'[1] The former FIFA President João Havelange, elided the notorious corruption and rigid stratification within the game in his native Brazil, when he opined, 'Football is not just a sport. It is the only universal link there is. It is the most democratic of all sports, we all talk to each other in a football stadium; everyone is equal. This feeling of democracy in the game is very important since football belongs to everybody' (*FIFA Magazine* April 1998: 3).

Notwithstanding their rather utopian elements, these and many other such observations by key decision-makers do provide sociologists with implicit reminders of the need to consider the *social* aspects of globalization in reference to the general cultural domain. In this discussion, we explore how football's contemporary social elements are constructed in transnational contexts, through processes of glocalization, with increasingly cosmopolitan consequences.

Our focus on the social reverses some recent trends in modern sociological theory. Some analyses of late modern Western societies have produced, in our view, rather 'asocietal' interpretations by reifying individualistic cultural obsessions with the self, personal identity, and autobiography (Giddens 1991; cf Robertson and Chirico 1985). Other analysts pronounce the 'death of the social', as executed by the advent of a media or information age. Lash (2002: 26–7), for example, states that a 'global information culture' procures the disintegration of the social, notably in institutional and structural terms. Harnessing Tönnies (1957, orig. 1887), he contends that the social realm (or *gesellschaftlich*) has been supplanted by cultural life (*gemeinschaftlich*); hence, in regard to religion, we witness the death of (social) churches and the rise of (cultural) sects. Most notoriously, Jean Baudrillard proffers a brazen insistence on the social's demise. Our hyperreal and simulated culture, Baudrillard (1983) imagines, implodes the social. The old social class structure disintegrates, to be replaced by the amorphous, asocial masses, the 'silent majorities', more preoccupied with cultural distraction than political emancipation. Baudrillard refers illustratively to the occasion when French citizens were far more absorbed by football than the politically controversial extradition of a German lawyer (Baudrillard 1983: 12–13). Thus, as the social dies, so too does its scientific contemplation, in the form of sociology (cf. Kellner 1989: 84–7).

Our reluctance to accept these and other premonitions of the global–social's demise is founded on analytical and methodological grounds. First, analysts such as Lash and Baudrillard do require us to reflect critically on how the social emerges from the interrelationships between information/media, globalization and 'post-modernity'. Yet, as Maffesoli (1996) has observed, the outcome may be the transmogrification and revitalization of the social (such as through neo-tribal sociality) rather than its generalized abolition, as Lash and Baudrillard separately submit. Other analysts, notably Knorr-Cetina (2001) and Wittel (2001), have made important contributions towards theorizing the nature of sociality and postsociality within networked environments. Second, there may be methodological rather than epistemological reasons for the relegation of the social in relation to the economic, cultural and political aspects of globalization. However, field work by anthropologists and scholarly fora such as *Global Networks* have aided the offsetting of this process through highlighting the everyday social construction and consequences of globalization.

In this article, we aim to contribute to the recovery of the social within globalization debates through very detailed reference to football. Our discussion locates the global–social with reference to the lodestar concept of 'glocalization', and through related sociological notions of cosmopolitanism, transnationalism and connectivity. We advance a relatively sociocultural reading of globalization that is attuned to the unevenness and complexity of global processes. Our discussion is separated into two general parts, beginning with a substantial theoretical statement, and followed by an empirical elaboration of these ideas within specific transnational football realms.

Richard Giulianotti and Roland Robertson

Theoretical framework

Glocalization

The concept of 'glocalization' underpins our analysis, and has been applied elsewhere to explain the globalization of football (Giulianotti and Robertson 2004, 2006, 2007). A conflation of globalization and localization, the term glocalization is derived from the Japanese word *dochakuka* (meaning 'global localization' or 'localized globalization') common in business circles since the late 1980s (Dicken and Miyamachi 1998: 73). The term has been conceptually substantiated in two general social scientific fields: among cultural social scientists, primarily by Robertson (1992, 1995; Robertson and White 2004); and among political economists and critical geographers, notably by Swyngedouw (1992, 2004). Notwithstanding significant divergences, analysts in both fields agree that glocalization encapsulates the quotidian complexity of local–global or universal–particular relations in the context of intensified global compression and transnational change.

We understand glocalization to refer to 'real world' endeavours to recontextualize global phenomena or macroscopic processes with respect to local cultures (Robertson 1992: 173–4; 1995). Glocalization critically transcends the banal binary oppositions associated with globalization, and so registers the societal *co-presence* of sameness and difference, and the intensified *interpenetration* of the local and the global, the universal and the particular, and homogeneity and heterogeneity.

Glocalization promotes critical sociological reflection on the axial principles of globalization, notably the interdependency of the local and the global. For example, some analyses assume that the global and the local are mutually exclusive, oppositional terms. Hence, it is assumed, globalization *a priori* involves the rejection or annihilation of 'local' cultures; if national cultures are sustained, then it is contended that globalization has somehow been 'repudiated' (cf. Rowe 2003). Conversely, we argue that globalization has been characterized in part by the global thematization of locality and nationality, by the global spread of differentiation along local and national lines. Otherwise stated, 'the local' is not simply a pre-given antinomy of the global, but is better understood as a transitional outcome of globalization (Robertson 1995: 40). As its etymological roots would suggest, glocalization highlights also the global visions and globalization projects of *non*-Western cultures, such as Korea, Japan and China. We may say that the projects of glocalization are now so advanced that they have become 'the constitutive features of contemporary globalization' (Robertson 1995: 41).

These observations have serious ramifications for the historical dimensions of globalization. In prior work, while recognizing that processes of proto-globalization have been apparent among ancient civilizations, Robertson (1992: 58–60) has identified five phases of globalization since the fifteenth century, culminating in the fifth 'uncertainty' period from the late 1960s to recent times. We would suggest that, since around 2000, the world has entered a sixth phase of globalization, which is chiefly characterized by this intensified local–global interpenetration, but whose broader features we are unable to expand upon within this specific context.[2]

Some analysts have associated glocalization with processes of sociocultural heterogenization (cf. Ritzer 2003, 2004). Such an approach has served the useful purpose of countermanding more reductive arguments regarding global homogenization, such as in simplified variants of the Americanization thesis. Nevertheless, glocalization is a dichotomous term that encapsulates the empirically verifiable interdependency of homogenizing and heterogenizing trends in globalization *tout court*. In that sense, we may talk of the *duality of glocality*. Sports such as football provide some basic illustrations.

In terms of heterogenization, the term 'football' refers not just to the sport of 'association football' or 'soccer', with which we are concerned here, for it applies further to various national sporting codes, such as 'American football' or 'Canadian football' in North America, Australian Rules football, Gaelic football in Ireland, and even rugby union or rugby league in parts of the British Commonwealth. Nor are these diverse football codes territorially sealed. Many have existed side-by-side since the late nineteenth century; intensified transnational migration since the mid-twentieth century has merely redoubled at least the heightened status of these games in different contexts. Moreover, despite its 'global' accolade, football has had a secondary sporting status within many public cultures, such as in the Indian sub-continent, Australasia and North America. Football also showcases technical and aesthetic heterogenization, as specific teams, regions and nations interpret and play the game in significantly varied ways.

On the other hand, football's homogenization is evidenced transnationally by isomorphic forms and institutional structures. For example, world sporting heterogeneity is reduced by football's global spread and the correlated displacement of many local games. Football is contested according to universal rules, and its systems of governance and administration are internationally standardized. Since the 1970s, there has been a general convergence in football tactics, as many teams use a 'classic' 4-4-2 formation and safeguard their competitiveness through standardized defensive play.

The social aspects of football display trends towards international homogenization and heterogenization. Among players, most cultures adhere to basic behavioural standards and ritual practices, such as handshakes after matches, respectfully observing anthems, and heeding the instructions of coaches. Greater cultural diversity is evidenced in terms of levels of 'acceptable' aggression, responses to being challenged or fouled, and in relations with referees during play. Such differences are magnified within transnational contexts. For example, in the UK, regular criticisms are voiced by migrant players from the European mainland about the excessive aggression or 'violence' in club football, while various stakeholders in the host society's game criticize the 'diving' or 'feigning injury' of these 'foreigners'.

Transnationalism

Despite some analytical limitations, the concept of transnationalism is particularly helpful for recovering the social in the analysis of globalization.[3] Transnationalism is

61

at heart a processual sociological term, and tends to be applied in regard to processes of migration and mediatization (Al-Ali and Koser 2002; Parreñas 2005; Purkayastha 2005; Smith 2006). Our focus here is on these dual, often interdependent processes, despite transnationalism's other, sometimes secondary applications (for example, regarding corporations or religious networks). We understand transnationalism in straightforward terms, as referring to processes that interconnect individuals and social groups across specific geo-political borders.

The period from the 1870s to the mid-1920s has been termed the 'take-off' period of globalization, when transnational relations expanded massively (notably through transport, trade, communications, education and migration), and the world underwent intensified 'sociocultural compression' (Robertson 1992). Illuminating this process, modern sports such as football underwent a very rapid transnational diffusion, notably in regions like Australasia and South America with 'homophilous' characteristics, in terms of sharing British or European languages, religions and cultural values (Rodgers 1962). These sports contributed significantly to the greater social and societal transnationalization of non-European peoples through stronger connectivity within the 'international community' (Holton 2005).

Transnational social relations became routinized within football, initially as British workers and settlers taught the game and established competitions among indigenous peoples. British teams such as Southampton, Everton and the Corinthians travelled to South America to contest challenge matches against local opponents while being hospitably entertained by Anglophile elites. South America established the football world's first continental governing body – the Confederación Sud American de Fútbol – in 1916 and numerous international tournaments were contested in the region. In turn, South American teams started to contest fixtures in Europe, notably through Uruguay's victories at the 1924 Olympics in France, and a year later when three club sides from Brazil, Uruguay and Argentina toured the continent (Mason 1995: 30–4).

Since that time, transnational processes in football have increased massively through intensified migration and advanced mediatization. Most football clubs have greater interconnections with other nations, such as through the recruitment of migrant players and the attraction of foreign fans. In terms of electronic media, the World Cup has reached larger cumulative global television audiences, rising from 13.5 billion in 1986 to 33.4 billion in 1998. Crucial to that advance is connectivity, a twin process to that of transnationalism.

Connectivity

The concept of connectivity registers the social 'electricity' of globalization. Indeed, Tomlinson (1999: 2) defines globalization in terms of 'complex connectivity', featuring 'the rapidly developing and ever-densening network of interconnections and interdependences that characterize modern social life'. An equally important feature of globalization is expanding global consciousness (Robertson 2007).

Connectivity is a Janus-headed facet of globalization; it is highly uneven, and serves to index major sociocultural differences and inequalities. First, it captures the routinization of transnational communication, such as through media, transport, and imagination. In football, it describes the intensification of transnational relations between football teams, such as through the expansion of tournaments like the World Cup finals, from 13 teams contesting 18 games in 1930 to 64 in 2006, or the European Cup/Champions League, from 29 fixtures in 1955/6 to 237 in 2002/3. Connectivity captures the elite socio-political transnationalism that has emerged among football officials. For example, during his 25-year FIFA Presidency, João Havelange claimed to have visited 192 nations at least three times, and to have spent around 20,000 hours on a plane; in one single year, his successor, Sepp Blatter, visited 50 nations (*FIFA Magazine*, January 2005).

Second, heightened connectivity gives rise to new and more acute forms of global *dis*connection. Indeed, *underdevelopment* was identified as the obverse of *development* during the 'uncertainty phase' of globalization, which ran from the 1960s to the 1990s (Nettl and Robertson 1968: 29; Robertson 1992: 59–60). We noted earlier the emergence of a sixth phase of globalization since about 2000. During this era it is possible to identify a similar antinomy, which involves *connectivity* and *disconnectivity*. Disconnected societies are unable or unwilling to establish many receptor points for global flows. In many instances, these societies have endured structural crises arising from neo-liberal economic reforms or downturns in commodity markets. In football, disconnection has been manifested in different ways. At club level, the political hegemony of the richest Western European clubs has resulted in the relative disconnection of sides based in smaller nations or in Eastern Europe. In the developing world, poverty, unemployment and forced migration have disconnected large populations from their sporting facilities and outlets. In some nations, 'structural adjustment' reforms have led to the privatization of state corporations and cutbacks in assistance to football sides that had previously enjoyed strong national and international competitiveness. In regard to televised access to elite football fixtures, peoples in the developed world easily establish such connectivity, whereas those in the developing world may be experiencing greater disconnectivity due to the excessive costs of pay-TV stations.[4]

Finally, a vital element of disconnectivity is reflexivity wherein the relevant communities, or at least their elite representatives, have an awareness of the heightened connectivity that arises elsewhere. Thus, the disconnection of many European clubs and nations from full competitive engagement has occurred while these competitions have acquired greater transnational exposure. Moreover, the developing football continents of Africa and Asia have been in recurring conflict with FIFA since the mid-1960s over their restricted allocation of qualifying places for the World Cup finals, just as the tournament's global popularity has soared.

Cosmopolitanism

Transnational processes and forms of connectivity facilitate intensified levels and kinds of cosmopolitanism. The ubiquity of discussions regarding cosmopolitanism in recent years suggests that this particular keyword is endangered by possible 'banalization'. Cosmopolitanism, like glocalization, is a portmanteau of the Greek words *cosmos* and *polis* (Beck 2004: 16). In contemporary culture, cosmopolitanism and localism have become a somewhat facile binary, often characterized misleadingly in class and national terms to differentiate a 'vacuous' worldliness from chauvinistic solidarities (Eagleton 2006). Such a standpoint ignores the analytical and empirical interdependencies of the two terms, rather in the same way that their sometime respective philosophical 'champions' (in the shape of Kant and Herder) have had their conceptual differences invented and exaggerated by subsequent commentators (cf. Dallmayr 1998). Cosmopolitanism has become a highly popular term in contemporary social science, and its understanding has acquired greater sophistication and maturity through some recent important conceptualizations that explore in part its diverse and non-European manifestations (Appiah 2006; Fine and Cohen 2002; Vertovec and Cohen 2002).

We understand forms of cosmopolitanism in two basic senses, in 'thin' and 'thick' terms. Both categories signify our agreement with various analysts on the complex interrelations between cosmopolitanism and glocalization (Beck 2004; Roudometof 2005; Tomlinson 1999). Indeed, the cosmopolitan outlook is essentially a glocal one, in terms of being able to reconcile the universal/global with the particular/local.

'Thin cosmopolitanism' involves a rudimentary politics of recognition, whereby the relatively 'equal-but-different' status of other cultures and social relations is acknowledged, though usually by implication rather than expression (Honneth 1995; Taylor 1994). Here, social actors rather instrumentally glocalize specific aspects of these other cultures, with the dialectical process heavily skewed towards sustaining the axial principles of the host culture. 'Thick cosmopolitanism' registers a decidedly more universalist orientation towards, and engagement with, other cultures. Here, social actors actively embrace and 'learn from' other cultures within the glocalization process, though local groundings and attachments remain evident.

Like Beck (2002, 2005), we have suggested the term 'banal cosmopolitanism' to describe the increasingly mundane nature of transnational social life (Giulianotti and Robertson 2006, 2007). In football, banal cosmopolitanism arises in multifarious ways: in the media, notably through the exponential growth of televised international games since the late 1980s; in employment, through routine transnational migration of players; and in general social interaction, through international travel, communications and friendships among supporters. In these and many other instances, a 'thin cosmopolitanism' is increasingly implied, as social actors routinely encounter other cultures according to particular circumstances. Longer-term trends towards 'thick cosmopolitanism' are possible, but not inevitable, through the cross-fertilization and hybridization of social practices across a transnational terrain.

However, just as we would argue that globalization is not incompatible with the strengthening of the nation-state, so banal cosmopolitanism does not eradicate more particularized forms of civic, ethno-national, ethno-linguistic or ethno-religious identification. Even in the most polyethnic 'world cities' (such as New York, Vancouver, Toronto, London), where visitors encounter a cornucopia of cosmopolitan experiences, we still find that very strong elements of ethno-national and ethno-linguistic identity are intrinsic to everyday life for residents, in terms of distinctive neighbourhoods, restaurants, bars, schools and social clubs. In football, this arises through the establishment of ethnically distinctive teams and clubs within these neighbourhoods. Moreover, most cities and nations still have special occasions and periods when forms of civic and national identification are strongly and routinely promoted. During major international football tournaments, for example, it is increasingly common throughout England to find banners and flags in support of the national side decorating homes, cars, businesses, major thoroughfares and other public spaces. In South American nations, support for the national sides remains intensive, particularly given the massive out-migration of players to European teams, which means that it is only during international fixtures that supporters may watch their greatest talents performing on home soil.

Despite their common binary juxtaposition, consideration of football identities highlights close interrelations of the local and the cosmopolitan. For example, supporters of most teams are socialized into a cosmopolitan commitment to appreciating the aesthetic qualities and possibilities of the game itself, even if these are realized by direct opponents in crucial fixtures. Such cosmopolitanism can have striking social irruptions, in what appear to be highly unlikely settings: witness, for instance, the applause of many Manchester United fans for the spectacular three goals scored against their team by Real Madrid's Ronaldo in April 2003; or the appreciation of Real Madrid fans for the brilliance of Barcelona's Ronaldinho at the Bernabéu Stadium in November 2003. On the other hand, football followers routinely profess that it is difficult to enjoy matches fully without having or developing some specific interest in the result or empathy for one team over another.

Indeed cosmopolitanism itself, by its own definition, will incline football followers to favour sides that best embody a cosmopolitan ethic. Moreover, as we noted in relation to glocalization, the local itself must be understood as an increasingly glocalized (and, by implication, cosmopolitan) entity. For example, the most avowedly localist of all clubs is replete with cosmopolitan influences, in terms of utilizing players, coaches, tactical systems, marketing methods, supporter practices that 'originated' previously in other cultural locations. Crucially, as social processes, cosmopolitan exchanges have some basic hermeneutic prerequisites regarding intelligibility and comprehensibility. If no such fusion of horizons occurs, then even thin cosmopolitanism becomes socially intangible.

Overall then, the concepts of glocalization, cosmopolitanism, connectivity and transnationalism enable us to explore a broad range of processes in the globalization of football. These concepts are particularly germane to our endeavour to elevate the social dimensions of globalization within debates on global processes. To explore their interrelationships more fully, we examine three substantive realms of the game that illuminate the social complexity of globalization. First, we discuss the most prominent subject over the past two decades within the international social scientific analysis of football: supporter subcultures. We divide this section into two parts to explore in turn the broad transnational relations of supporters and the particular case of diasporic fan communities. Second, we examine an important professional grouping within football that has been relatively under-explored by social scientists: sport journalists. Third, by drawing upon secondary sources, we provide a short study of Japanese football culture. Our discussion illuminates the close relationship of the national game to indigenous values and customs within the global context; it also returns the concept of glocalization to its point of origin, to explore how the Japanese themselves 'glocalize' with football as a case study. The sections on supporter subcultures and sport journalists draw significantly upon our primary research (notably participant observation, interviews and textual analysis) with these groups in the UK and overseas, most recently while undertaking an ESRC project on football and globalization.[5]

Football Worlds

Supporter subcultures 1: transnational relations

'Militant' or 'hardcore' supporter subcultures are established at almost all professional clubs in Europe, Latin America and Asia. These formations, as with most football crowds, tend to have informal, relatively open, social characteristics, while displaying a duality of glocality. In terms of homogenization, these groups are transnationally isomorphic, in having collective names and song repertoires that prioritize the favoured team. Alternatively, self-identifying hooligan groups converge upon a collective commitment to competing successfully and violently with rival peers.

In terms of heterogenization, significant variations are evident. 'Militant' fan identities in northern Europe, notably the UK, have been relatively more associated with subcultural hooliganism. In southern Europe, *ultras* are more formally institutionalized (such as through having headquarters and social clubs), have more complex friendships or rivalries with other fan groups, deploy more spectacular displays of support to their team, cherish stronger loyalties to their *curva* (or stand) where they gather, and often have more uniform (sometimes extremist) political identities. In Latin America, supporter subcultures such as the *hinchas* (or *barras bravas*) in Argentina and Uruguay share many of these characteristics, but also have more complex historical conflicts with security forces and relatively closer sociopolitical relations with club officials.

There are also dual forms of heterogenization and homogenization in the transnational experiences of supporter subcultures. We may consider the Tartan Army, which follows the Scotland national team to fixtures overseas, as a case in point. In terms of heterogenization (or variegated cosmopolitanization), overseas fixtures attract greater numbers of Scotland fans, from a wider geographical spread, than in the previous decades, enabling more opportunities for transnational social engagement. The disintegration of the Soviet complex has created many new football 'nations', such as the Baltic Republics, for Scottish fans to visit. Intensified transport and telecommunications connectivity ensures that diverse social friendships are more easily sustained. Some Scottish fans are more socially universalistic, in initiating charitable exercises to assist needy local people.

Yet some long-term participants in the Tartan Army indicate that increasing homogenization (or standardized cosmopolitanization) in transnational social experiences is more evident. For example, older fans in the Tartan Army perceive a convergence in the social spaces encountered abroad. Supporters congregate typically in standard 'Irish' pubs and interact mainly with English-speaking and Anglophile locals. The adventurous risks of foreign trips have been greatly reduced: flights and hotels are readily booked through the internet; visas are rare or easily accessed; the post-Communist East harbours fewer 'unknown' qualities; and mobile phones generally ensure that getting lost in incomprehensible surroundings is almost impossible.

The banal cosmopolitanism of football fan subcultures has intensified significantly since the late 1980s. Thin cosmopolitanism is routinely facilitated by varied, more intensified connectivity, such as transnational travel to European fixtures or increased television coverage of foreign leagues. Thick cosmopolitanism is more evident in the voluntaristic transnational practices of network-building militant fans. Thus, for example, militant groups at leading European clubs often reciprocally 'host' transnational visitors associated with other fan subcultures.

Thick cosmopolitanism helps to describe the significant kinds of transnational glocalization that have occurred since the 1960s in regard to supporter styles and social practices. In Europe, stronger forms of connectivity were established from this time, in terms of migration, transnational club fixtures, and mediatization. Northern Italian supporters established the *ultras* subcultural identity at their various clubs during the 1960s, and this fan form quickly spread across Italy, then into southern France, Yugoslavia, and (following democratization) Portugal and Spain. The *ultras* borrowed significantly from UK fan styles, in terms of singing, congregating at ground 'ends', and displaying team colours; but they further 'glocalized' these traditions to create more organized, systematic and visually spectacular modes of support.

In the UK from the late 1970s onwards, the connections of militant fandom with violence were hardened, as self-identifying hooligan groups came to evolve the 'casual' style, which was particularly distinctive for disporting relatively upmarket sportswear and branded fashions. Followers of the casual style drew variously from continental Europe in utilizing fashion outlets (for example, Sergio Tacchini, Lacoste, Armani), borrowing from the Italian *paninari* youth style, and visiting (or raiding) department stores during sorties abroad. In turn, at the 1990 World Cup finals in Italy and afterwards, the *ultras* style influenced some non-hooligan fans in the UK. Some transnational friendships were established between particular supporters; connectivity intensified as UK television and football magazines paid increasing attention to Italian football and its popular culture. To inject fresh atmosphere into stadiums, some UK fan formations borrowed directly from the *ultras* to create more colourful and raucous modes of support for their teams.

As these glocalization practices confirm, football fandom continues to display very strong forms of civic, regional and national pride. Such differentiation is promoted by security practices within stadiums, as supporters are segregated into ground sections where they may only intermingle with followers of their own team, thereby serving to heighten forms of collective identification and effervescence.

In line with the categorizations of Georg Simmel, we may say that some fan subcultures construct their own globalisms in the shape of 'world forms'. These higher forms arise when 'the main type of formative capacity of the human spirit is able to shape the *totality* of contents into a self-contained, irreducible world of experience' (Levine 1971: xvii). 'Worlds' are ideal types, and constitute 'great forms' 'through which, as it were, each particular part of the content of the world can, or should, pass'(Simmel 1959: 288). Religious belief systems, for example, serve to organize all experiences and to locate the human condition within a totalizing vision. In Wittgensteinian terms, these world forms appear as highly cultivated 'language games' that absorb all content.

We would suggest that some world forms occur in football when supporter formations seek to establish global identity and statuses for themselves or their teams. Fans of specific club or national teams seem to construct a global ideal in their own collective images, for example by consciously portraying themselves transnationally as 'the world's best supporters' (for example Brazil's 'carnival' fans, or Scotland's 'Tartan Army'). Similarly, some fan cultures have emerged organically out of particular 'world forms', wherein very strong kinds of shared ethno-national or ethno-religious identity provide a critical orthodoxy for collectively interpreting the world. In this way, specific supporter groups (such as some Scottish/Northern Irish Protestant-Unionists following Rangers from Glasgow, or some Basques who follow Athletic Bilbao) develop their football-ethnic habitus into worldviews that enable critical and homologous understandings to arise regarding national and international politics (for example the Middle East conflict).

Supporter subcultures 2: diasporic formations

A further subject for increasing consideration in regard to transnational fandom concerns those diasporic supporter communities who live away from their team's home nation.[6] For example, leading club sides from Europe, Mexico and South America have large worldwide followings that can exceed 50 million. There are two general kinds of these transnational formations. First, 'self-inventing transnational fandoms' are comprised of followers with little or no biographical attachment to the team and its home city or nation. Yet these followers adopt a thick cosmopolitan social relationship to the team, enabling its particular habitus to shape significant aspects of their personal identities. Such fandom is facilitated principally by media connectivity (for example satellite television coverage) or indirect socio-symbolic ties, such as when a favoured player joins this specific club. Leading European clubs in the wealthiest national leagues (notably England, Spain and Italy) cultivate this fandom through their integral presence in the banal cosmopolitanization of football, in terms of competing regularly in the world's biggest tournaments, signing or developing 'celebrity' players, conducting summer tours of new fan 'markets', capitalizing on strong transnational television exposure, and heightening their historical mythology.

Second, 'diasporic self-sustaining communities' are comprised of supporters living abroad with long-standing biographical attachments to the team or its associated region and nation. While some allegiances may have abated during emigration, global media connectivity has furnished greater opportunities for rekindling their 'long-distance love'. Such fandom is particularly strong at leading clubs from large migratory societies, such as Italy, Turkey, Greece and Mexico.

Our research has considered Scotland's leading football sides – Celtic and Rangers, both from Glasgow – which have large transnational supporter networks, primarily across the main seats of British colonization and Irish migration, such as North America, Australasia, Singapore, and South Africa (Giulianotti and Robertson 2006, 2007). The two teams (but primarily Celtic) have over 120 supporters' clubs sprinkled across North America, which are largely comprised of migrants who arrived between 1960 and 1980. Many clubs were founded in the late 1990s with the express intention of combining their members to receive live satellite coverage of their team's football fixtures from a small network provider.

These supporters' clubs operate in transnational contexts where banal cosmopolitanism is very evident: in the Toronto area, for example, there are over 150 nationalities with diverse linguistic, culinary and sporting traditions. Yet strong forms of civic, national and ethno-religious identity are nurtured by diasporic fans, as evidenced by the very existence of these clubs, and the members' keen retention of their Scottishness.

The supporters' clubs display significant degrees of transnational homogenization and heterogenization. Each club is formally instituted with office-bearers, has a 'home' location where members congregate, and is affiliated to a continental supporters' association. Yet the clubs diverge in various ways: in terms of scale, member demographics, and frequency of gatherings; the nature of their general relationships with supporters of other teams; and the kinds of social ties between members. Most club members maintain strong transnational ties with Scotland, through friends, family and 'home-based' fellow supporters.

Two major transnational processes threaten the long-term future of many clubs. First, the ageing membership is not being replenished by their more assimilated children or grandchildren, or by new Scottish migrants. Second, the greater availability of internet football may encourage members to stay at home to watch live games. In response to the latter, however, many club members insist that they do not intend to lose the Simmelian sociability of watching transnational games in familiar social surroundings, where club members congregate and construct match-day atmospheres, by wearing team colours and behaving as they would inside Scottish football stadiums.

While the transnational transmission of Scottish football fixtures has obvious benefits in terms of connectivity, some major new forms of disconnectivity also arise. A 'digital divide' is opened transnationally in cultural not class terms. Fans of smaller Scottish clubs report their frustration at receiving only irregular television or internet coverage of their teams when based overseas. Yet Celtic and Rangers fans too are aware of their underprivileged Scottish status. Many express frustration at the exclusion of their teams from the more glamorous European leagues and competition, which receive intensive coverage by global media corporations. In part consequence, many Celtic and Rangers fans in North America would favour their club moving to join a revamped English league.

Football media

In regard to the media's relationship to globalization processes, research by Hannerz (2004) has demonstrated the importance of examining the practices of foreign correspondents. An equivalent point might be extended to include sport journalists when addressing the social aspects of football and globalization. The social transnationalism of sport journalism is dependent upon three factors: *context, contacts* and *content.*

First, in terms of context, there are two inter-related processes at play, within football and its media. Football has become increasingly transnational, in terms of player migration, team competitions, supporter association, and the educational backgrounds and global connectivity of football's various stakeholders. The game's media has become similarly transnational for various reasons. Transnational media corporations provide the technical and business infrastructure for the global flow of football information, and for the exponential increase in specialist television channels and magazines devoted to the game. Interconnecting ties between football clubs, associations and media broadcasters have become increasingly complex since the late 1980s. Yet clubs are increasingly equipped to establish their own media outlets – notably television channels and websites – to control information outputs and reach directly their global audiences. Again, this precipitates forms of disconnection, as smaller clubs or weaker national teams cannot sustain sophisticated websites or television stations to reach their fan bases.

Second, the banal cosmopolitanization of football is indexed chiefly by its far greater volume of exposure in the mainstream mass media. Hence, football journalists are required to produce far greater volumes of reporting to fill these column inches or television schedules. In turn, these journalists are able to assume higher levels of thin cosmopolitanization among their audiences, in terms of harbouring far stronger 'stocks of knowledge' and empathetic orientations regarding transnational football.

Third, in terms of contacts, the transnational social networks of football journalists have multiplied in recent years. Many contacts are developed informally at international fixtures, as journalists establish reciprocal relationships with foreign reporters. Player migration encourages transnational ties, so that stories from one nation are communicated to journalists in another. These stories incline towards thin rather than thick cosmopolitanism, in terms of communicating gossipy information to home audiences rather than promoting deeper transnational interrelations. For example, in the UK, foreign players find to their chagrin that, if they conduct frank interviews with journalists at home, transnational contacts allow British journalists to obtain and 'spin' the story in more sensationalist tones for UK audiences.

Additionally, many UK media outlets employ multilingual journalists who can access information about star foreign players from transnational sources.

The duality of glocality is evidenced through aspects of social homogenization and heterogenization in the football media. Thick cosmopolitanism among UK football audiences, regarding growing interest in the game overseas, has facilitated significant forms of heterogenization, for example, as more transnational social ties are made with players and journalists. Trends towards significant homogenization are apparent in the relatively isomorphic banks of specialist 'foreign' journalists, who typically specialize in nation-specific stories and cultural knowledge, and in the select list of freelance UK reporters who have migrated to nations like Spain and Italy. The latter are particularly busy during peak thin cosmopolitanism periods, when self-interested UK audiences have direct concerns with these nations, such as prior to European fixtures against overseas sides, or whilst transfer speculation links specific players to UK teams. One significant element of heterogenization concerns the journalists' identification of significant sociocultural differences between UK and other international football media. European journalists, notably those in the north, are under significantly less editorial pressure than their UK counterparts to obtain background stories on players and to fill vast numbers of pages on a daily basis.

Finally, many journalists report that they have generally far weaker social relationships with players than in the past. In large part, this is attributed to the proliferation of players from overseas, who have a more instrumental relationship with the domestic football culture. Alternatively, it is easier for journalists to develop long-term social ties with homegrown players and coaches, who are considered to be more approachable for interviews, and to have a more homologous habitus in terms of recreational tastes, senses of humour, and cultural and political viewpoints.

Football in Japan

As the etymological cradle of glocalization, Japan reflected the duality of glocality *avant la lettre*. Modernization of Japanese society occurred during the Meiji period (1868–1912), the principle philosophy of which was encapsulated in the implicitly glocalist aphorism, *wakon yosai* ('Japanese spirit, Western learning'). Japanese football reflects a similarly glocalist relationship to *gaijin* influences.

The game's initial diffusion was facilitated by increasing transnational connectivity, enabling in-migration of British workers and settlers who played football. Japanese responses to the game were glocally ambivalent, with local college students enjoying participation while many teachers considered football's roughness contrary to civilized social mores (Guttmann and Thompson 2001: 70–1). In the post-war period up to the 1990s, Japanese football was glocalized further as a reflection of the state corporatist economic model. Company teams were founded and established a national league in 1965. Thick cosmopolitanism was indexed by Japan's emerging football system establishing football links with world leaders, notably West Germany and then Brazil, through conducting tours, hiring coaches, and sending players to training camps (Horne with Bleakley 2002; Moffett 2003).

Increasing media and competitive connectivity during the 1980s and 1990s underpinned Japanese senses of relative disconnection to football's globalization, notably through the national team's failures to qualify for the ever more global World Cup finals. As football's corporate support and mass audiences increased, a fully professional league – the J-League – was launched in 1993, featuring ten clubs. In terms of homogenization, J-League marketing borrowed heavily from North American sports, notably the NFL. J-League clubs followed standard practice in world football by substituting their corporate nomenclature with civic titles. Yet, in terms of heterogenization, the distinctly creolistic practices of Japanese society were also actuated, as team names blended local and transnational signifiers:

> Nissan FC became Yokohama Marinos, using the Spanish word for sailor, because Yokohama was a port. Yomiuri Football Club called its first team 'Verdy' from *verde*, Portuguese for green, because they played in green and had several Brazilian players. Gamba Osaka came from the Italian word for leg, which also sounded like the way Osakans say *ganbaru*, a Japanese word for 'try hard'. And Sumimoto Metals FC became Kashima Antlers, as Kashima literally meant 'Deer Island'.
>
> (Moffett 2003: 23–4)

The most transnational name belongs to Yokohama AS Flügels. Flügel is the German for 'wing', reflecting the club's backing by the All Nippon Airways (ANA) group. But the 's' at the end is an English, not German, plural. The 'AS' refers to the names of the club's owners (ANA, and the Sato Kogyo construction firm), but in football these abbreviations have other connotations, such as to Italian clubs like AS Roma (Moffett 2003: 54).

Japanese teams looked strongly to South American and European stars, notably Dunga and Zico of Brazil, to accelerate national football development, homogenizing the indigenous game to transnational standards. Since the early 1970s, several Brazil-born players have become naturalized Japanese citizens and represented the Japan national team, for example Ruy Ramos, Wagner Lopes and 'Alex'. Around 40 Brazilian players join Japanese clubs annually, and a similar number is spread across the J-League's 18 teams.

The continuing heterogenization of Japanese football is largely underpinned by the concept of *nihonjinron*, which points towards the alleged uniqueness of Japan that is strongly cultivated by the Japanese themselves. In a variation of modernization theory, overseas coaches and players complain, for example, that individual Japanese players are technically advanced, but unable to homogenize their competitive practices and psychology to a global level. Asian social hierarchies, deference to authority, commitment to harmonious relations, and preference for collectivism over individualism, are viewed by foreign professionals as distinctive indigenous values that are inimical to competitive success. In some instances, for example, age stratification can mean that players refuse to eat, share accommodation or give passes to younger, technically superior teammates. Similarly, Japanese coaches have been criticized for their corporatist reluctance to discard senior players, and for failing to instil a highly competitive psychology in their teams. Intense public criticism can be directed at Japanese players such as Hidetoshi Nakata who reveal strong individualism through assertive and self-orientated opinions.

Japanese fan culture displays similar glocal mixtures of indigenous and transnational processes. Early J-League fan groups borrowed from the traditional *oendan* spectator culture, which had originated in Japanese college sports and later moved into baseball.[7] Unlike most other football cultures, J-League fans typically applauded the endeavours of both teams, refused to rebuke their team for poor performances, and even staged post-match congratulatory displays for their team when it lost, to the bemusement of overseas players and coaches (Birchall 2000: 59–60). J-League club officials tended to be far more influential than their European or South American counterparts in shaping the practices of 'militant' fan subcultures.

In transnational terms, both club officials and supporters examined closely and selectively copied the fan practices in European and Latin American stadiums. Yet, as in baseball, it would be wrong to assume that Japanese football crowds 'conform too neatly to certain stereotypes about an alleged Japanese character of mindless collectivism' (Kelly 2004: 83). From the mid-1990s onwards, fans at club and national levels were involved in fractious and disorderly incidents that still reflected, in part, particularly Japanese responses to match events. On some occasions – notably the 1997 defeat of Japan in Tokyo by the United Arab Emirates – serious public disorder and rioting occurred. In other incidents, some club fans have demanded more respect or apologies from their players following poor performances (Nogawa and Maeda 1998: 231–3; Satoshi 2002).

In recent times, intensified connectivity has enabled Japanese league and international football to enter the banal cosmopolitanism of global audiences. The self-understandings and ambitions of Japanese football are increasingly dominated by this global looking-glass and transnational relations. Qualification for the 1998 World Cup finals enabled ordinary Japanese to suspend their patriotic ambivalence, and to celebrate intensively their national identities. Co-hosting the 2002 tournament with Korea enabled Japan to cement its global football status. The 'mega-event' accelerated the thin cosmopolitanism of Japanese football followers, for example in measuring transnationally their players' standards, such as by monitoring the fortunes of national players in European leagues. Moreover, the 2002 World Cup placed Korea and Japan – with their long histories of political conflict and Japanese military occupation – in a more integrationist and universalist political location, by being popularly illustrative of football's capacity to promote peace and social reconciliation between divided societies.

Concluding comments

To sum up, we have sought to demonstrate here that football is the cultural form *par excellence* for tracing the social electrification of contemporary global processes. Detailed consideration of supporters, journalists, and football in Japan provided the highly relevant empirical domains for elaborating our analysis. The discussion has built significantly upon our earlier work on football and globalization (see, for example, Giulianotti and Robertson 2004, 2006, 2007). We have advanced a variety of fresh thinking and arguments: for example, by forwarding the concept of the 'duality of glocality'; by differentiating 'thin' and 'thick' forms of cosmopolitanism; by developing the connectivity–disconnectivity couplet; and, by focusing concertedly upon the social and transnational aspects of globality. While football has provided the critical sociocultural focus for discussion, other sporting realms would be equally suitable venues for the deployment and elaboration of our theoretical claims. Additionally, our analysis may be extended historically to examine global processes in sport since at least the nineteenth century.

More specifically, we have endeavoured to illuminate three main aspects of social globalization. First, we understand the duality of glocality as capturing the complex and highly variable interrelations between homogenizing and heterogenizing impulses in globalization. In general terms, homogenization is commonly associated with societal forms, while heterogenization is more evident in regard to sociocultural content. For example, homogenization is evident in the technical thresholds and coaching of Japanese players, the formal identification of supporter subcultures, or the national-based professional statuses of 'foreign correspondents' in the football media. Heterogenization is evident in the creolized styles of team names and supporter practices in Japan, the diverse transnational social relationships established by football journalists, and the varied cultural politics of supporter subcultures.

Second, cosmopolitanism is characterized by thick and thin variants, and has become increasingly mundane or banal in recent times. Thick cosmopolitanism is evidenced, for example, by supporter subcultures whose institutional forms or chief social practices are largely inspired by transnational influences. Thin cosmopolitanism is evidenced by the national newspapers which utilize overseas sources to gain stories on imported players. Banal cosmopolitanism is evidenced by the increasingly routine accessibility of Japanese and other international football for Western television audiences. Cosmopolitanization does not abolish 'the local', but germinates more varied relations with forms of particularity, as illustrated, to pick one example, by diasporic communities of club supporters. Cosmopolitanization also facilitates periodic irruptions of identity-differentiation, such as during major international fixtures.

Third, the twin processes of transnationalism and connectivity are highly uneven, and thus give rise to disconnectivity, which is understood and experienced in relational terms. Connectivity is most obvious in regard to the transnational communication channels of contemporary football media. Disconnectivity is a principal pathology of the current phase of globalization. It is evidenced in football through stronger senses of social exclusion, such as in regard to non-participation in major tournaments, or relatively weaker access to the benefits of digital or satellite communications.

Our analysis has two principal intentions in regard to social scientific analysis of globalization. First, there remains the importance of locating sport, and especially the global game, at the heart of sociological scrutiny of globalization. Football, as we have argued, is a core feature of transnational social relations. During the World Cup finals in particular, we find that exceptional levels of global connectivity arise while forms of disconnectivity become ever more acute. In recent years, sport has been harnessed by transnational corporations, international NGOs and governing institutions, to play a highly important role in promoting social universalism, such as in war-torn regions and impoverished societies. In the longer term, as glocalization becomes more intensive, football's significance to globalization processes will intensify.

Second, the interrelationships between glocalization and cosmopolitanism warrant closer empirical and analytical examination by social scientists. Our initial comment is that cosmopolitanism is one of many outcomes of glocalization processes. The social empowerment and engagement of everyday actors serve to determine the kinds of thick or thin cosmopolitanism that are evident in their glocalization projects. In accordance with the duality of glocality, the banal variants of cosmopolitanism must be counterpoised with the continuation of mundane forms of civic, regional and national identity.

Some analysts have advocated a normative fusion of cosmopolitanism and glocalization. For example, Tomlinson (1999: 194–5) argues for an 'ethical glocalism' that transcends local chauvinisms, while Ritzer (2004) believes that 'glocal' cultures may be a final refuge from the oppressive omnipresence of 'nothing' cultural products (cf. Beck 2004; Roudometof 2005). Our emphasis is on the complexity and uncertainties of glocalization *qua* cosmopolitanism. We observe too that glocalization is perhaps more diverse than these analysts would suggest, giving rise to forms of homogenization and heterogenization, and to universalism and chauvinism.

Football provides one crucial venue for considering normatively the potential outcomes of cosmopolitan glocality. There is great scope for critically scrutinizing the utopian universalism that often surrounds the game, as set out by Havelange and Chirac at the start of our discussion. In this regard also, we need to examine the everyday potentialities of football in facilitating stronger social relations within difficult circumstances.

Acknowledgements

The research for this paper was financially assisted through a grant from the UK ESRC (award number R000239833). We benefited from the insightful comments and constructive criticisms of the three journal referees on an earlier draft of this paper; and the excellent guidance, patience and diligence of the *Global Networks* editors, particularly Alisdair Rogers with whom we have had most correspondence.

Notes

1. See http://www.clysce.fr/elysee/anglais/speeches_and_documents/2004/address_by_mr_
   jacques_chirac_president_of_the_french_republic_on_the_occasion_of_the_decoration_of_
   mr_joseph_s_blatter_president_of_fifa_and_the_centennial_year_of_fifa.1904.html

2. Robertson is now proposing that the present phase be conceptualized as the *millennial* phase.
3. Certainly, the term harbours important analytical limitations. It may become a very widespread term, applicable to so many international processes, to the point that it appears somewhat meaningless. Its usage tends to be in relation to post-1945 global processes, but that obscures the fact that transnationalism, and globalization in general, have far older and more varied histories (Kennedy and Roudometof 2002: 2–3).
4. The social uses and consequences of internet connectivity, particularly in facilitating diverse products and niche markets, are highlighted by Anderson (2006).
5. UK ESRC award number R000239833.
6. On diasporas in general, see Cohen (1997).
7. *Oendan* in educational institutions were highly organized, being strong on internal stratification, choreographed displays of support, and uniform attire. *Oendan* were primarily male, but also featured some pom pom girls (Moffett 2003: 53).

References

Al-Ali, N. and K. Koser (eds) (2002) *New approaches to migration? Transnational communities and the transformation of home*, Routledge: London.

Anderson, C. (2006) *The long tail*, London: Random House Business.

Appiah, K. A. (2006) *Cosmopolitanism: ethics in a world of strangers*, London: Allen Lane.

Baudrillard, J. (1983) *In the shadow of the silent majorities*, New York: Semiotext(e).

Beck, U. (2002) The cosmopolitan perspective: sociology in the second age of modernity, in S. Vertovec and R. Cohen (eds) (2002) *Conceiving cosmopolitanism: theory, context, and practice*, Oxford: Oxford University Press, 61–85.

Beck, U. (2004) 'Rooted cosmopolitanism: emerging from a rivalry of distinctions', in U. Beck, N. Sznaider and R. Winter (eds) *Global America? The cultural consequences of globalization*, Liverpool, Liverpool University Press, 15–29.

Beck, U. (2005) 'Cosmopolitical realism: on the distinction between cosmopolitanism in philosophy and the social sciences', *Global Networks*, 4, 131–56.

Birchall, J. (2000) *Ultra Nippon: how Japan reinvented football*, London: Headline.

Cohen, R. (1997) *Global diasporas*, Seattle: University of Washington Press.

Dallmayr, F. (1998) *Alternative visions*, Lanham, MD: Rowman and Littlefield.

Dicken, P. and Y. Miyamachi (1998) 'From noodles to satellites: the changing geography of the Japanese *Sogo Shosha*', *Transactions of the Institute of British Geographers*, 23, 55–78.

Eagleton, T. (2006) '*Homo loquax*: talking bodies', *Globalizations*, 3, 1–4.

Fine, R. and R. Cohen (2002) 'Four cosmopolitanism moments', in S. Vertovec and R. Cohen (eds) (2002) *Conceiving cosmopolitanism: theory, context, and practice*, Oxford: Oxford University Press, 137–64.

Giddens, A. (1991) *Modernity and self-identity*, Cambridge: Polity.

Giulianotti, R. and R. Robertson (2004) 'The globalization of football: a study in the glocalization of the "serious life"', *British Journal of Sociology*, 55, 545–68.

Giulianotti, R. and R. Robertson (2006) 'Glocalization, globalization and migration: the case of Scottish football supporters in North America', *International Sociology*, 21, 171–98.

Giulianotti, R. and R. Robertson (2007) 'Forms of glocalization: globalization and the migration strategies of Scottish football fans in North America', *Sociology*, 41, 133–52.

Guttmann, A. and L. Thompson (2001) *Japanese sports: a history*, Honolulu: University of Hawaii Press.

Hannerz, U. (2004) *Foreign news: exploring the world of foreign correspondents*, Chicago: University of Chicago Press.

Holton, R. (2005) 'The inclusion of the non-European world in international society, 1870–1920: evidence from global networks', *Global Networks*, 5, 239–59.

Honneth, A. (1995) *The struggle for recognition: the moral grammar of social conflicts*, Cambridge: Polity.

Horne, J. with D. Bleakley (2002) 'The development of football in Japan', in J. Horne and W. Manzenreiter (eds) *Japan, Korea and the 2002 World Cup*, London: Routledge, 89–105.

Kellner, D. (1989) *Jean Baudrillard: from Marxism to postmodernism and beyond*, Cambridge: Polity.

Kelly, W. W. (2004) 'Sense and sensibility at the ball park: what Japanese fans make of professional baseball', in W. W. Kelly (ed.) *Fanning the flames: what Japanese fans make of professional baseball*, Albany: SUNY Press, 79–105.

Kennedy, P. and V. Roudometof (2002) 'Transnationalism in a Global Age', in P. Kennedy and V. Roudometof (eds) *Communities across borders: new immigrants and transnational cultures*, London: Routledge, 1–26.

Knorr-Cetina, K. (2001) 'Postsocial relations: theorizing sociality in a postsocial environment', in G. Ritzer and B. Smart (eds) *Handbook of social theory*, London: Sage, 520–34.

Lash, S. (2002) *Critique of information*, London: Sage.

Levine, D. N. (1971) 'Introduction', to G. Simmel, *On individuality and social forms: selected writings*, edited by D. N. Levine, Chicago: University of Chicago Press, ix-lxv.

Maffesoli, M. (1996) *The time of the tribes*, London: Sage.

Mason, T. (1995) *Passion of the people? Football in South America*, London: Verso.

Moffett, S. (2003) *Japanese rules*, London: Yellow Jersey Press.

Nettl, J. P. and R. Robertson (1968) *International systems and the modernisation of societies*, London: Faber & Faber.

Nogawa, H. and H. Maeda (1998) 'The Japanese dream: soccer culture towards the new millennium', in G. Armstrong and R. Giulianotti (eds) *Football cultures and identities*, Basingstoke: Macmillan, 223–33.

Parreñas, R. S. (2005) *Children of global migration: transnational families and gendered woes*, Stanford: Stanford University Press.

Purkayastha, B. (2005) *Negotiating ethnicity: second-generation South Asian Americans traverse a transnational world*, New Brunswick: Rutgers University Press.

Ritzer, G. (2003) 'Rethinking globalization: glocalization/grobalization and something/ nothing', *Sociological Theory*, 21, 193–209.

Ritzer, G. (2004) *The globalization of nothing*, London: Sage.

Robertson, R. (1992) *Globalization: social theory and global culture*, London: Sage.

Robertson, R. (1995) 'Glocalization: time-space and homogeneity-heterogeneity', in M. Featherstone, S. Lash and R. Robertson (eds) *Global modernities*, London: Sage, 25–44.

Robertson, R. and J. A. Chirico (1985) 'Humanity, globalization and worldwide religious resurgence', *Sociological Analysis*, 46, 219–42.

Robertson, R. and K. E. White (2004) 'La Glocalizzazione Rivisitata ed Elaborata', in F. Sedda (ed.) *Glocal*, Roma: Luca Sossella Editore, 13–41.

Robertson, R. (2007) 'Global consciousness', in R. Robertson and J. A. Scholte (eds) *Encyclopaedia of globalization*, volume 2, New York: MTM/Routledge, 502–6.

Rodgers, E. (1962) *The diffusion of innovations*, New York: Free Press.

Roudometof, V. (2005) 'Transnationalism, cosmopolitanism and glocalization', *Current Sociology*, 53, 113–35.

Rowe, D. (2003) 'Sport and the repudiation of the global', *International Review for the Sociology of Sport*, 38, 281–94.

Satoshi, S. (2002) 'Japanese soccer fans: following the local and the national team', in J. Horne and W. Manzenreiter (eds) *Japan, Korea and the 2002 World Cup*, London: Routledge, 133–46.

Simmel, G. (1959) *Essays on sociology, philosophy and aesthetics by Georg Simmel et al.*, edited by K. H. Wolff, Ohio: Ohio State University Press.

Smith, R. C. (2006) *Mexican New York: transnational lives of new immigrants*, Berkeley: University of California Press.

Richard Giulianotti and Roland Robertson

Swyngedouw, E. (1992) 'The Mammon quest: "glocalization", interspatial competition and the monetary order: the construction of new scales', in M. Dunford and G. Kafkalis (eds) *Cities and regions in the new Europe: the global-local interplay and spatial development strategies*, London: Belhaven Press, 137–66.

Swyngedouw, E. (2004) 'Globalisation or "glocalisation"? Networks, territories and re-scaling', *Cambridge Review of International Affairs*, 17, 25–48.

Taylor, C. (1994) 'The politics of recognition', in A. Gutmann (ed.) *Multiculturalism*, Princeton, NJ: Princeton University Press, 107–48.

Tomlinson, J. (1999) *Globalization and culture*, Cambridge: Polity.

Tönnies, F. (1957) *Community and society: Gemeinschaft und Gesellschaft*, East Lansing: Michigan State University Press.

Vertovec, S. and R. Cohen (2002) 'Introduction: conceiving cosmopolitanism', *Conceiving cosmopolitanism: theory, context, and practice*, Oxford: Oxford University Press, 1–24.

Wittel, A. (2001) 'Toward a network sociality', *Theory, Culture & Society*, 18(6), 51–76.

6

Is baseball a global sport? America's 'national pastime' as global field and international sport

WILLIAM W. KELLY

I claim that Base Ball owes its prestige as our National Game to the fact that as no other form of sport it is the exponent of American Courage, Confidence, Combativeness; American Dash, Discipline, Determination; American Energy, Eagerness, Enthusiasm; American Pluck, Persistency, Performance; American Spirit, Sagacity, Success; American Vim, Vigor, Virility.

Base Ball is the American Game par excellence because its playing demands Brain and Brawn, and American manhood supplies these ingredients in quantity sufficient to spread over the entire continent.

(Spalding 1911: 12)

The articles of this special issue are but the latest to demonstrate how powerfully sports have been a connective tissue of modern life on imperial, international and global scales. Soccer, cricket and baseball were at the core of a myriad of organized sports and physical leisure activities that were formalized in the nineteenth century and spread quickly from the West to the Rest. From the second half of that century, they travelled the colonial, military and mercantile circuits of the world as organizational complexes of skills, rules, equipment and players, creating a global sportscape of local followings, national pastimes and international rivalries. What happened when they arrived in locations around the world has produced a fascinating, rich literature about the dynamics of domestication that often these days goes under the catch-all notion of 'glocalization'. The term captures the sense that local appropriation is seldom simply assimilating and imitating. Rather, it is generally a process of indigenization – of appropriating the foreign objects and practices by recontextualizing them into local matrices of meaning and value.

However, the differences in the world histories of the three sports are as significant as their commonalities, and in this article I begin with some of the distinctive features of baseball's development in the USA and its move through the Caribbean and western Pacific regions, with special reference to Japan. Unlike soccer and cricket (and American football), baseball in the USA developed wholly outside elite schools and, perhaps for that reason, was fully commercialized and profession-alized much earlier than soccer and cricket. The professional game was never antagonistic to amateur or school forms of the sport, no doubt because baseball as sport never had very strong ideological associations with a personal 'character' ethic. At least by the 1860s, baseball was already explicitly 'nationalized' as the American pastime, and in that image it was emulated and resisted in the locations in which it took root. There has been a transnational world of baseball for almost a century and a half. From the 1860s, and over time this has linked several circuits of the game within the USA (including Major League Baseball or MLB, the Negro Leagues, and various minor league systems), across the Caribbean and Central America (especially the Cuban, Dominican Republic and Mexican leagues), and through East Asia (especially Japan, Taiwan and South Korea).

Because of these and other related factors, I argue that baseball has never developed the global character of soccer. Despite Albert Spalding's tireless proselytizing, it is not even the equal of cricket, which became a fully Commonwealth sport with an inter-national competitive balance that disrupted (and de-classed) early English dominance. In the sportscape of world baseball, the US professional association (MLB) has always remained the dominant centre, and this has significantly determined (and distorted) the sport's local histories, its regional forms and its cross-national linkages. Baseball is, as my subtitle suggests, a sport regarded as the national pastime of several countries in the Americas and Asia that are linked internationally and transnationally, but whose domestic games are far more important than international competition.

The year 2006 illustrated the contrast between soccer and baseball quite instructively. The 18th FIFA World Cup final pool and championship rounds in Germany, after two years of qualifying by its 207 member national federations, demonstrated once again that soccer is the only truly global team sport (just as athletics, under IAAF, is our only really global individual sport). This is true in several senses. There was extensive participation and spectatorship across the North–South divide. FIFA exercises powerful supranational governance in establishing standards and adjudicating disputes. This was a genuinely open world championship competition. There are now in professional soccer generally only limited controls on the movements of transnational players and there was relatively open competitive bidding for media rights and extensive coverage.

Of course, one may point out that traditional powerhouse teams from Europe and South America dominated the championship rounds, that FIFA is a crony-ridden headquarters pursuing narrow self-interest, that financial clout has replaced legal restrictions in controlling the soccer labour movement, and that only a few powerful multinational corporations can vie for primary commercial sponsorship and media rights. Nonetheless, for at least half a century since the 1950 tournament, the FIFA World Cup has been one of the few titles deserving of its name, and FIFA can rightly claim to be in the vanguard of supranational sports governance.

The global scale and transnational nature of soccer stood out starkly against the events of three months earlier, in March 2006. For 17 days, the first 'World Baseball Classic' was held in several venues among 16 national teams, grouped into four first-round pools. It was less the scale of participation than the hegemony of US organizational power that revealed world baseball's skewed landscape. Four of the seven tournament venues were on the US mainland, and two were in Puerto Rico; only the Asian first round pool was played beyond the American flag in Tokyo. The WBC was organized by the US Major League Baseball (MLB) and the MLB Players' Association, which reserved for themselves a major share of the proceeds. The Classic had been delayed a year over objections by the Commissioners' Office of Japanese professional baseball (NPB for Nippon Professional Baseball) precisely because NPB felt that the scheduling, logistics, rules and finances of the event had been established by and for MLB. Moreover, the Classic was threatened with cancellation in the winter of 2005 over the US government's unwillingness to grant visas to members of the Cuban national team.

Of course, in this case too, there are factors that some feel mitigate a simple conclusion that US domination has kept baseball as a parochial sport. It was not lost on many who followed the tournament that Japan and Cuba, the two teams that met in the single-game championship, are the two nations with the most vibrant and autonomous baseball cultures. The US national team advanced to the second round but after winning a close game with Japan that was decided by a controversial call by an American umpire, it was routed by Korea and closed out by Mexico and was relegated to spectatorship.

We may also note that this World Baseball Classic was not the beginning of broad international competition but more precisely an effort by MLB to graft itself onto longstanding and multi-level international baseball organizations and competitions. Though little known, there has been a Baseball World Cup since 1938 – the first was held in Great Britain with only two teams, from Britain and the USA, and was a five-game series won by Great Britain (thus, England participated in and won a baseball World Cup before joining the soccer World Cup). The organization that has evolved into the International Baseball Federation (IBAF) was formed that year to promote these competitions. With 112 national member units, it now administers several levels of world championship tournaments, including youth, junior, university and 'inter-continental'; a Women's Baseball World Cup has been held twice since 2004. The Baseball World Cup itself has been held 35 times since 1938, with Cuba winning the last nine titles (25 of 36 overall, despite not participating several times for political reasons).

Baseball has an Olympic history in that it was played as an exhibition sport first in 1912 and again in 1936 in Berlin before 125,000 spectators at the Olympic Stadium, still the largest crowd ever to watch a baseball game. It was a demonstration sport in the 1984 and 1988 Games before gaining official designation in 1992. To associate it even more directly with the Olympic movement, the IBAF moved its headquarters to Lausanne, Switzerland in 1993.

However, a litany of amateur and professional international competitions and a growing global audience for MLB satellite broadcasts do not make a global sport. Most of the important baseball scholars talk about baseball 'globalization', but hesitate to label it a global sport. Peter Bjarkman's valuable *Diamonds around the globe: the encyclopedia of world baseball* profiles the distinct but intertwined histories of the sport in a dozen or so countries that together characterize what he most frequently terms 'international baseball' (Bjarkman 2005). Alan Klein's new book details 'the globalization of major league baseball', by which he means international sources of players and an aggressive marketing of MLB games and products to foreign markets (Klein 2006). And at the end of his new edited collection, *Baseball without borders: the international pastime*, George Gmelch (2006) asks 'is baseball really global?' While he tries hard to answer the question affirmatively, he too concludes with an emphasis on the diversification of US professional baseball.

Their caution is appropriate. Baseball is a significant international sport with rich and well-documented autonomous histories in several countries. It is also a trans-national sport because, among these national spheres, organizational templates, players, techniques, strategies and spectatorships have continuously circulated. It is not a global sport as measured by what Giulianotti and Robertson astutely identified as globalization's core process, namely that it 'relativizes all particularisms' (Giulianotti and Robertson 2004: 547). There is a single centre to the baseball world and it is in New York, not Lausanne, at the MLB Commissioner's Office. Baseball has many local vernaculars of a single dominant language, and that is the particular language of US baseball. Throughout its history, US professional baseball has successfully subordinated all challenges to its popularity and profitability (at least from within the sport). For example, early on, Albert Spalding and the National League engineered the collapse of a rival Players League in 1889; and the National League absorbed a second rival American Association several years later and finally, in the early twentieth century, forced a détente with the American League to form Major League Baseball. Then, in the mid-twentieth century, it turned back a renegade Mexican league (Klein 1997), undermined the Negro Leagues with its own integration, embraced Caribbean players, made a labour peace with its own players' union, and forced an agreement with the Japanese professional leagues that has created a posting system to facilitate the MLB signing of Japanese stars.

Even at the amateur level, the IBAF remains a minor world federation, for bi-national politics (namely the continuing baseball cold war between Cuba and the USA) has been overshadowing and undermining its championships for 50 years. The world's highest profile amateur competition is actually the Little League World Series, carefully managed by 'Little League International', the decidedly American organization that also puts on seven other similar 'world series' championships of youth baseball and softball. The current format of dividing teams into the United States Bracket and the International Bracket ensures that an American team will reach the finals and this is symptomatic of uneven power in the baseball world, which at all levels tilts towards the United States.

In all this, precisely what has not happened has been a relativizing of the particular shaping force of MLB baseball, to recall Giulianotti and Robertson's standard. Their measure, applied to sport, does not to reduce globality to relative strength (does the MLB always win?) or geographical dispersion (in how many countries are MLB broadcasts popular?). It draws attention, more significantly, to patterns of governance, vectors of player movement, and flows of media attention and sports capital. In baseball, the centre still holds.

Baseball, besuboru, and beisbol

Why is this so? Baseball's emergence as an organized sport and its diffusion beyond the USA began even earlier than the English sports of soccer and rugby (the spread of cricket predated all three). Even as baseball was spreading across the USA from its New England and mid-Atlantic beginnings in the 1860s, during and after the Civil War, it was simultaneously moving abroad – to Cuba in 1860, to elsewhere in the Caribbean and Central America soon after, to China in 1863, and to Japan and Korea in the early 1870s. Given this, we might have expected it to have assumed a more global rather than international form in the ensuing century. Albert Spalding certainly did, as he expressed triumphantly in the magazine piece he wrote on his return from leading an exhibition tour of baseball stars around the world from December 1888 to March 1889 (Spalding 1889; see also Lamster 2006). Instead, baseball's further advance was much slower and in fact depended more on Japan, which promoted baseball in its empire in Korea, Taiwan (Morris 2004), Southeast Asia, and then Oceania (for example, Murdock 1948) as it moved across the Pacific. Japanese immigrants to Brazil and Hawaii promoted the game there in the early twentieth century.

Soccer's diffusion was slightly later, but it sustained a momentum of promotion and appropriation. Certainly, European continental interest and British imperial circuits gave the sport a far wider zone of contact than baseball. Much is made of the 'simplicity' of soccer as responsible for its global reach – its minimal rules, basic equipment, and fundamental skills necessary to play and watch knowledgably. What is more immediately approachable than a round ball propelled gracefully about an open flat rectangle by a balanced number of players? Baseball, by contrast, seems so idiosyncratically complicated. It has an oddly configured field with a diamond infield and non-converging foul lines, base paths and pitcher's mound. It has arbitrary dimensions and positional skills; gloves, masks, bats and bases must accompany the ball; it has arcane statistics; the intervals on interruption entice coaches, managers and umpires to interject authority and expertise: it is too quirky and arcane to appeal popularly.

Perhaps the features of the two sports do account for some of their differential reach, as Appadurai (1995) and others argue, but other sport cases suggest this is at best incomplete. Basketball, for example, matches soccer in its pace and elegant simplicity (it is but soccer on a smaller scale, by hand rather than by foot and head), but basketball was vastly slower to spread since its invention in 1891. Basketball leads some to find cause in an American parochial disinterest in promoting its own sports abroad. This not only applies to baseball and basketball but also to American football and lacrosse – none of America's four indigenous modern sports gained any world standing like soccer and athletics.

This too runs against the historical experience. In fact, I would argue three features of baseball's early international history shaped and ultimately limited its spread. The first was its precocious professionalization in the USA in a league format that created powerful commercial interests and incentives for team ownership, stadium, transport and baseball goods. Of course, much nineteenth-century sporting activity became professional in terms of paying performers, charging for admissions and gambling revenues. This applied to pedestrianism, cycling, bare-knuckle fighting and a host of 'blood sports', but baseball was different. People played baseball as much as they watched it and it rapidly stabilized into regular seasons, stadium fixtures, continuing player contracts and monopolistic associations of owner-operators. That is, more than the other early professional sports, it systematized and stabilized its business foundations as a small monopoly of individual owners.

At the same time, and as a way of consolidating and expanding its business potential, baseball was promoted in highly nationalistic terms as embodying American values and inculcating an American character. Much of this national pastime discourse was exhortative and aimed at domestic conditions through decades of massive waves of foreign immigration and internal population movements. The playable spectator sport was a powerful solvent, even though the game perpetuated racial, ethnic and gender exclusions. The same coding of baseball practices as culturally American was the idiom by which the sport was so fervently promoted abroad as a surrogate for more direct political control. Most notably, this was through Spalding's own tireless efforts, and his 1911 proclamation of 'America's national game' has been a central text in several explications of national sports diplomacy waged through baseball (especially Brown 1990, 1991; Crepeau 1982; and Dyreson 2003, 2005). 'It has followed the flag to the Hawaiian islands', Spalding boasted, 'and at once supplanted every other form of athletics in popularity. It has followed the flag to the Philippines, to Porto Rice and to Cuba, and wherever a ship flying the Stars and Stripes finds anchorage today, somewhere on nearby shore the American National Game is in Progress' (Spalding 1911: 14; see Elfers 2003 for the 1913–14 world tour).

These are strong claims, but misleading history. Cuban students returning from the USA brought the game to the island and, while baseball's origins in Hawaii have mainland roots, its popularity and strength was borne much more by Japanese immigrant labour (Nakagawa 2001). American sailors on shore playing the game in ports of call had important demonstration effects on local populations, but it was actually several resounding defeats of such a team in the late 1890s by Japanese schoolboys that boosted the popularity of the sport and shaped it in a direction quite different from Spalding's American style. A third feature of baseball's early international history is that the countries in which it was most enthusiastically adopted fell within the political and economic orbit of the USA but were not under its direct colonial rule. Missionaries, educators, YMCA instructors, merchants, and others were teachers and models of the American game (Bjarkman 1994; Gems 2006; Reaves

2002), but local players and promoters could and did respond with considerable creativity and even irreverence.

In short, the consequence of the specific political conditions of baseball's spread was that the distinctiveness of the various national baseball cultures was framed in dialectic with the sport's central power, the USA. The form of this dialectic is what I turn to now.

Uncanny mimicry: the ideological dynamic of world baseball

Sports of course are among a vast array of institutional complexes and commercial products that form the political economy of globalization (political constitutions, film industries, scientific technologies and fast-food franchises). What sets sports apart is that they are by definition contests, and this has made them inevitable and compelling frameworks for organizing social solidarities and rivalries, emotional attachments, and ideological polarities at intra-societal and inter-societal levels. One cultural idiom for expressing relations of affinity and opposition is that of sporting 'style', generally taken to be a distinctive albeit elusive configuration of coaching philosophy, game strategy, player attitudes, and team social relations. Individual players and coaches have styles; teams have style, but the notion is used most broadly (and most problematically) as national styles of sports. Participants, spectators and commentators invest much in defining and defending the style of Brazilian soccer, Indian cricket, Pakistani field hockey, Romanian gymnastics, Soviet ice hockey and so forth. Sports styling is, in effect, a core grammatical construction of sports glocalization.

Styling, though, assumes a different syntax in the world of soccer – an ever-shifting polyglot of continental, national and club styles – than in baseball's circuits, where for much of its century and a half, styling becomes a response to American claims of authenticity and authority. Under these conditions, what has most frequently developed is appropriation in the form of an 'uncanny mimicry' – a condition, to put it tongue in cheek, in which Sigmund Freud meets Homi Bhabha. By uncanny, I mean Freud's original sense of the unnerving sensation of encountering something both familiar and foreign at the same time. As I argued above, since the 1860s, Americans have exuberantly exported the game, all the while worrying constantly if those beyond the smell of hot dogs and the strains of our national anthem can and should play it properly. Two of the most enthusiastic promoters of American baseball, Albert G. Spalding and Henry Chadwick, both wrote with messianic zeal about spreading the 'American game' (and its American values) to what Spalding once labelled the 'little brown skin peoples'. It was 'gratifying', he observed, to see them playing the American national pastime, but disappointingly inevitable that they could never quite 'get it' and 'extremely unsettling' whenever they beat us! From Albert Spalding to the latest high-priced and under-performing American star for the Japanese professional teams, the effect of seeing 'our' and 'not our' baseball at the same time is just that sensation captured by Freud's uncanny meeting.

What does baseball glocalization look like from the other side? Baseball was taken to Japan and elsewhere in a spirit of enthusiastic *mimicry*, at least as Homi Bhabha

(1984) used the term for how colonial and neo-colonial subjects appropriated their master's practices with equal measure of anxiety and anger. 'Mimicry' is both the pale copy destined to fall short of an original and an aggressive appropriation that imaginatively exceeds the model. It is playful disruption and intentional distortion.

What I am suggesting is that the dynamics of uncanny mimicry have been one significant form of sports glocalization, especially in the case of baseball, a sportscape of plural manifestations across a global playing field but with a single centre that continues to claim the aura and authority of authenticity. I turn to the fate of baseball in Japan to illustrate these dynamics, although I believe we can find equal demonstration in all corners of the baseball world (see especially, Eastman 2005 for Cuba; Klein 1991 for the Dominican Republic; Klein 1997 for Mexico; and Morris 2004 for Taiwan).

Samurai sporting style in an international sportscape

Japan is a strategic case of uncanny mimicry because it is the nation beyond the USA with the longest history of the sport, the largest spectatorship, the most extensive media coverage, and the most elaborated administrative organizations at the amateur and professional levels. Baseball has been regarded as the national pastime sport at least since the mid-twentieth century. Even during the 70 years prior to that, it had no rival in popularity.

The many forms of baseball in Japan, from children's sandlot through national high school tournaments, university and industrial leagues, to the professional leagues are nonetheless most often reduced to (or essentialized as) a single dominant image. Japanese baseball is samurai baseball. To commentators, both foreign and domestic, it looks just like US baseball but it is really completely different. The same field dimensions and rule book seems to have spawned radically divergent cultures of performance. Free-spirited, hard-hitting, fun-loving, independent-minded American baseball players are pitted symbolically against team-spirited, cautious, self-sacrificing, deeply deferential, intensely loyal samurai with bats. As *The Economist* (1996) opined several years ago:

> To Americans, baseball is all about enjoyment and sudden surprises; of spectacular hits, dexterous fielding and cheeky running between the bases. Not so in Japan. When introduced in the late 19th century, baseball was widely interpreted by the former samurai elite to be a kind of spiritual training – a discipline for shaping young minds and bodies. To the Japanese, *yakyū* (field ball) is seen to this day as a martial art to be practised remorselessly to perfection and then grimly executed with the sole purpose of crushing the opposition.

Such portraits as this form a thick file of media stories stretching over many decades, by visitors and locals alike. An American reporter, for instance, captured his own discomfort at the uncanniness of Japanese baseball in the following report:

'Japanese Baseball: A Whole New Ballgame'
Orange County (CA) Register, Sunday, Sept. 28, 1997
By Gary A. Warner, Orange County Register

> *Oh, take me out to the besuboru game*
> *Take me out to the dome*
> *Buy me some dried squid and yakitori on a stick*
> *The orange-colored rabbit mascot is really a kick*
> *For it's bang the taiko drum for the home team*
> *But if they tie the other team, it'd be great.*
> *One, two, three "sanshin", bow to the ump, and you're out*
> *At the old besuboru game.*

They do not sing that song during the seventh-inning stretch at Japanese baseball games. In fact, they do not sing anything at all. Oh, the insanely loud home-team rooters in the right-field seats screeching on their whistles and pounding on a big taiko drum will occasionally break into a toe-tapper such as 'To the Sky with Fighting Soul, Ah Giants'. But that can happen any time. Or rather all the time. From an hour before the game until the final out.

Still, it's baseball all the same. Nine players. Nine innings. Three outs. A full count is still 3-and-2.

No wait, it is 2-and-3. In Japan, the strikes are called first. But otherwise, it is just like a night at Seattle's Kingdome or at Dodger Stadium.

Except for players bowing to the umpire instead of kicking dirt on him. And the cheerleaders dancing on the field between innings. The young women with pony kegs of beer strapped to their backs serving draft from a spigot. The vendors hawking cigarettes or the couples sharing a 'bento box' of deep-fried asparagus and raw fish on rice wrapped with seaweed. The players throwing stuffed animals to the crowd after a home run.

Same pastime. Different nations. Baseball in Japan is a game familiar, yet exotic. Unchanged, yet with more twists than a Fernando Valenzuela screwball.

'There's fewer fastballs. More full counts. Strategy is what it's about – bunting, hit and run, moving the man over. Giving yourself up for the good of the team', said John De Bellis, an American expatriate who covers baseball for the *Asahi Evening News*, a major Tokyo-based newspaper. 'It's baseball, but not the same baseball Americans know.'

Or, as a somewhat less charitable Reggie Smith, the former Dodger slugger, put it after his first year with the Yomiuri Giants in 1983: 'This isn't baseball – it only looks like it.'

Indeed, the dominant image of Japanese baseball is that of a society that has actively and forcefully reshaped baseball's original forms and spirit to fit a set of purposes that turn play into pedagogy, that subordinate the excitement of contest for the demands of character building. Americans gleefully play baseball; Japanese grimly work baseball – and they are worse for it.

Warrior players giving their all for the team has been potent imagery, especially in the international world of baseball, because it is a vividly oppositional metaphor (setting the Japanese East against the US West) that simplifies the often confusing task of sorting out what is common and what is different. That is, as a singular image and a universal label for baseball in Japan, it allows us to ignore important and intriguing differences across teams, across levels of play and across history (precisely, the differences and changes that Japanese fans often find most absorbing about the sport in their own society). It is also conveniently all-purpose. In one simple opposition (group work versus individual play), it purports to describe Japanese baseball (this is how they play it over there), to explain it (they play it that way because they are samurai), and to judge it (usually negatively, because although Americans idealize cowboys, we are far more dubious of samurai). This is sport reduced to eternal, essential national verities.

However, this is only half of the dynamic of uncanny mimicry. American players and commentators may view the repositioning of the sport in Japan – its glocalization – in deprecating terms, but local appropriation of American forms has a very different and decidedly positive valence for many Japanese. The most crucial inversion in the introduction of American baseball into Japan in the late nineteenth century was its positioning within the elite boys' schools of the time. This happened in the 1880s and 1890s when it became one of a number of Western sports (sharing popularity with cricket, rowing and rugby) that were encouraged as student-run club activities at the so-called higher schools, the narrow conduits to the single national university in Tokyo. In this regard, it was less like baseball in the USA and more like American football or like cricket and rugby in Great Britain. All of these school-based sports generated an ethic that games-playing inspired virtue, formed character and developed manliness.

Although these sports quickly found enthusiasts among the elite students who developed organized clubs and spirited inter-scholastic competitions, the associations of school sports with personal character training and a samurai identity were not inevitable. In fact, baseball was highly unusual, and its emergence as school sport *par excellence* depended on the fortuitous circumstances of a series of challenge games that the baseball club of First Higher School played against Americans resident in the treaty port of Yokohama augmented by fleet sailors. These games have been recounted frequently in the literature (for example, in English, see Guthrie-Shimizu 2004; Guttmann and Thompson 2001; Kelly 2000; and Roden 1980); from 1896 to 1904, First Higher played 13 games against the Yokohama Americans, winning 11 and losing only twice. The repeated victories reinforced the prominence of the baseball club among other sports clubs at the school, the status of Ichiko in the world of elite education, and the spread of baseball as a popular sport upwards to the universities and downwards into the national secondary school system.

The particular styling of baseball as embodying a samurai 'fighting spirit' owed much to the way this baseball club conducted itself, revelling in punishing practices and proclaiming a rhetoric of self-sacrifice. It no doubt saw its ethic vindicated by the considerable success it enjoyed on the field. However, this was also a decade when elite youth fell under the critical gaze of a populace suspicious of their moral and physical fitness for the prestigious positions soon to be theirs. The ostentatious exertions of the First Higher School Baseball Club and its articulation of 'fighting spirit' was in part an attempt to answer these suspicions.

Then, in the late 1910s and 1920s, 'fighting spirit' found another influential ideologue – and a slightly different formulation – in the Waseda University player, coach, manager and later newspaper commentator, Suishū Tobita. Like the First Higher club, Tobita stressed a spiritualized and self-sacrificing playing commitment explicitly likened to a warrior code. However, baseball clubs had now come under adult supervision, both at the university and high school levels, and not surprisingly, Tobita insisted on the unquestioned authority of the manager and his coaches in controlling the team. The lines of discipline and hierarchy were redrawn.

Although there were other coaching styles and philosophies, Tobita's proved compelling at a time, in the second and third decades of the century, when newspapers and transport companies rushed to sponsor sports events and to fan sports fever for corporate profit. Tobita's stern amateurism was used to temper this emerging commercialized popularity, especially of middle school and Tokyo area college baseball. Tobita's spiritualization of sport performance also dovetailed the Japanese state's efforts in mobilizing athletics to counter what it targeted as 'subversive' elements among educators and university students in the 1920s and 1930s. Thus, in the mid-1930s, when a professional league was organized, it adopted some of this amateur fighting spirit into its own image in order to make itself palatable and profitable with a public warmed to sports as character building. Famous managers, star players and leading teams have all appealed to reputed samurai qualities to explain themselves, to exhort others and to distinguish themselves from those foreigners who fall outside this noble heritage.

To be sure, the genealogy of 'samurai baseball' is much more complicated than this (as others and I have tried to delineate elsewhere) and this ideologically charged imagery cannot account for the fuller history of the sport in Japan and its multiple attractions to sponsors and spectatorships (Kelly 1998). The symbol of the samurai was deployed to baseball as much to associate the sport as a vehicle for training and displaying certain codes of citizen-worker conduct in Japan, as it was to establish a contrast set with its American counterpart. The baseball player as samurai warrior was but one of many extensions of the image to define and discipline social roles in twentieth-century Japan (especially soldiers, students and workers). The virtues of samurai baseball have shifted since the early days of solidarity with the autonomous student team, to deference to the single adult manager, to the more impersonal loyalty demanded of contemporary players, to the large organization of professional clubs (each with rosters of 70 players, coaching staffs of 20 or more, and front offices of 50–70).

Finally, it is essential to note that part of the lasting fascination in Japanese baseball with the samurai imagery is the sheer difficulty of coaching and performing 'samurai' baseball, especially at the professional level. For every legendary example of 1000-fungo drills, of pitchers overextending their innings, of absolute obedience to managerial whims, there are undercurrents and counter-examples of petulance, irreverence, and outright resistance to these practices and demands. As is often the case with moral injunctions, the frequency with which they are demanded is a clue to how difficult it is to elicit their acceptance. Japanese players and fans alike have always been able to distinguish the practices of a sport from its ideology. Much of the continuing fascination of Japanese baseball has been in savouring this gap between saying and playing (W. Kelly 2006).

Future prospects

Among the dominant American professional sports, both the National Football League and MLB have watched enviously through the 1980s and 1990s as the National Basketball Association succeeded in a highly profitable international campaign to advertise its games and stars and sell its products in markets around the world (LaFeber 2002). Both the NFL and MLB sought to emulate this expansion, but there are few analysts who share Spalding's conviction in the destiny of any of the three to attain global standing. In the case of baseball, several factors severely limit such a prospect.

First, the very organization of sport obstructs sustained multinational league competition. Of the major sports, baseball has the longest seasons; an American professional ball team plays 162 regular season games a year (Japanese teams play a 140-game schedule) plus pre-season exhibitions and post-season playoffs. Moreover, post season tournament play in baseball at the university and professional levels are multi-game series (for example, best-of-seven for the World Series and Japan Series). The logistics of international travel would require substantial truncation of its format, which is highly unlikely. Cricket's compression of multi-day test matches to single-day competitions had its analogue at the 2006 WBC in a single-game championship – which was widely criticized as one of the worst features of the Classic.

Even more importantly, as with the NBA and the NFL, MLB financial interests lie much more with marketing its 'product' to the rest of the world rather than promoting autonomous zones of baseball and ceding some jurisdictional powers to other national federations and an international body like IBAF. In fact, MLB has joined with USA Baseball, the national federation that administers US participation in world championships at all levels, in part to protect its control (for an extended discussion, see John Kelly's brief but pungent 2006 account).

Its extension to other parts of the world is also intended to developed foreign sources of new player talent, and in this MLB has been strikingly successful. The

MLB team baseball academies in the Dominican Republic have become critical channels for recruiting young and inexpensive prospects, the machinations in enticing Cuban players to defect and sign with MLB clubs, and the extensive scouting efforts in Japan and other East Asian countries have resulted in the increasingly multi-ethnic composition of MLB teams. The effect is to draw the best players to the USA rather than to nurture elite level competition elsewhere. The consequences of such asset stripping were long ago evident in the Dominican Republic, where only an abbreviated Winter League remains of what had been robust year-round league play that rivalled the MLB and attracted some of its players during their off-season (Klein 1991). The costs of the accelerating bright flight of Japanese stars for the long-term prospects of the professional leagues in Japan is uncertain, but attendance and television market share of NPB are in decline and JPB has been unable to negotiate an equitable bi-national agreement with MLB over player movements.

Ironically, the continuing internationalization of baseball in the form of current MLB initiatives will only undermine its prospects of ever becoming a global sport. Many think that anti-American politics (unrelated to baseball) within the International Olympic Committee has precipitated the dropping of the sport (and softball) from the official Olympic roster. Whatever the cause, its absence from the only meaningful supranational multi-sports organization will consolidate the present configuration of the baseball world as a dominant centre of economic clout, jurisdictional authority, and ideological aura constraining though never wholly dominating a penumbra of baseball nations that have fashioned some space for autonomous development through the dynamics of uncanny mimicry. Indeed, the American reporter in the Japanese stadium was not watching 'a whole new ballgame', but had come upon a sibling form of the sport that had been raised under different historical conditions and whose mimicry of its older sibling was so uncannily discomforting to him.

References

Appadurai, A. (1995) 'Playing with modernity: the decolonization of Indian cricket', in C. A. Breckenridge (ed.) *Consuming modernity: public culture in a South Asian world*, Minneapolis: University of Minnesota Press, 23–48.

Bhabha, H. (1984) 'Of mimicry and man: the ambivalence of colonial discourse', *October*, 28, 125–33.

Bjarkman, P. C. (1994) *Baseball with a Latin beat: a history of the Latin American game*, Jefferson, NC: McFarland & Company.

Bjarkman, P. C. (2005) *Diamonds around the globe: the encyclopedia of international baseball*, Westport, CT: Greenwood Press.

Brown, B. (1990) 'Waging baseball, playing war: games of American imperialism', *Cultural Critique*, 17, 51–78.

Brown, B. (1991) 'The meaning of baseball in 1992 (with notes on the post-American)', *Public Culture*, 4, 43–69.

Crepeau, R. C. (1982) 'Pearl Harbor: a failure of baseball?' *Journal of Popular Culture*, 15 (4), 67–74.

Dyreson, M. (2003) 'Globalizing the nation-making process: modern sport in world history', *International Journal of the History of Sports*, 20, 91–106.

Dyreson, M. (2005) 'Prologue: the paradoxes of American insularity, exceptionalism and imperialism,' *International Journal of the History of Sport*, 22, 938–45.

Eastman, B. (2005) 'Rejected America: Adolfo Luque, American interventionism and Cubanidad', *International Journal of the History of Sport*, 22, 1136–72.

Economist (1996) 'Throw till your arm drops off', *The Economist*, 28 September.

Elfers, J. E. (2003) *The tour to end all tours: the story of Major League Baseball's 1913–1914 World Tour*, Lincoln: University of Nebraska Press.

Gems, G. R. (2006) *The athletic crusade: sport and American cultural imperialism*, Lincoln: University of Nebraska Press.

Giulianotti, R. and R. Robertson (2004) 'The globalization of football: a study in the glocalization of the "serious life"', *British Journal of Sociology*, 55, 545–68.

Gmelch, G. (ed.) (2006) *Baseball without borders: the international pastime*, Lincoln: University of Nebraska Press.

Guthrie-Shimizu, S. (2004) 'For love of the game: baseball in early US–Japanese encounters and the rise of a transnational sporting fraternity', *Diplomatic History*, 28, 637–62.

Guttmann, A. and L. Thompson (2001) *Japanese sport: a history*, Honolulu: University of Hawaii Press.

Kelly, J. D. (2006) *The American game: capitalism, decolonization, world domination, and baseball*, Chicago: Prickly Paradigm Press.

Kelly, W. W. (1998) 'Blood and guts in Japanese professional baseball', in S. Linhart and S. Fruhstuck (eds) *The culture of Japan as seen through its leisure*, Albany: State University of New York Press, 95–112.

Kelly, W. W. (2000) 'The spirit and spectacle of school baseball: mass media, statemaking, and "edu-tainment" in Japan, 1905–1935', in T. Umesao, W. W. Kelly and M. Kubo (eds) *Japanese civilization in the modern world XIV: information and communication*, Senri: National Museum of Ethnology, 105–16.

Kelly, W. W. (2006) 'Japan: the Hanshin Tigers and professional baseball in Japan', in G. Gmelch (ed.) *Baseball without borders: the international pastime*, Lincoln: University of Nebraska Press, 22–42.

Klein, A. M. (1991) *Sugarball: the American game, the Dominican dream*, New Haven: Yale University Press.

Klein, A. M. (1997) *Baseball on the border: a tale of two Laredos*, Princeton: Princeton University Press.

Klein, A. M. (2006) *Growing the game: the globalization of Major League Baseball*, New Haven: Yale University Press.

LaFeber, W. (2002) *Michael Jordan and the new global capitalism*, New York: W. W. Norton.

Lamster, M. (2006) *Spalding's world tour: the epic adventure that took baseball around the globe – and made it America's game*, New York: Public Affairs Press.

Morris, A. D. (2004) 'Baseball, history, the local and the global in Taiwan', in D. K. Jordan, A. D. Morris and M. L. Moskowitz (eds) *The minor arts of daily life: popular culture in Taiwan*, Honolulu: University of Hawaii Press, 326–81.

Murdock, G. P. (1948) 'Waging baseball on Truk', *Newsweek*, 32 (9), 69–70.

Nakagawa, K. Y. (2001) *Through a diamond: 100 years of Japanese American baseball*, San Francisco: Rudi Publications.

Reaves, J. A. (2002) *Taking in a game: a history of baseball in Asia*, Lincoln: University of Nebraska Press.

Roden, D. F. (1980) 'Baseball and the quest for national dignity in Meiji Japan', *American Historical Review*, 85, 511–34.

Spalding, A. G. (1889) 'In the field papers. Base-ball', *The Cosmopolitan*, 7 (6), 603–12.

Spalding, A. G. (1911) *America's national game: historic facts concerning the beginning, evolution, development and popularity of base ball: with personal reminiscences of its vicissitudes, its victories and its votaries*, New York: American Sports Publishing Company.

Warner, G. A. (1997) 'Japanese baseball: a whole new ballgame', *Orange County (CA) Register*, Section 1, page 7, 28 September.

7

More than a game: globalization and the post-Westernization of world cricket

CHRIS RUMFORD

Consider these two images of cricket as a global sport. First, the announcement by the International Cricket Council (ICC) that it will open a global cricket academy in Dubai. Facilities will include, 'a 30,000-capacity stadium, three other cricket grounds, indoor training and fitness facilities. The project will open in 2007 and will be available to all of the ICC's 92 member countries' (BBC News 29 September 2004). Second, the Taliban seeking ICC recognition for cricket in Afghanistan (back in 2001), a country with little tradition of domestic cricket and where the majority of current players have lived in exile in Pakistan for many years (McCarthy 2001). Afghanistan is now an affiliate member of the ICC and in 2006 its national team completed a first tour of England (BBC News 11 June 2006).

The first image conforms to a familiar pattern associated with the globalization of sport: a world governing body; a high proportion of the world's nation-states being members; location of the administrative centre in a global city – Dubai (for commercial rather than sporting reasons); the professionalization and standardization of the game – the global academy 'will be a focal point for the training and development of cricket players, coaches, umpires, curators and administrators' (Long 2005). The second image points to the importance of global culture in shaping national expectations (Lechner and Boli 2005). For the Taliban, sporting participation was viewed as a vehicle for wider international diplomatic recognition. The conventional interpretation of Islamic fundamentalism poses it in opposition to globalization. The Taliban's policies have certainly been viewed in this way, with its efforts to ban recorded music, preventing its people from watching TV, and outlawing the education of women, for example. But the Taliban did not attempt to avoid global modernity, rather it sought to create a space for itself within global culture. As Beyer points out, writing about Islam and globalization more generally rather than the Taliban, 'the central thrust is to make Islam and Muslims more determinate in the world system, not to reverse globalization. The intent is to shape global reality, not to negate it'

(Beyer, quoted in Robins 1997: 42). For the Taliban, cricket was considered a sport that could be compatible with both Islam *and* its global aspirations, and therefore a port of entry into the wider world of international relations. Cricket benefited from this global cultural imperative in large part because it satisfied the Taliban's strict interpretation of the Islamic dress code; 'Mullah Omar had decreed that, unlike athletics, football or swimming, playing cricket did not require any part of the body to be revealed to the public' (Guha 2001).

Both images point to an important aspect of the globalization of cricket, namely its post-Westernization. Recent years have seen a power shift in cricket administration away from the traditional 'Western' centres of power towards the Asian countries (symbolized by the relocation of the ICC headquarters from London to Dubai) fuelled by the increasing importance of one-day cricket and the prominence of the one-day international match (ODI) as both a televisual cricketing spectacular and a major revenue generator. If globalization has its 'winners and losers' then India has emerged as a winner in recent years, while places such as South Africa and the West Indies can be considered losers (Gupta 2004). In many ways, India is the focal point for both the globalization of cricket – a new focus for generating cricket finance through massive TV audiences and administrative leadership – and for the post-Westernization of the game. As the themes of globalization and post-Westernization are central to the account in this article it is to these theoretical constructs to which we must first turn.

Globalization and post-Westernization

The relationship between globalization and sport is often seen as contradictory. On the one hand, a world championship competition is pivotal to most major sports (football, rugby, boxing) and the Olympic Games is still the pre-eminent tournament for many other sports, especially track and field athletics. However, it is worth noting that two of the most 'global' sports, golf and tennis, manage quite nicely without a world championship as such, organized instead around four 'major' tournaments. World Cups can be considered a key vehicle for globalization in the Robertsonian sense, namely the 'compression of the world and the intensification of consciousness of the world as a whole' (Robertson 2002: 8). During a World Cup competition the world becomes a single space of competition within which competitors and supporters aim for their team to be the world's best, acknowledged as such by the rest of the world. World championships and world cups thereby reinforce globalization; the world becomes more interconnected and is viewed in organizational terms as a single place.

At the same time, sport is often seen as reinforcing national identification; the biggest championships are competed for by national teams, or are organized in such a way that individuals represent their nation-states. This has led to interpretations that emphasize the potential for resisting globalization inherent in organized sport (Rowe 2003), or that more commonly assert the necessity of nationalist sentiment for the success of global competition. It is fair to say that one of the central issues in the literature on globalization and sport is the tension between the nationalist dimension of competitive sport and its globalization, the first dimension not necessarily constituting a barrier to the second. For example, for Scholte, 'global spectacles like the Olympic Games and various World Cups have also thrived on nationalist sentiment' (Scholte 2000: 163). For Hedetoft (2003), that sport can easily be utilized as a vehicle for national identity is due to its competitive nature. International competition can take on an importance symbolic dimension: 'in this world of competing sovereigns, the playing-field is much more level than in the reality of military, political or economic competitive processes. Here all stand a chance, even the smaller nation-states, who can occasionally enjoy the compensatory pleasure of defeating their bigger brothers' (Hedetoft 2003: 71–2).

However, it would be a mistake not to interrogate the national–global nexus a little further. In recent years national sport has also developed a marked post-national dimension. For example, in England premiership football has become post-national in many respects: leading clubs have fielded teams containing 11 'foreign' players (in other words, players not qualified to play for the national team); top premiership teams play in the European Champions League, which has created a strong non-national focus for domestic football; foreign ownership of leading clubs is increasing; the Bosman ruling has created a greater, EU-derived, mobility for players; leading clubs such as Manchester United and Chelsea promote themselves as global brands (Roche 2007). Thus, globalization is not only to be equated with the global scope of the game, or the fact that the World Cup is a global televisual event, or that footballers can become global icons. The structure and orientation of the domestic game has also been transformed by globalization.

English cricket has been subject to the same global forces and the domestic game has experienced a similar form of 'globalization from within', and a post-national game has emerged as one consequence of globalization. More so than in the case of football, cricketers are tempted to qualify to play for a country other than that of their birth (in the current England team that is true of several players, Andrew Strauss and Kevin Pietersen – both South African born – and Geraint Jones – born in Papua New Guinea, raised in Australia), although this is certainly not just a recent phenomenon. Cricket also has its equivalent of the 'Bosman affair' and 'Kolpak' players are an increasing feature of the English game. Maros Kolpak was a Slovakian handball player in the German league who lost his place in the team because of a league quota on non-EU players. He disputed the ruling as unfair and won his case at the European Court of Justice. The implication of the decision for English cricket is that players from non-European countries that possess trade agreements with the EU are now protected by EU employment law. This means that in England a foreign player with a work permit must, if coming from a 'Kolpak' country (such as South Africa, Zimbabwe, and the Caribbean islands), be treated the same as a domestic-qualified player and not be subject to the quota of overseas players (currently two per team) that applies in the English domestic game. In this sense, English cricket, like football before it, demonstrates a strong post-national dimension, although this situation is by no means replicated in other cricket-playing countries to anything like the same extent (in Australia rugby has a much stronger post-national dimension than cricket). 'In theory county teams in the future could have no England-qualified players' (Mark Newton, chief executive of Worcestershire County Cricket Club, quoted in Gough 2004).

The idea of post-Westernization has become an important one in recent years (Delanty 2003, 2006), and cannot simply be equated with the ending of the cold war, the bipolar world order, and the decreasing salience of the idea of the 'West' as a reference point for political identification and global leadership. Post-Westernization is a process or series of processes with a number of key dimensions. First, post-Westernization signals the increasing lack of unity within those countries formerly considered to have a common 'Western' world view (such as divisions over the invasion of Iraq in 2003, or action on climate change). In the cricketing context this can be related to the divisions between the ICC and England over playing matches in Zimbabwe during the 2003 World Cup. Against a background of domestic political protest urging England not to play in Mugabe's Zimbabwe the England team chose to frame its concerns in terms of security, and England's players, backed by the England and Wales Cricket Board (ECB), refused to travel to Zimbabwe. 'The ECB had hoped that the death-threat letter they received from an organization called Sons and Daughters of Zimbabwe, would act as the key evidence to support their case' (BBC News, 15 February 2003). However, the ICC ruled that the venue was safe and that England should play. England forfeited the match and, in the process, seriously reduced its chances of qualifying for the next stage of the competition. During the same tournament New Zealand forfeited a match scheduled to be played in Nairobi, Kenya, also citing security concerns. Significantly, Sri Lanka took a different approach and played its match in Nairobi as scheduled.

Second, post-Westernization involves the recognition that there is no one single global modernity. What we have instead is a mélange of different modernities – Western, post-communist, Islamic – rather than the expansion of a singular Western modernity (Karagiannis and Wagner 2006; Therborn 2003). When applied to cricket this calls into question the assumption that what needs to be explained, in relation to globalization, is the global diffusion of the sport and the reasons why the game has been more successfully transplanted/adopted in some countries than others. Thus, while cricket is rightfully associated with British colonialist expansion and was successfully 'exported' to many colonies (Australia, India, South Africa) it did not become established in Canada and the USA, for example, at least not after the end of the nineteenth century (Kaufman and Patterson 2005). Third, post-Westernization alerts us to the emergence of a new East capable of shaping global affairs, previously seen as the preserve of the West. In cricketing terms, the balance within ICC membership has shifted, 'non-Western nations now prevail and their numbers continue to grow with Bangladesh already a new Test playing nation' (Gupta 2004: 268).

The post-Westernization of cricket is closely related to the growing tensions between the two versions of the game. The traditional 'first class' version played over three, four and, in the case of international or 'Test' matches, five days, exists alongside the newer, and in many ways more marketable and therefore revenue-generating, 'one-day' or limited-overs version of the game (it should be noted that the same professional players participate in both versions of the game). The two formats, while existing to a certain extent in a state of tension (in the sense of competing for space within busy schedules), are organized in parallel by a common governing body, the ICC. The growth of the ODI has been dramatic (after a slow start – the first ODI was played in 1971, the second not until 18 months later). In 1976 there were 6 ODIs, by 1986 this figure had risen to 62, by 1996 127, and in 2006 159 ODIs were played. There are also more Test matches scheduled nowadays: in 1976 there were 23 Tests, 30 in 1986, and 28 in 1996. In recent years the figures have increased sharply with 46 in 2006. The figures were even higher in 2005 (48) and 2004 (51).

It is argued that the existence of two formats for the game of cricket, and the rapid expansion of ODIs in recent years (assisted by the establishment of major one-day tournaments – especially the World Cup and Champions Trophy – which have also permitted a greater range of counties to play international cricket, for example Hong Kong, Ireland, the Netherlands, Canada and Kenya) has allowed for the globalization of the game and, of particular importance, has allowed for the former British colonies, in Asia especially, to become more equal players in this nascent global sport; a crucial aspect of what I have termed post-Westernization. It could be argued that the globalization of cricket consists in the struggle between the Asian cricketing countries (especially India) and the traditional centres for control of the game, the crux of which is the issue of the balance between Test matches and ODIs.

Rethinking globalization and cricket

Cricket is a sport not normally thought of as having a strong global dimension, despite being played on five continents. It is played mainly in the countries of the British Commonwealth but because it is not an Olympic sport it maintains a low profile outside of the circuit of cricket playing nations. Cricket does have a world governing body, the ICC, and a World Cup competition every four years, a key marker of global aspirations, as in other sports but does not possess global superstars, players known widely outside the game, although the exploits of great players such as Don Bradman, Garry Sobers, and Imran Khan have eventually filtered through to a wider public. Current cricketing greats such as Shane Warne, Sachin Tendulkar and Brian Lara will never achieve the global recognition of leading figures from other sports: Tiger Woods, Ronaldinho, Roger Federer. Thus, cricket cannot easily claim to capture the global sporting imagination and because of its many peculiarities, not least of which is that a match can be played over five days without necessarily producing a winner, it is commonly seen as a sport for aficionados rather than a sport with mass appeal. The rules can seem complex, the progression of play incomprehensible: it is not always possible easily to answer the question 'who's winning?', a definite turn-off for the casual spectator. There are other apparent limitations: cricket is conventionally thought of as a quintessentially English summer sport, a game of the upper-classes exported around the world through colonialism, and limited to a few countries that have little claim to international sporting excellence (India, Pakistan, Sri Lanka). For all of these reasons it is easy to conclude that it will never 'go global'.

Accounts of cricket as a global game, or more commonly why cricket must fail in an attempt to globalize, tend to centre on the extent to which it has become 'indigenized' and accepted in different settings (or not). Thus, the key to globalization is thought to be the ability of recipient countries to nationalize, naturalize and otherwise make the sport culturally authentic in a colonial/post-colonial setting. In countries where it has become embedded as a national sport, cricket is no longer 'an English mystery. It is an Australian game and as much at home in Africa or Asia or the Caribbean as in Canterbury and Hove' (Reynolds 1975: 242). It has been said that 'Indians have indigenized cricket and that it is more Indian than English' (Sethi 2004). Nandy expresses this sentiment more strongly, opening his book *The Tao of cricket* with the provocative assertion that 'Cricket is an Indian game accidentally discovered by the English' (Nandy 2000: 1). This section will critically evaluate a number of approaches to understanding the spread of cricket in various parts of the world before elaborating on the central issue in relation to the globalization of cricket: the emergence of India as one of 'cricket's superpowers' (Runciman 2005), and the shifting balance in the world game between Test and one-day cricket.

In their historical account of the global spread of cricket, Kaufman and Patterson argue that cricket became 'successfully diffused to most but not all countries with close cultural ties to England' (Kaufman and Patterson 2005: 82). They focus on the cases of Canada and the United States and aim to explain the failure of cricket to become properly established in these countries. Their account emphasizes the role of cricket in the diffusion of colonial values from England to its colonies and highlights the role of local elites and cultural entrepreneurs in popularizing and indigenizing the sport. In the case of Canada and the USA, despite early successes in establishing the game in the 1800s, 'cricket became a marker of high social status, and the game was not promoted among the population at large (Kaufman and Patterson 2005: 99). A key element in the global cultural diffusion of cricket is the 'ability of some groups of recipients to dominate or otherwise limit access to cultural imports, thereby "capturing" such imports for themselves' (Kaufman and Patterson 2005: 106). In the USA and Canada access was 'overprotected' by elites, thus preventing cricket from becoming part of the cultural landscape. In contrast, in many other colonial societies cricket became attractive to all major social strata: 'In India, for example, love for the game was spread through the organization of matches between ethno-religious groups, each of which welcomed talented players from within their communities regardless of rank' (Kaufman and Patterson 2005: 99).

The ability of cricket to become part of the 'national patrimony', to use a phrase employed by Kaufman and Patterson, has been remarked upon by many commentators in the case of India. The work of Arjun Appadurai (1996) is important in this regard, and the best (perhaps only) example of a leading theorist of globalization turning his attention to cricket. He is drawn to question how cricket has become 'Indian'. This question has been 'answered' in different ways, including the explanation associated with Ashis Nandy that was alluded to above and that is inherent in the idea that there is a 'mythical structure beneath the surface of the sport that makes it profoundly Indian in spite of its Western historical origins' (Appadurai 1996: 90).

Appaduarai's own explanation proceeds from the idea that indigenization is the result of nationalist experimentation with modernity (entry into the wider community of nation-states), rather than the adoption of imported cultural norms *per se*. For Appadurai a key moment in Indian cricket was the transcendence of traditional cricketing norms and values – the primacy of Test matches, traditional codes of on-field behaviour associated with amateur or 'Victorian values', nationalist struggles against former colonial masters – when cricket 'moved into yet another, post-national phase, in which entertainment value, media coverage, and the commercialization of players' (Appadurai 1996: 108) would dominate. In this new world of one-day cricket (ushered in by Australian media magnate Kerry Packer's 'World Series Cricket' in the late 1970s) 'the Victorian code and nationalist concerns are subordinated to the transnational flow of talent, celebrity, and money' (Appadurai 1996: 108).

While this development certainly helps us to understand the pivotal role of one-day cricket in transforming the world game in a way that the argument by Kaufman and Patterson does not, Appaduarai recognizes that it does not by itself account for the Indian passion for cricket, or why, in his words, 'it is not just indigenized but the very symbol of a sporting practice that seems to embody India' (Appadurai 1996: 110). The answer to the question of why cricket became 'so profoundly Indianized' (Appadurai 1996: 111) is complex, but consists of several key components. It became an emblem of Indian nationhood and allowed many different groups within Indian society to experiment with the 'means of modernity': state bureaucrats could manipulate nationalist sentiment, entrepreneurs could master the media through advertising, the viewing public could engage with national competition, the working classes could exercise group belonging. In sum, the 'producers and consumers of cricket can share the excitement of Indianness without its many, divisive scars' (Appadurai 1996: 112–13).

The key theme to emerge from Appadurai's account is the changing nature of cricket during the 1970s – the onset of one-day cricket, commercialization, pro-fessionalization – and the way in which these changes allowed for a shift in power, away from the traditional cricket establishment towards both commercial concerns and the Asian cricketing nations, especially India. Writing in the mid-1990s Appaduarai could discern the emerging patterns in world cricket but was not able to witness their full development; a decade further on, the new world order of cricket has crystallized around the increasingly global image of the ODI.

Gupta makes the point that for most sports globalization has typically followed the patterns witnessed in most areas of international relations – control of wealth, technology and marketing leading to the domination of 'Western' nations over the rest. Cricket is different: 'it is a game where the non-Western countries have begun to dominate not just on the field, but more importantly, in shaping the economies and politics of the game' (Gupta 2004: 257). Central to this argument is the idea that while cricket is on the rise in the traditional peripheries of the game, it is in decline in the core countries. This aspect of cricket's transformation can be overstated. For example, Gupta argues that the power shift has been aided by the fact that cricket 'has a diminishing status as a sport in the country of its origin –

England' (Gupta 2004: 274) and is very much second to football as a national game. It is worth noting that the idea that English cricket (stereotyped as an upper middle-class or elitist sport) never enjoyed the mass appeal of football (with its working-class associations) can easily be challenged. According to John Arlott (1975: 29–30) cricket enjoyed its 'pop' age in the immediate postwar period, filled with glamorous sporting figures and national heroes (Hutton, Compton, Trueman, Laker). However, the next generation of players had less mass appeal. According to Arlott, 'Cricket fell upon hard times. In 1966, when England's footballers won the World Cup, soccer finally superseded cricket in the majority public imagination' (Arlott 1975: 29). It is true that English cricket lost ground against other sports in the 1970s and 1980s due to its perception as a tradition-bound relic of a former age coupled with the often woeful performances of the national team, but has since enjoyed a period of stability, even prosperity. This has been made possible by stronger financial foundations throughout the county game (through the revenues generated by the one-day game), the professionalization of coaching and administration of the national team, and the multiculturalism of the domestic game (the current England team contains one player from a Sikh background, Monty Panesar, and another from a Muslim community, Sajid Mahmood). In the past few years the England team has become one of the best in the world (at the time of writing ranked the second best Test team in the world by the ICC). Moreover, England has pioneered a new cricket format, 20/20, an even shorter version of the one-day game that has proved to be very popular (and financially lucrative) at both domestic and international level since its introduction in 2003. International 20/20 matches are becoming a significant part of the ODI calendar and 20/20 looks set to become an even more important component of the globalization of the game: inclusion at the 2010 Commonwealth Games in Delhi has already been mooted.

Gupta makes a strong case for the transformation of cricket under conditions of globalization, particularly the non-Western countries shaping the economics and politics of the game. Television and modern information and communication of technology have created the possibility for cricket to be a global game, feeding 'diaporas that support their team across frontiers [through] technology that provides real-time global coverage of the sport' (Gupta 2002). What is clear from this account is that the central feature of the globalization of cricket has been the shift of decision-making power to the non-Western, former peripheries of the game. The Asian cricketing nations, led by India, have managed to wrest much control from the traditional centres. This power shift has been driven by political ambition, new communication and media technologies, and the market power of large TV audiences, and has only been held back by the political tensions between India and Pakistan, which prevent a 'common front' being constructed among Asian cricketing countries.

Despite this lack of unity, 'South Asia, with its tens of millions of enthusiastic supporters, its super-rich internationals, its strong financial base and its over-compensating administrators, has gradually begun to replace Western control with Eastern control' (Majumdar 2006). One reason for this is that TV audiences for cricket (both domestic and among expatriates) is huge. According to Marqusee, 'cricket in the subcontinent is an ideal vehicle for multinational corporations seeking to penetrate "emerging markets". And, thanks to satellite television, subcontinental cricket can be used to sell goods in Europe, North America, the Middle East and South-East Asia' (Marqusee 2004, quoted in Gupta 2004: 265). India alone 'produces 60 per cent of world cricket's income' (Bose 2005) and draws the largest TV audiences. Moreover, India has emerged as a major superpower in world cricket, in both the sense that its national team is among the world's best and also because India, through its financial and media influence on the game, has shifted the centre of gravity of cricket from Test matches to ODIs. Not everyone sees this as a positive development. From Runciman's (2005) point of view, 'the rise of India as the centre of the cricketing world does not bode well for test cricket, for the simple reason that in India the one-day game remains much more popular. Most Indian cricket fans would far rather their team win the next World Cup than that they become the number one team in test cricket'.

The ICC as global entrepreneur

The ICC has recently moved its headquarters from Lord's (in London) to Dubai. It has calculated that this move will bring benefits other than tax concessions. According to Malcolm Speed, chief executive, cricket's biggest audiences are in the Indian sub-continent: 'In those four countries [India, Pakistan, Sri Lanka and Bangladesh] there is a great passion for cricket. That is 22 per cent of the world's population. They are huge economies that are growing rapidly. ... Much of our revenue now comes from that region. ... We moved to Asia. It was a deliberate move' (*Cricinfo News*, 17 June 2006). For most of its existence the ICC has not had anything like this level of global awareness.

The International Cricket Council, established in 1907 as the Imperial Cricket Conference, has until recently been 'dominated by the white nations of the Commonwealth. Thus it was England, Australia, South Africa and even tiny New Zealand that set the rules for the game and guided its economics and marketing' (Gupta 2004: 260). For most of its existence it has acted as traditionalist and gate-keeper, promoting a conservative view of the game (ODIs were not played until 1971, with the first World Cup staged in 1975, despite the fact that competitive one-day cricket had been part of the English domestic game since 1963), and restricting access to new Test playing nations, keeping Sri Lanka out of the Test arena until the 1980s, for example (Gupta 2004: 261). Indeed, Marqusee argues that it was a combination of the amateurism and parochialism of the ICC, subsumed as it was to the imperialistic MCC, that prevented cricket from developing as a truly global sport during the twentieth century, 'unlike football, cricket's spread remained confined to societies under the direct rule of the British Empire' (Marqusee 2005).

Until recently the ICC has been anything but a force for the globalization of the game. It failed to encourage Test playing nations to play against each other, leaving matches to be organized bilaterally. For example, it allowed apartheid-era South

Africa to avoid playing the West Indies, India or Pakistan (Marqusee 2005). However, recent years have seen important changes. The modernization of the game, which has accelerated since the 1980s (as Marqusee points out, neutral umpires did not stand in Test matches until the late 1980s when they were introduced by Pakistan) has created new divisions within the game. Put simply, 'the ICC has been riven by conflict between the South Asian and Anglo-Australian blocs. The South Asian bloc's economic and political clout is formidable and the Anglo-Australians have found that reality hard to swallow' (Marqusee 2005). The 'power shift' has encountered further problems – allegations of match-fixing and corruption, particularly surrounding matches played in Sharjah (United Arab Emirates), and political tensions between India and Pakistan, which have limited sporting contacts between the two nations.

Earlier, it was commented that cricket has been incapable of producing globally-recognized sportsmen, even from the ranks of the truly great performers. It has, however, recently thrown up a major figure who has earned a global reputation. Jagmohan Dalmiya has had a huge impact on world cricket over the past two decades both in terms of placing India at the forefront of the global game and in the wider sense of modernizing cricket and its finances to an unprecedented degree. He has been recognized by the *International Journal of the History of Sport* as one of its three 'foremost statesmen of modern sport in the last quarter century' (Taylor & Francis press release, undated), the others being Sepp Blatter (football) and Juan Samaranch (Olympic movement). He was thus recognized for having 'helped to change the face of the world in the last 25 years through sport', his 'lead in making South Asia the hub of cricketing activity', and for playing a 'substantial role in ensuring the shift of power, prestige and prominence of the sport to South Asia from where it was before' (*The Hindu*, 17 July 2005). Although he was a controversial ICC president (and continues to be a controversial cricket administrator in India) Dalmiya shaped the game decisively during his term of office between 1997 and 2000. In particular, he was instrumental in expanding the ICC's pro-grammes around the world – the globalization of the game, as it became known in ICC parlance – and generated greater revenue from sponsorship and television rights. One key to achieving this was to create a coherent programme of international cricket. As Malik (2006) writes:

> One of Dalmiya's gifts to cricket was the five-year international cricket calendar. Till the early 1990s, cricket matches were negotiated bilaterally. The Indian cricket board met the Pakistani board and agreed to tour in month X; then it met the New Zealand board and agreed to host their team in month Y. Gaps were filled in with *ad hoc* tournaments, and tours conceived or cancelled at short notice. A certainly hierarchy was built into this. England, for instance, toured the subcontinent on sufferance. Australia gave India a series down under once a decade. ... The ICC calendar changed all that. It made it incumbent for every team to play every other at regular intervals, home and away.

Another of Dalmiya's achievements prior to his stint at the ICC was to bring the 1987 and 1996 World Cups to the subcontinent, and in doing so start to unsettle the balance of power between the traditional centres and the subcontinent. This also helped to consolidate the important status of the ODI in India (following on from their World Cup triumph in 1983) and generate the economic power base that has done so much to shift the balance of power. In the case of the 1996 World Cup Dalmiya, negotiating on behalf of India, managed to out-manoeuvre England and Australia by winning the support of the ICC associate members (non-Test playing members) by promising them a greater share of the financial rewards from the event.

Concluding comments: cricket – more than a game

One of my favourite cricket books when I was a teenager was entitled *Cricket: more than a game* (Sheppard 1975). The subtitle refers to the way sporting values associated with cricket transcend the status of mere 'games' and can offer guidelines for 'playing by the rules' in life more generally. It also alludes to the way in which an understanding of cricket – how it is played and by whom – can help us understand the complexities of English, Australian, or Indian society, for example. The book appears quite dated now, especially since it was 'designed to be published on the eve of the first-ever one day series between international teams for the Prudential Cup' (jacket blurb) – the first World Cup, in other words – and yet it fails to devote a single section to one-day cricket. This neglect is ironic because the intervening 30 or so years have indeed shown international cricket to be 'more than a game'. In fact, it is two games – Test matches and ODIs. Globalization has driven the two formats further apart and created two circuits of international cricket, both of which are so heavily scheduled that there is barely enough time in the calendar year to fit some 50 Test matches and 150 ODIs.

In this article I have highlighted the important developments associated with the post-Westernization of cricket, a series of developments that point to more than the reorganization of the administration of the game away from the imperial centres of cricket. The shift in the balance of power towards the Asian cricketing countries has helped to keep within bounds major disputes that have upset the smooth operation of the global game over the past decade or so and helps us understand how a game that could have been riven by colonial and post-colonial suspicions and inequalities has survived into the twenty-first century. One such point of contention surrounds accusations of 'chucking' (an infringement of the rules whereby the bowler throws rather than bowls the ball, this being a difficult accusation to prove or disprove). Several leading players from Asian countries have found it extremely difficult to remove the stigma of 'chucking', including two of the world's leading bowlers, Shoaib Akhtar of Pakistan and Muttiah Muralitharan of Sri Lanka. There is suspicion in the Asian cricketing world that the authorities have unfairly singled out Asian cricketers, while non-Asian bowlers have had their actions approved much more readily. At the same time, the Anglo-Australian cricketing world remains suspicious of the motives of the ICC in relaxing the rules concerning the straightening of the arm so central to allegations of 'chucking'.

Other disputes have the ability to drive further a wedge between West and East. One such incident took place during the series between England and Pakistan in August 2006. Pakistan forfeited the fourth and final Test of the series (the first time a forfeiture had occurred in 129 years of Test cricket) as a result of its players' unwillingness to retake the field of play following a ruling by the match umpires that they had 'tampered' with the ball (namely changed its condition intentionally and for their own advantage). The Pakistan team's refusal to take to the field was designed to register a protest against the allegation of cheating. An ICC hearing subsequently cleared the Pakistan captain Inzamam-Ul-Haq of ball-tampering but he was banned for four matches for 'bringing the game into disrepute'.

The success of cricket in transcending the East–West divide is often under-estimated, according to Andrew Miller. In his reflections on the 'ball-tampering incident' (Miller 2006) he makes a valuable point:

> But I'll tell you what cricket really is. It's a bridge between cultures that might otherwise have drifted apart with scarcely a backwards glance. OK, so it's rooted in its colonial heritage, which is right at the crux of the issue that is eating the game this morning, but how grateful is the world right now for even the slightest insight into the psyche of the other?

It is also worth bearing in mind that it is likely that a dispute such as this can be resolved more easily, any injustice felt by Pakistan addressed more convincingly, and any lingering resentment of prejudicial treatment ameliorated by a global cricketing context in which, until 2006, the president of the ICC was a Pakistani, Ehsan Mani. Cricket now operates within a global frame, and its success in 'bridging East and West' pointed to by Miller is in reality evidence of the post-Westernization of the sport. Cricket could not have become a global sport while it was structured according to the hierarchies of imperial legacy. Divisions in the game arising from 'chucking', ball-tampering, match fixing, sledging, walking, time-wasting, and the balance between Test cricket and ODIs, all of which have been issues central to the running or the playing of the game in recent years are thus best understood, not in a post-colonial context, but in a post-Western one.

References

Appadurai, A. (1996) *Modernity at large: cultural dimensions of globalization,* Minneapolis: University of Minnesota Press.

Arlott, J. (1975) 'England', in J. Sheppard (ed.) *Cricket: more than a game*, London: Angus & Robertson, 19–36.

Bose, M. (2005) 'Coming of age' [review of 'Twenty-two yards to freedom: a social history of Indian cricket' by Boria Majumdar], *The Wisden Cricketer,* 18 March.

Delanty, G. (2003) 'The making of a post-Western Europe: a civilizational analysis', *Thesis Eleven,* 72, 8–25.

Delanty, G. (2006) 'Introduction: the idea of a post-Western Europe', in G. Delanty (ed.) *Europe and Asia beyond East and West*, London: Routledge, 1–7.

Gough, M. (2004) 'Counties fear Kolpak', BBC News, 3 March.

Guha, R. (2001) 'A man from Kabul', *The Hindu*, 2 September.

Gupta, A. (2002) 'South Asia dominates cricket', *Daily Times*, 13 December.

Gupta, A. (2004) 'The globalization of cricket: the rise of the non-West', *International Journal of the History of Sport*, 21, 257–76.

Hedetoft, U. (2003) *The global turn: national encounters with the world*, Aalborg: Aalborg University Press.

Karagiannis, N. and P. Wagner (2006) 'Introduction: globalization or world-making', in N. Karagiannis and P. Wagner (eds) *Varieties of world-making: beyond globalization*, Liverpool: Liverpool University Press.

Kaufman, J. and O. Patterson (2005) 'Cross-national cultural diffusion: the global spread of cricket', *American Sociological Review*, 70, February, 82–110.

Lechner, F. and J. Boli (2005) *World culture: origins and consequences*, Oxford: Blackwell.

Long, J. (2005) 'Rod Marsh appointed a Director of Coaching at ICC Global Cricket Academy', www.icc-cricket.com/icc-media/content/story/218368.html

McCarthy, R. (2001) 'Afghan applause just isn't cricket', *Guardian*, 18 May.

Majumdar, B. (2006) 'Cricket cultures in conflict', BBC News, 28 February.

Malik, A. (2006) 'Of money and muscle', *Cricinfo Magazine*, February.

Marqusee, M. (2004) 'A magnet for long-distance nationalism', *The Hindu*, 17 September.

Marqusee, M. (2005) 'The ambush clause: globalization, corporate power and the governance of world cricket', in S. Wagg (ed.) *Following on: cricket and national identity in the postcolonial age*, London: Routledge.

Miller, A. (2006) 'What a horrible mess', *Cricinfo Magazine*, 21 August.

Nandy, A. (2000) *The Tao of cricket*, Oxford: Oxford University Press.

Reynolds, S. (1975) 'The grand old limey game', in J. Sheppard (ed.) *Cricket: more than a game*, London: Angus & Robertson, 241–7.

Robertson, R. (2002) *Globalization: social theory and global culture*, London: Sage.

Robins, K. (1997) 'What in the world's going on?', in P. Du Gay (ed.) *Production of culture/cultures of production*, London: Sage, 11–47.

Roche, M. (2007, forthcoming) 'Europe, the "cosmopolitan condition" and European sport', in C. Rumford (ed.) *Cosmopolitanism and Europe*, Liverpool: Liverpool University Press.

Rowe, D. (2003) 'Sport and the repudiation of the global', *International Review for the Sociology of Sport*, 38, 281–94.

Runciman, D. (2005) 'Cricket's superpowers', *London Review of Books*, 27(18), 22 September.

Scholte, J. A. (2000) *Globalization: a critical introduction*, Houndmills: Palgrave.

Sethi, R. (2004) 'Diaspora and the global market', *Tribune*, 28 November.

Sheppard, J. (ed.) (1975) *Cricket: more than a game*, London: Angus & Robertson.

Therborn, G. (2003) 'Entangled modernities', *European Journal of Social Theory*, 6, 293–305.

8

Imagined communities in the global game: soccer and the development of Dutch national identity

FRANK J. LECHNER

In preparation for the 2006 World Cup, the Dutch soccer federation selected Marco van Basten, former European player of the year and star of the Netherlands' 1988 European championship team, to coach the national selection. Though he had little coaching experience, he had been recommended by Johan Cruyff, Dutch soccer icon and star of an earlier generation. Van Basten's job was to correct the lapses the national team had suffered under a previous coach and return to playing the 'right' way, that is, to 'play according to the laws of the so-called *Hollandse* school' and find the players to match the style (Kok 2006: 166), to 'combat globalization' by making his team '*Hollands*' again (Kuper 2006a). Van Basten's assistant, John van 't Schip, expressed their joint commitment when he said that 'our way of playing is more important than the result' (Van 't Schip 2005). After the team played just well enough to advance to the second round in the 2006 World Cup but failed to show the expected flair, foreign experts like the German inter-national Günter Netzer voiced disappointment at the Dutch failure to display 'their' style and domestic commentators quickly complained that 'this is not our soccer' (H. Camps in NOS 2006a). 'Our' soccer had always been different – different, especially, from the dour, mechanical version attributed to the Germans, who in this regard, as in others (Boterman 1999), served as a major foil. These examples convey the widespread notion that, like other nations prominent in the game, the Dutch have enriched global soccer with a distinct style that reflects their special virtues. 'Total soccer' is their claim to global fame, the way the nation made its mark on the world at large.

The sociology of sports approaches such claims with scepticism. Drawing on the idea that nations are 'imagined communities' that have 'invented' their presumed national traditions, it has developed a way of thinking about national sporting traditions that leads us to expect any imagined distinction to break down on closer inspection, both because the actual soccer record does not match the idealized national style and because any country's national myth-making is bound to resemble that of many other nations. The Dutch may just be constructing another 'fantasy shield' (Maguire 1999: 187) in a defence against global pressure. Such a critique has merit, and the Dutch do indeed use soccer in re-imagining the nation, but it overlooks another side of Dutch soccer discourse. Conventional wisdom regards the 1974 World Cup tournament as the high point of Dutch soccer distinction, but one of the stars of that time, Willem van Hanegem, has said that no one planned the team's style and that total soccer 'just developed' by chance (van Hanegem in NOS 2006b). Another star of 1974, Arie Haan, has played down the virtues of total soccer itself, saying that 'prizes you win in a different way' (Haan in NOS 2006b). Dutch reporters have gone further, calling the whole idea of a distinct national soccer tradition a 'myth'; they advocate greater appreciation of the real requirements for success in the international game (Onkenhout and Vissers 2001; Visser 2006). Such examples indicate that in their soccer discourse the Dutch are not uniformly in thrall to 'brilliant orange' and argue the merits of a myth they understand as myth. Generalizing from such examples, I suggest that the standard critique of the use of soccer in the defensive and particularist re-imagining of a national community underestimates the complexity, reflexivity, and fluidity in the way the Dutch experience soccer. This record fits a line of thought about globalization in which the process is not seen as a threat to be met by national bulwarks and in which creative engagement with new networks leads to a layering of identities.

How to position the nation in a globalizing world is an important issue for the Dutch, as it is for many others, beyond the sports arena. After a period of relative neglect, the who-are-we question has returned to the public agenda in the Netherlands (cf. Koch and Scheffer 1996). According to recent literature on globalization, that is only to be expected: deterritorialization calls into question any group's collective attachment to place, border-crossing flows undermine any state's hold on loyalty, and in the global cultural economy, according to Held et al. (1999: 328), the significance of national culture remains to be deciphered. In the Dutch case, immigration and EU integration – two quasi-global trends – served as triggers for an intensifying debate. In that debate, the sociologist and populist leader Pim Fortuyn (2002) as well as others, such as the former leader of the liberal VVD, Josias Van Aartsen (Peeperkorn and Remarque 2004), argued for restoring Dutch pride in national history and heroes as a way to achieve greater national cohesion. From this standpoint, Dutch soccer embodies a unique tradition and the rituals surrounding it nicely promote cohesion. This strand of discourse had an affinity – causal links are more difficult to assess – with the soccer fervour of previous decades and displayed a nostalgic essentialism of the sort sociologists typically question. In the Dutch debates, however, critics brought to bear sceptical insights from the postmodern literature on nations and nationalism to suggest that the Netherlands 'doesn't exist anymore' (Van der Veer 2000). From this standpoint, Dutch soccer discourse is just a form of entertaining but practically futile myth-making and ostensibly nationalist rituals, such as fans elaborately decked out in orange garb, have an ironic quality – while some are die-hard supporters, others play at the role in the manner of typically more middle-class 'post-fans' (Giulianotti 1999: 148–9). Still others searched for a middle ground I call cosmopolitan nationalism, characterized by a revived attachment to things national that remains at the same time outwardly oriented, a position of which intellectuals have offered competing versions. In this strand of identity discourse, the nation is neither bulwark nor empty shell but one type of communal identity in need of renegotiation. From this standpoint, both the self-affirming and ironic, both the self-critical and globally engaged dimensions of the Dutch soccer tradition appear significant. While this latter reading 'fits' a line of thought in globalization studies, it is only one among others. As I will reiterate, the meaning of Dutch soccer achievements, like the meaning of Dutch national identity, is contested. 'The' tradition does not have an unequivocal meaning but rather can be read different ways from the different vantage points in Dutch identity debates. That variation itself serves as one piece of evidence against common scenarios about the national implications of globalization.

Reading the Dutch soccer record as intertwined with transformations in the 'real' national identity is instructive but also risky. Such a reading assumes that the national soccer experience has a certain natural coherence – that it makes sense to talk as if '*the Dutch* feel ...' even though it may well be the reading itself, as carried out by predominantly male Dutch soccer interpreters or by sociologists, that creates the unity of its presumed national subject. Strictly speaking, as sociologists are wont to do, there is no single Dutch soccer experience: many games played by diverse teams experienced by publics at different times are at best virtually united via an imaginative construction of an ongoing tradition. However great the passions soccer inspires among fans, the ideas that frame those passions also need not carry over to the serious business of the nation. Though soccer features prominently in the public space of many modern nations – especially when 'our' team happens to be playing well – it does not shape national affection and self-understanding in any constant fashion; rather, as the Dutch case illustrates, its significance varies. The work of recreating a national identity in response to, and using resources drawn from, globalizing processes takes many forms, as would-be representatives of the nation construe it in numerous settings ranging from debates about how to teach history to devising programmes for immigrant integration to deciding on how to position the country within transnational structures like the EU. At best, in the Netherlands as elsewhere, soccer provides one answer among others to the who-are-we question. That answer is important in itself, and it pervades public discourse thanks to ever-increasing media coverage of sports, but it does not carry over easily to other spheres.

With those caveats in mind, I next examine more closely the way the Dutch imagine themselves as a national sporting community, then interpret this as fitting a global pattern described by sports scholars, next review sceptical responses to Dutch national identity work, and conclude by returning to the prospect of a cosmopolitan nationalism.

Soccer style as national self-definition

In Dutch soccer memory, the early 1970s stand out as a critical period. In 1970, Feyenoord was the first Dutch club to win the grand prize for club teams on the European stage, what was then called the European Cup. Ajax followed with three European club championships in a row. In the 1974 World Cup tournament in Germany, the Dutch team reached the finals for the first time, defeating traditional powers like Argentina and Brazil along the way but in the end falling short against Germany. While the club achievements stirred the passions of soccer fans, the World Cup, televised live, produced a truly national emotional outpouring, an 'orange transformation' subsequently considered 'typical' of the Netherlands (Stouwdam 2005). The losers of 1974 were treated to an unprecedented welcome upon their return, receiving the adulation of huge crowds. At a festive reception with the queen and cabinet, the otherwise restrained prime minister famously danced with the players. The nation celebrated its team's heroic accomplishments via intense displays of collective sentiment. National pride derived precisely from the global setting of the World Cup, where a small county had shown how great it was. 'We' could play with anyone.

The key player of the period, Johan Cruyff, proved to be an exemplary figure on and off the field. Though he had departed for Barcelona, which he later also coached to a European club championship, he was critical to Dutch soccer discourse as it unfolded after 1974. A movie about 'Number 14' (always worn by Cruyff) had already enshrined him as a soccer genius. Images of his exploits were so ubiquitous that he was seen as a 'place of memory' in his own right, the embodiment of the Dutch sense of being a 'chosen nation' (Bommeljé 1995). Through a series of columns in the most popular newspaper, the *Telegraaf*, he commented extensively on the shortcomings of clubs and players. As technical adviser to Ajax after his playing days, he tried, as he saw it, to have the club stay true to its tradition. Ajax, he claimed, had played 'technical, visually appealing soccer, based on beauty' throughout the history of the game (Cruyff in Davidse 2006: 37). Few televised international matches were complete without Cruyff's analysis and oracular pronouncements. In the 1980s he served as a mentor to rising stars such as Marco van Basten, who in 2004, as mentioned, became national team coach on Cruyff's recommendation. In all these roles, Cruyff advocated a distinct vision of 'the' Dutch style of soccer (Cruyff in Van Zoest 2000 and in Verkamman 1989) – an adventurous, attacking style in which all players move continuously. This style, he argued, reflects essential qualities of Dutch players and is therefore necessary for the Dutch to be successful internationally. Not surprisingly, many viewed him as the 'keeper [*herder*] of the national heritage' (Lex Muller in Davidse 2006: 73).

The media keep the memory of past achievement alive. In the run-up to any major tournament, comparisons with teams past are inevitable, complete with repeat showings of key episodes on television. The Dutch soccer record is now virtually available, a shared 'memory' even to those too young to witness the actual games of old. For example, in the context of a series of history programmes retrieving the feel of 'other times,' a documentary on 1974, first broadcast in 2004, illustrates legendary Dutch soccer greatness by retelling the story of the team's heroics, showing clips of critical game events, and interviewing nostalgic journalists and fans (Andere Tijden 2004). In the same year, a marvellously evocative history of the team and the times became a best-selling book in the Netherlands (Kok 2004). Weaving player biographies into social history, it shows how the team's experience reflected broader changes in society and came to symbolize how the Dutch liked to imagine themselves. Soccer success galvanized the nation. Of course, the book's title, *We were the best*, appealed to Dutch sensibilities.

Already in the early 1970s, in Ajax's 'golden' age, soccer aficionados began to attribute to the Dutch a distinct style of play (De Galan 2006). Ajax stressed offence, allowing defensive players to move to the opponent's half. At the same time, forwards always had to fight for the ball and derail the other team's offensive manoeuvres. Use of the wings created space, enabling forwards to outwit the opposing backs. Players in constant motion, taking each other's place when necessary, kept the ball circulating. This was dubbed 'total soccer,' a style demonstrated to perfection by the 1974 national team and subsequently celebrated at home and abroad. The term captures the 'idea of Dutch football,' described in loving detail even – or perhaps especially – by foreign fans like the journalist David Winner (Winner 2000: 1). In such accounts, fluid motion, offensive quality, and intricate team effort mark the 'neurotic genius' of Dutch soccer, a 'brilliant orange' approach to the game. This style presumably mirrors Dutch culture: according to Winner, Cruyff and his colleagues changed the dimensions of the football field just as the Dutch had always sought to alter the physical dimensions of Holland itself (Winner 2000: 44). Just as the Dutch 'are at their best when we can combine the system with individual creativity,' so Cruyff demonstrated the power of 'creative individualism' within a team context (H. Smeets, cited in Winner 2000: 26–7). Cruyff's 'deep and original' conception of the field is 'essentially Dutch,' reminiscent of the artistic vision of great Dutch painters (Winner 2000: 59). Committed as they are to their own soccer aesthetic, the desire to win means nothing to them: as Winner (2000: 130) quotes fellow journalist Simon Kuper, 'To go down with honour is all the Dutch want' – a sentiment assistant national team coach Van 't Schip appeared to second in his comment to the effect that playing the right way mattered more than the result. The point resonates with Dutch conceptions of their role in the world, as a small nation with a conscience unwilling to play by the cynical rules of the great-power game.

Notwithstanding their supposed indifference to losing, the Dutch seek affirmation of their soccer prowess in their international record. 'Brilliant orange' players, clubs, national teams, and coaches have proven themselves in international competition, enhancing the Dutch sense of soccer distinction. The 1988 European championship showed the strength of a new generation of players that continued the tradition of the 1970s, and some of these players helped AC Milan achieve European dominance. In later years, others had a major impact on top clubs like Barcelona and Manchester United. When Ajax won the European club championship in 1995, it recaptured the glory of its illustrious predecessors. PSV Eindhoven could boast some similar accomplishments. Elimination in the semi-finals of the 2004 European Cup hurt the Dutch self-image though it also showed that the Dutch continued to compete with the best. Former players like Gullit and Rijkaard have coached abroad. Professional Dutch coaches like Van Gaal, Hiddink, and others have been even more successful, illustrated by their role in guiding the teams of Australia, South Korea, and Trinidad and Tobago to the 2006 World Cup. Like modern 'VOC captains,' they have had an impact on the world at large (Van der Steen 2006) by establishing a 'Dutch school' in coaching (Camps 2006). Such international achievement became essential to maintaining national soccer pride.

In short, over the last several decades the Dutch have created a 'football culture' of their own (Finn and Giulianotti 2000), fed by the memory of past achievements, fostered by influential exemplars, reproduced by mediated reconstructions of the past, ritualized in the way the Dutch participate in and talk about their role in international competition, framed as a distinct style that reflects essential national qualities, and celebrated as a mark of Dutch greatness in the global soccer arena.

Dutch imagination in global context

For all their imagined distinctiveness, the Dutch follow a familiar global pattern. All soccer nations define themselves in relation to the global game, notably the World Cup tournament (Sugden and Tomlinson 1994). By claiming particular identities within soccer's universal framework, they turn 'the global game' into the 'glocal game' (Giulianotti and Robertson 2004: 547). But the ingredients of that self-definition are standard (cf. Archetti 1994): media representations of critical events, embellished by continuous soccer talk, reproduce the collective memory and reinforce a sense of national distinction, usually focused on a set of assumptions about 'the' national style held to reflect long-standing national characteristics. Nations, if we may represent them as a single actor for the sake of convenience, like to think of themselves as distinct, superior, and whole. They express that uniquely superior wholeness in remarkably similar fashion. The global sporting system (Van Bottenburg 2000) not only standardizes forms of play but also moulds the identities of participants in isomorphic ways. Due to such global constraints, nations are alike in the way they claim distinction.

The Dutch also fit other patterns stressed in sports scholarship. One of these is to argue that in modern nation-states sports serve to shape and cement national identities (Giulianotti 1999: 23), provide an 'arena' in which people can 'articulate' such identities (Blain et al. 1993: 12), help to create a symbolic sense of stability and pride (Maguire 1999: 181), and offer a means to generate new habits among citizens (Miller et al. 2001: 3). Thus, ritual preparations for major tournaments produce national senti-ment, as in the Dutch orange craze, soccer narratives assist in national self-imagining (Archetti 1996: 201), media coverage captivates the nation while exacerbating cross-national contrasts (Blain et al. 1993), and sports facilitate representations of the nation as 'one sentient being' (Blain et al. 1993: 15). Durkheim would have been pleased to see the expressive and integrative function of sports emphasized in this way.

Another line of argument extends a now-conventional way of thinking about the nation to sports. If the nation is an 'imagined' community, if national traditions are typically 'invented,' if nations are modern constructs used to sustain industrializing societies, then soccer must 'express' identities it helps to manufacture in the first place. Soccer nationalists engage in a kind of intellectual bootstrapping. Their myth-making may not be a 'delusion' but it nevertheless hides the real political 'conditions of its own existence' (Miller et al. 2001). It is typically an exercise in 'willful nostalgia' that creates a 'fantasy image' of the nation, so that all sports are in some sense 'patriot games' (Maguire 1999). Essentialist accounts of the national record stress continuity and contrast in highly stylized histories (Archetti 1994, 1996). Sports reproduce, in emotionally charged fashion, many of the tropes of nation-building. This constructionist view underlies sociological scepticism with regard to claims about distinct national styles.

Current accounts interpret the integrative constructionism of national self-definitions in soccer as a reaction to threatening globalization. Intense globalization dulls the former 'radiance' of the nation, and this is what triggers a defensive nostalgic response (Maguire 1999: 180, 206). The sporting nation is a 'counter-sign' to the 'universal signage,' a riposte to the 'juggernaut' of capitalist globalization (Miller et al. 2001). The 'Network' of global soccer, the transnational media-MNC-sporting complex that commodifies the game, 'overrides' the powers of the nation-state (Sugden 2002: 63), but, far from being a 'spent force,' nations mobilize 'endogenous' cultural resources to 'counteract' globalization by restoring themselves as 'bulwarks' (Hargreaves 2002). Put differently, as Richard Giulianotti has suggested, nations and their national soccer organizations may engage in a 'neo-mercantilist' response to the 'neo-liberal' strategies of global clubs and media groups. Globalization spells identity loss (Croci and Ammirante 1999) but resistance fortifies local identities (Ben-Porat and Ben-Porat 2004). By practically demonstrating the 'operational strength' of the nation (Blain et al. 1993: 197), soccer helps to create a home in a homeless world. In the Dutch case, scholars have noted, globalization increases 'the need for feelings of community' while soccer 'compensates for the loss' of national identity especially among the losers in globalization (L. van Zoonen and M. van Bottenburg in Olgun 2004). The common denominator in all such accounts, which differ in other respects, is the reactive and defensive quality of soccer nationalism.

A critique of soccer style as national self-definition

In claiming soccer distinction, the Dutch resemble others. This fact suggests that, like many such claims, the Dutch one may in fact embellish a collective memory, idealize a particular view of Dutch soccer, distort its actual record, and turn extraordinary events and people into emblems of perennial Dutch qualities. Conventional sociological wisdom reinforces this critique by alerting us to the myth-making involved in the construction of any imagined sporting community and to the use of such myths in cementing national identities at a time when they are under global threat. The soccer connoisseur and the sociological sceptic thus converge on the view that 'total soccer,' construed as an 'essentially Dutch' style that reflects national qualities, must be an ahistorical fantasy. They have a point, yet, as I will show, they also miss other aspects of Dutch soccer discourse and experience.

Winner's celebration of 'brilliant orange,' unusually fervent and romantic even for Dutch fans, provides one example of ahistorical, essentializing redescription of 'the' nation. An approach to soccer that was 'unrefined' until the 1960s suddenly gives way to a 'typically Dutch' new style (Winner 2000: 6). The characteristically Dutch approach to space, dormant until that time, suddenly revealed itself on Dutch soccer fields. Such accounts read into the soccer record only selected qualities of the overall national culture – a culture often defined by foreigners, for foreigners. Foreigners also played an oft-forgotten role in creating 'Dutch' traditions – Ajax had a British coach for many years, and the Austrian coach Ernst Happel brought to Feyenoord his knowledge of Hugo Meisl's pioneering, attacking 'whirl' style (later described by his brother Willy Meisl in *Soccer revolution*). In the haze of national memory, to mention another instance of ahistorical distortion, the Dutch like to forget that the miracle team sent to Germany in 1974 lacked a number of key defensive players due to injury (Van Eeden 1994: 7). Though offensive vigour masked defensive problems for much of the tournament, the Germans took advantage of such weaknesses in the final to score two goals, as noted in the best-seller mentioned above (Kok 2004). Contrary to the demands of total soccer, the exemplary Johan Cruyff never played much defence, as one of his Ajax team-mates has pointed out (Winner 2000: 33). The vaunted beauty of total soccer in part depended on a ruthlessly physical, even cruel, attitude towards opponents, reflected in numerous fouls (Kok 2004). The victims may have had cause to doubt the 'deep' Dutch decency fans like Winner consider a basis for total soccer (Winner 2000: 130, 144). Many such national virtues, of course, are in the eye of the biased beholder.

The selectivity in national soccer imagination also appears in what is left unsaid. For example, outside the domain of sports Dutch identity discourse often singles out the tendency to resolve problems via extensive consultation as a Dutch trait. But in this regard the great teams of the 1970s were not very Dutch, managed as they were by a taciturn coach not given to sharing and led by a player whose nickname was 'the general.' Presumably essential traits of the 'real' national identity, as construed in conventional political discourse and scholarship, did not carry over to the sports arena. When they did, as on teams of the 1990s given to excessive 'dialogue', this was widely viewed as the dysfunctional downside of Dutch-style deliberation. That the Dutch feel no great need to win would come as a surprise to Dick Advocaat, national scapegoat after failing to coach his team to the European championship in 2004, and to the numerous coaches dismissed by Ajax in recent years. In 2006, national coaches Van Basten and Van 't Schip gained moral support from their commitment to playing the right way but were judged entirely on their record. The presumed commitment to maintaining a proper style easily gives way to the desire to win. The repeated recriminations about 'unexpected' failure are themselves a feature of Dutch soccer discourse but, for soccer nationalists, do not call into question the merits of total soccer.

The Dutch imagine that 'their' brand of soccer is unusually beautiful and effective, and therefore like to consider themselves a global soccer power, but this reputation is not entirely secure. Even in 1974, they could not convert their presumed superiority into actual victory. When they finished second again in 1978, this gave rise to a 'bad luck culture' (Bloembergen 2005), a tendency to attribute failure at crucial moments to a lack of nerve or external factors. Premature elimination by Portugal in the 2006 World Cup, in a game notable for rough play, red cards, and the absence of sparkling soccer, added another trauma. With only a few exceptions, Dutch club teams have suffered a drought of international successes since the 1970s, in part due to well-known changes in the European soccer market. There is good reason to think that the problem is a structural one, since domestic teams can no longer hold on to emerging homegrown stars (Kuper 2006b). While some Dutch coaches have been successful abroad, their role in maintaining the Dutch global soccer reputation is ambiguous since they do not appear, or claim, to follow any consistently 'Dutch' coaching philosophy. As in other nations, the actual record thus dulls the lustre of brilliant orange.

Such a sceptical take on the Dutch soccer record would not surprise most Dutch fans who are well aware that the myth is a myth. The TV documentary on 1974 half-ironically refers to the 'legend' of 1974, of a team that symbolized what the nation 'wanted to be,' and proceeds to show how it was manufactured into existence. As mentioned, former player Willem van Hanegem has questioned the whole idea of a distinct style that was somehow deeply ingrained in his generation of players. Many reporters take pleasure in correcting such 'widespread misunderstandings' about Dutch soccer traditions (Bloembergen 2005). '*We were the best*' is both description and critique of national nostalgia, placing the presumed symbolic qualities of the 1974 team in context without claiming that it in fact 'represents' the nation. Though Cruyff's reputation as a player is quite secure, his role as defender of 'the' Ajax house style and 'the' Dutch national style is more controversial: 'down with Cruyff and his sect,' say critics who deride his influence as a Bhagwan for addled brains (Van Holland 2006), while others question whether his pronouncements, issued in idiosyncratic language, are even understandable (Wieldraaijer 2006). Thus several elements of the national myth have come under critical fire. In the Netherlands, even nostalgia is not what it used to be.

The very idea of a single Dutch soccer style is contested: the presumed style, according to critics of the 'orange myth,' depended on Cruyff's presence, evolved by chance, and no longer suits the requirements of a more physical international game (Visser 2006). In domestic competition, club styles depend on available personnel, including foreign players. Judged by the demands of the modern game, 'the' national style does not hold up in any case, as top players have argued. For example, Edgar Davids, a star in Italy who was left out of the 2006 national selection, criticized Van Basten after the World Cup for being too 'romantic' and not sufficiently realistic in choosing and preparing the team (Davids 2006). Even disregarding the grudge behind the critique, the point is a common one, namely that the viability of total soccer in an era of new defensive strategies is in doubt (Onkenhout and Vissers 2001). As such examples show, a highly reflexive form of self-criticism runs through Dutch soccer discourse.

Though it might go too far to say that Dutch soccer has witnessed a battle of soccer philosophies similar to that between Menotti traditionalists and Bilardo modernists in Argentina (Archetti 1994, 1996; Alabarces and Rodríguez 2000), the approach advocated by Cruyff and his 'sect' has not gone unchallenged. For example, the more disciplined, less free-flowing style advocated by Louis van Gaal, successful Ajax coach in 1995, contrasts with Cruyff's traditionalism. The best coaches, such as Guus Hiddink guiding South Korea and Australia through the World Cup, adapt their approach to the players they have to work with instead of consistently preaching 'Dutch school' soccer. The experience of playing in foreign leagues shaped the views of several players who became prominent coaches, like Rijkaard and Van Basten, especially by showing the virtues of tough-minded, defensively oriented, 'typically Italian' *catenaccio*-style soccer (Missèt 2000). Though they may stress offensive strategies, as Rijkaard did in coaching Barcelona to a Champions League victory, they are, in a quite literal sense, global players who adopt hybrid styles rather than purveyors of one national tradition – and Rijkaard, not surprisingly, describes himself as a 'world citizen' who happens to have a 'warm spot' for several specific places (Greven 2006). Soccer historians might push the point further to suggest that most traditions are composites that arise from the transnational circulation of ideas, as illustrated by the way *catenaccio* evolved from experiments in Spain by a South American coach who drew on Swiss precedent.

How well the functional view of soccer as integrative experience applies to the Netherlands is also up for debate. In the early 1970s, to be sure, soccer stirred national passions that could not otherwise be expressed in the public sphere at a time when attention to national identity was widely considered unduly nationalist. It 'took the place of nationalism' (Winner 2000: 107). Ever since, major tournaments in which the Netherlands participated have created a sense of commonality. The function is hardly latent, as demonstrated when in the run-up to the 2006 World Cup the major news show on Dutch public television interviewed a foreign observer to make the point that '*Oranje*' had become a binding element in a nation that had lost many others (NOS 2006c). But whether it lives up to Durkheimian expectations is less clear. The periodicity in collective attention implies that soccer style does not bolster national self-imagining in any continuous way – the soccer nation crystallizes at tournament time and otherwise leads a mostly virtual existence. Soccer fans may enjoy the communal passion but perhaps take the 'ritual' slightly less seriously than Durkheimian sociologists, as illustrated by the title of a prominent journalistic account of Dutch soccer, 'All my strings vibrate for *Oranje*' (Scheepmaker 1994) or, more prosaically, by the deliberately outrageous outfits donned by fans at major international matches. Some rituals of the orange craze display a tongue-in-cheek patriotism, illustrated by the way fans have turned a serious nineteenth-century song about naval hero Piet Hein, originally intended to stir pride in the Dutch golden age, into a mechanically repeated single-line celebration of how the Dutch team wins the '*Zilvervloot*'. The craze is deliberately played up as a commodified media spectacle, incorporated as a form of entertainment into the national party culture by knowing consumers untroubled by the 'fever' or 'tribal instincts' attributed to them by concerned intellectuals (Ribbens and Van der Walle 2006). Soccer turns the self-display of the nation into diverting entertainment. Watching, on TV or in person, is time set apart for pleasure. Soccer does constitute a 'communal passion' (Stouwdam 2005), but self-aware consumption, irony, and contestation qualify the notion that the Dutch engage in just another form of ritualized national myth-making.

It is difficult at any rate to judge the integrative or expressive role of soccer without assessing how it functions in a wider context of national identity work, both in discourse and state policy. In the Dutch case, this identity work has greatly intensified in past decades, triggered most notably by the fall-out of immigration and European integration. Yet in the collective soul-searching about the state of the nation since the late 1990s, expressed in dire diagnoses of the 'crisis' and 'confusion' in the country, few looked to soccer as a means of national renewal. Occasionally, a politician might refer to 'orange' sentiment to invoke national pride, but in arguments about what the nation does or should stand for, or in debates about what historical canon, if any, to teach in schools, soccer played no role. Though the national team became more ethnically diverse, and the success of players of Surinamese origin may have smoothed the inclusion of their ethnic minority, this did little to resolve the actual dilemmas of national integration. At times, the tension surrounding these dilemmas affected the national selection, a point I cannot pursue here. As in the case of France, where the World Cup triumph of a diverse team temporarily seemed to herald a new national spirit (Dauncey and Hare 1999), newly imagined unity depends on extraordinary success and even then rarely carries over to the everyday life of a state-managed national community. The very fact that soccer helps to generate communal passion and a sense of national tradition matters, at least as common background in other spheres. But beyond the game, soccer does little to cement collective identity. Integration through sports only goes so far.

Globalization does present challenges to Dutch soccer. When the national team loses in major tournaments, or star players depart for lucrative careers abroad, or storied clubs suffer declines, it is easy to blame the standardization of soccer strategy or the impact of market forces that work to the detriment of small powers. In the founding period of the presumed Dutch style, however, the international stage represented an opportunity as much as a threat. The Dutch showed who they were by proving themselves 'globally,' without at all appearing to restore a lost sense of superiority. The market worked to the advantage of players and coaches. The expansion of media offerings enabled fans to follow their home teams as well as select players abroad and also the national team. The global, especially the intra-European, scene enriched the experience of fans. Few, if any, complained, for example, that a majority of Dutch players on the 2004 European championship team played abroad while a majority of Ajax players at the time were foreigners (Lechner 2004). Dutch fans betrayed little anxiety in having to juggle multiple interests and identities. To all appearances, they can live with globalization.

Beyond the critique

The way the Dutch view themselves as a unique soccer nation fits familiar global patterns. A sociologically informed critique of their romantic soccer self-image displays the myth as myth. The Dutch do indeed engage in some conventional myth-making and parts of Dutch soccer discourse fit the expectations of sceptical scholars. But an exercise in deconstruction fails to capture some important aspects of the way soccer feeds Dutch national self-definitions. To some extent, as the previous section has illustrated, the critique is part of the discourse, which is more than an ahistorical expressive myth erected as a defence against globalization. It is more complex, more reflexive, more fluid than standard accounts of soccer nationalism would lead us to expect or than straightforwardly nostalgic neopatriots might prefer.

This critique of a standard critique of national sports image-making fits a promising thrust in soccer and globalization scholarship. As the Dutch case illustrates, the place of the nation is undergoing 'renegotiation' (King 2001: 248). Its attraction may not be permanent but rather periodic. National claims may be more plausible in some contexts than in others. The strength of the nation's centripetal action constantly fluctuates in response to centrifugal forces within and without. This response is no mere defence. Soccer shows how multiple identities develop within global processes (Bairner 2001: 13), how the nation functions as just one identity within the 'new medievalism' of overlapping identities (King 2001: 247; also Scholte 2005), how the 'national' and the 'global' can be complementary (Holton 2005). Sporting events carry multiple meanings, often symbolizing layers of identity, as illustrated most notably by the Barcelona Olympics (Hargreaves 2002). Globalization, construed as 'deterritorialization' (Scholte 2005), nevertheless 'takes place' in and through nations. Far from being a uniform threat, global flows in national settings produce 'unique mixtures,' due in part to the active involvement of ostensibly national actors themselves (Ben-Porat and Ben-Porat 2004). Postmodern nations engage complex globalization to produce new identities, defining their particularity in relation to universal standards (Giulianotti and Robertson 2004).

The Dutch are at the forefront of global struggles to find a new balance of identities, to renegotiate the place of the nation in the world, a theme further explored elsewhere (Lechner forthcoming). Outside the soccer arena, public intellectuals have proposed new ways of imagining the nation as multicultural haven, as platform from which to explore the world, as incarnation of liberal values, and so on. Much of this identity work aiming to re-place the nation has a postmodern cosmopolitan thrust: it relativizes national exclusivity, sees the nation as part of a larger whole, advocates liberal values, and discounts claims to superiority. Thus far, it lacks sentiment, solidarity, and particularity. It is mostly 'civic,' not very 'ethnic.' At the risk of suggesting another 'half-baked' soccer-as-national-character interpretation, ignoring a warning against doing so by the journalist Simon Kuper, perhaps Dutch soccer, as experienced by fans and as discussed in the public sphere, strikes a balance not yet evident in other arenas, suggesting a model of sorts for what the Dutch may strive to achieve – a combination of knowing nostalgia, occasional commonality, and outwardly oriented nationalism (cf. Pels 2005). It would ironically reinstate a national myth of sorts to suggest that the Dutch are unique in this regard. Some aspects of their tradition may indeed favour a certain way of handling the pressures of globalization, a point also pursued elsewhere, but if the recent thrust in soccer and globalization scholarship is correct, further comparative analysis would show that the Dutch also have much in common with other soccer nations.

Apart from occasional invocations of soccer passion and tradition in other spheres, and notwithstanding the clear common awareness of the Dutch as a 'soccer nation,' there is little explicit 'soccer creep' into those other areas. Whether a model of enlightened yet sentimental, reflexive yet passionate national self-imagining can carry over to domains more closely tied to state functioning – minority integration, the welfare state, the media, and education – remains to be seen. Recent literature on globalization suggests that renegotiation of national identities along these lines is at least viable but, of course, it cannot prescribe such an outcome. Ambitious states still require some conception of national identity to frame their policies but as state sovereignty atrophies so does societal demand for national identity, leaving the outcome of identity work in doubt. Even in a place like the Netherlands that ostensibly takes pride in the search for consensus, cosmopolitan views of national identity contend with neopatriotic claims about national distinction and with sceptics for whom any national project is implausible. Reflecting on the Dutch soccer experience thus raises the question under what conditions a 'cosmopolitan nationalism,' in and beyond soccer, of the sort implied by recent work on globalization might flourish. Answering it is a task for another paper – and for the Dutch themselves.

Acknowledgments

I thank the Institute for Comparative and International Studies at Emory University for funding research related to this article, Richard Giulianotti for his detailed response to a draft, and two reviewers and Alisdair Rogers for their helpful comments.

References

Alabarces, P. and M. G. Rodríguez (2000) 'Football and Fatherland: the crisis of national representation in Argentinian soccer', in G. P. T. Finn and R. Giulianotti (eds) *Football culture: local contests, global visions*, London: Frank Cass, 118–22.

Andere Tijden (2004) 'Oranje 1974' (TV broadcast), geschiedenis.vpro.nl.

Archetti, E. P. (1994) 'Argentina and the World Cup: in search of national identity,' in J. Sugden and A. Tomlinson (eds) *Hosts and champions: soccer cultures, national identities and the USA World Cup*, Aldershot: Ashgate, 37–64.

Archetti, E. P. (1996) 'In search of national identity: Argentinian Football and Europe', in J. A. Mangan (ed.) *Tribal identities: nationalism, Europe, sport*, London: Frank Cass, 201–19.

Bairner, A. (2001) *Sport, nationalism, and globalization: European and North American perspectives*, Albany: State University of New York Press.

Ben-Porat, G. and A. Ben-Porat (2004) '(Un)bounded soccer: globalization and localization of the game in Israel', *International Review for the Sociology of Sport*, 39, 421–36.

Blain, N., R. Boyle and H. O'Donnell (1993) *Sport and national identity in the European media*, Leicester: Leicester University Press.

Bloembergen, J. (2005) 'Verlies AZ en PSV Niet Meer Dan Toeval', *NRC Handelsblad*, 6 May.

Bommeljé, B. (1995) 'Johan Cruijff: Twintig Jaar, en God', in N.C.F. Van Sas (ed.) *Waar de Blanke Top der Duinen en Andere Vaderlandse Herinneringen*, Amsterdam: Contact, 151–8.

Boterman, F. W. (1999) *Duitsland als Nederlands Probleem (Duitsland Cahier 4)*, Amsterdam: Duitsland Instituut Universiteit van Amsterdam.

Camps, H. (2006) 'De Hollandse School', *Elsevier*, 10 June, 28–32

Croci, O. and J. Ammirante (1999) 'Soccer in the age of globalization', *Peace Review* 11, 499–504.

Dauncey, H. and G. Hare (1999) 'Conclusion: the impact of France 98', in H. Dauncey and G. Hare (eds) *France and the 1998 World Cup: the national impact of a world sporting event*, London: Frank Cass, 205–21.

Davids, E. (2006) 'Van Basten Overschreed Grens Fatsoen', *Voetbal International*, 5 July.

Davidse, H. (ed.) (2006) *Je Moet Schieten, Anders Kun Je Niet Scoren, en Andere Citaten van Johan Cruijff*, 's-Gravenhage: BZZTôH.

De Galan, M. (2006) *De Trots van de Wereld: Michels, Cruijff en het Gouden Ajax van 1964–1974*, Amsterdam: Bert Bakker.

Finn, G. P. T. and R. Giulianotti (eds) (2000) *Football culture: local contests, global visions*, London: Frank Cass.

Fortuyn, P. (2002) *De Verweesde Samenleving: Een Religieus-Sociologisch Traktaat*, Uithoorn: Karakter.

Giulianotti, R. (1999) *Football: a sociology of the global game*, Cambridge: Polity Press.

Giulianotti, R. and R. Robertson (2004) 'The globalization of football: a study in the glocalization of the "serious life"', *The British Journal of Sociology*, 55, 545–68.

Greven, K. (2006) 'Wereldburger Zonder Dromen (Interview)', *NRC Handelsblad*, 16 December.

Hargreaves, J. (2002) *Freedom for Catalonia? Catalan nationalism, Spanish identity and the Barcelona Olympic Games*, Cambridge: Cambridge University Press.

Held, D., A. McGrew, D. Goldblatt and J. Perraton (1999) *Global transformations: politics, economics and culture*, Stanford: Stanford University Press.

Holton, R. J. (2005) *Making globalization*, New York: Palgrave Macmillan.

King, A. (2001) *The European ritual: football in the New Europe*, Aldershot: Ashgate.

Koch, K. and P. Scheffer (eds) (1996) *Het Nut van Nederland: Opstellen over Sovereiniteit en Identiteit*, Amsterdam: Bert Bakker.

Kok, A. (2004) *1974: Wij Waren de Besten*, Amsterdam: Thomas Rap.

Kok, A. (2006) *Onze Jongens: De Nieuwe Helden van Oranje*, Amsterdam: Thomas Rap.

Kuper, S. (2006a) 'Oranje Heeft Te Weinig Klasse', *NRC Handelsblad*, 6 June.

Kuper, S. (2006b) 'Op de Divan in de Watergraafsmeer', *NRC Handelsblad*, 17 March.

Lechner, A. D. (2004) Personal communication.

Lechner, F. J. (forthcoming) *The Netherlands: national identity and globalization*, London: Routledge.

Maguire, J. (1999) *Global sport: identities, societies, civilizations*, Cambridge: Polity Press.

Miller, T., G. Lawrence, J. McKay, and D. Rowe (2001) *Globalization and sport: playing the world*, London: Sage.

Missèt, R. (2000) 'Oranje-Fan met Italiaanse Passie', *NRC Handelsblad*, 1 July.

NOS (2006a) 'Studio Sportzomer', TV show, 17 June.

NOS (2006b) 'Studio Sportzomer', TV show, 6 June.

NOS (2006c) 'NOS Journaal', news broadcast, 8 June.

Olgun, A. (2004) 'Oranje Zit Vooral van Buiten', *NRC Handelsblad*, 15 June.

Onkenhout, P. and W. Vissers (2001) 'Het Voetbal Krijgt een Ander Gezicht', *De Volkskrant*, 15 September.

Peeperkorn, M. and P. Remarque (2004) 'Je Moet een Samenleving Vullen met Emotie (Interview)', *De Volkskrant*, 30 December.

Pels, D. (2005) *Een Zwak voor Nederland: Ideeën voor een Nieuwe Politiek*, Amsterdam: Anthos.

Ribbens, A. and E. Van der Walle (2006) 'Met Leeuwenhosen op de Tribune', *NRC Handelsblad*, 7 June.

Scheepmaker, N. (1994) *Voor Oranje Trillen Al Mijn Snaren*, Utrecht: Scheffers.

Scholte, J. A. (2005) *Globalization: a critical introduction*, New York: Palgrave Macmillan.

Stouwdam, H. (2005) 'Communal passion', *NRC Handelsblad*, 24 June.

Sugden, J. (2002) 'Network football', in J. Sugden and A. Tomlinson (eds) *Power games: a critical sociology of sport*, London: Routledge, 61–80.

Sugden, J. and A. Tomlinson (eds) (1994) *Hosts and champions: soccer cultures, national identities and the USA World Cup*, Aldershot: Ashgate.

Van 't Schip, J. (2005) Interview, *Nummer 14* (May), 10–15.

Van Bottenburg, M. (2001) *Global games*, Urbana: University of Illinois Press.

Van der Steen, H. (2006) 'Coaches als Moderne VOC Schippers', *Eindhovens Dagblad*, 14 June.

Van der Veer, P. (2000) 'Nederland Bestaat Niet Meer', *De Gids* (December), 742–9.

Van Eeden, E. (1994) *Totaalvoetbal: Elf Interviews met Spelers uit het Legendarische Team van de WK '74*, Amsterdam: Forum.

Van Holland, G. (2006) 'Weg met Cruijff en Zijn Sekte', *NRC.nl Weblog*, 1 July.

Van Zoest, R. (2000) *Ajax 1900–2000*, Bussum: THOTH.

Verkamman, M. (1989) *Het Nederlands Elftal: De Historie van Oranje 1905–1989*, Amsterdam: Weekbladpers.

Visser, J. (2006) 'De Mythe van het Oranje-systeem', *Nieuwe Revu*, 14–21 June, 46–9.

Wieldraaijer, E. (2006) 'Johan Cruijff Spreekt een Taal die Voetbalkenners Soms Zelfs Niet Snappen', *KRO Magazine* (June), 18–19.

Winner, D. (2001) *Brilliant Orange: the neurotic genius of Dutch football*, London: Bloomsbury.

9

The global footballer and the local war-zone: George Weah and transnational networks in Liberia, West Africa

GARY ARMSTRONG

Sport has been integral to global processes since the nineteenth century. Games have been disseminated and imitated for over 150 years for their intrinsic worth, alongside their extrinsic – and parallel – globalizing forces based in commerce and communications (Allison 1986, 2002; Aris 1990; Budd and Levermore 2004; Crawford 2004; Guttmann 1994; Maguire 1994, 2005). Sporting practices have facilitated a variety of identities – real, imagined and submerged – and inculcated a variety of disciplines based on the requirements made both on the individual body and collectively via team efforts (Allison 2002; Bale and Maguire 1994).

The sporting hero has been synonymous with notions around heroic masculinities since antiquity. Sports stars are authentic individuals who can inspire many an admirer or onlooker (Gilchrist 2005; Smart 2005). The political, economic and technological forces that produce such celebrity have been subject to a number of recent analyses (Andrews 2001; Cashmore and Parker 2003; Klausen 1999; Marshall 1997; Nalapat and Parker 2005; Turner 2004; Whannel 2002). In parallel to this, the sporting migrant has become the object of both sporting and transnational curiosity (Andrews and Jackson 2001; Maguire 1999). The recent corporatization of sport and its parallel televised obsessions (often synonymous with 'Americanization'[1]) have seen in many instances the demise of local influences and the rise of the global sporting celebrity (Forster and Pope 2004; Jarvie 2005; Lines 2002; Miller et al. 2001; Vertinsky and Bale 2004). In the final decade of the twentieth century the Liberian-born George Weah was a global sporting celebrity *par excellence*.

Football has proven useful in African political campaigns, and has played a defining role in how African nations globally situate themselves (Armstrong and Giulianotti 2004; Giulianotti 1999; Goldblatt 2006). The game has become increasingly central to the negotiations and interventionist policies of charities and non-governmental organizations, and to the politics and universalism of FIFA, football's world governing body (Darby 2003; Sudgen and Tomlinson 1998). This article considers the roots of Weah's celebrity, and his iconic status in Liberia. It also illustrates the fragility of the hero; in sport, such heroes are objectified through a variety of narratives based on performance, masculinity and the sublime, but in the post-career scenario, such local status and transnational celebrity is more fluid and negotiable.

Liberia: freedom, 'Big Man' politics and football

Africa is a continent that has historically seen European empires systematically conquer every nation, with one exception; Liberia. Despite this, Western influences impinged upon this sovereign society founded after the abolition of slavery in the northern territories of the United States in the 1790s. Freedom was offered to some 160,000 Black Africans, a number that increased to 250,000 by the 1820s. Tens of thousands were assisted in their departure 'home' and those that survived the transatlantic journey found themselves on the West Coast of Africa in a land given the nomenclature 'Liberia' (Clapham 1989; Jubwe 1997). Thus, Liberia experienced Americanization some 150 years before university campuses discovered the term. The new arrivals set up an imitative American system of government with a Senate and House of Representatives headed by a president and cabinet, and symbolized by a national flag that borrowed from the Stars and Stripes. More poignant in this neo-colonial situation was the willingness of the ersatz-colonists to perpetuate a system of slavery upon the indigenous peoples (Jubwe 1997).

The nation of Liberia has thus always manifested what Robertson (1992) has termed 'glocalisation' and 'indigenization'. Its national identity has been confused and contested since its mid-nineteenth century origin, and its practices dependent on complex relations of ethnicity, religious identity, and relative proximity to the dominant core. Liberia's proximity to European colonial empires, its 400 mile-long seaboard and its emotional ties with the USA have provided a constant interaction with the cultural 'Other'.

Football had come to Liberia in the early 1930s via West African sailors working on the ships that travelled from the Gold Coast along the Atlantic seaboard of Portugal and ultimately to Liverpool. The game was obviously witnessed in these footballing cities and brought back to West Africa. Further diffusion of football resulted from fishermen bringing the game inland via river fishing (Armstrong 2002). The distant and the exotic have been enhanced in recent times by global football images being made available through satellite television and telecommunications.

Liberian football generates strong domestic interest and attachment to local clubs, while satellite television generates fascination for the big teams of Europe and South America. International football might be watched on televisions powered by car batteries or, in more status-giving terms, by privately-owned generators; thus, one can observe the game being studied by the destitute as, eating peanuts, they enjoy the travails of millionaire players in programmes from the Middle East and South Africa. By the mid-1990s, the migrating professional footballer had taken on a role in Liberia – that of the 'returning hero' – which had not existed two decades earlier. Paid astronomical salaries by most national standards (let alone Liberia where most people exist on less then $1 per day), foreign-based footballers were thus feted on their return by hangers-on and well-wishers. Such social celebration has clear parallels with the classic form of supplication or even client-patronage in a society of acute economic scarcity, but it was performed also out of genuine, heartfelt admiration for football ability and personal courage in seeking new pastures.

The nation at play

Given their neo-colonial context, Liberian politicians have had endemic problems in creating a single national consciousness amongst their diverse peoples. In pursuit of this elusive sentiment, politicians have turned to football, domesticating the global game to local political projects. In 1964, President William Tubman organized a nation-building football tournament known then and now as the 'County Meet'. The annual, two-week Monrovia-based tournament sought to bring together teams from the 16 counties that then constituted Liberia. The Antoinette Tubman Stadium (ATS), named in honour of his wife, hosted the tournament, its final attracting some 30,000 spectators; the event generally inculcated a tradition of playing, watching and enjoying the game.

Tubman's successor William Tolbert was instrumental in building the national sport stadium a few miles outside Monrovia; the work was done by the Taiwanese in return for iron-ore concessions. However, Tolbert became entrenched in party squabbles and his ostentatious nepotism infuriated observers. He was executed by Samuel K. Doe's soldiers in Liberia's first military coup in 1980. An enthusiastic amateur footballer, Doe assumed the role of armed forces Commander-in-Chief, and named the subsequently completed stadium in his own honour. The Samuel K. Doe (SKD) Stadium thus stands as a tribute to his power, vanity and murderous reign; for many, it is a fitting structural emblem of the *realpolitik* of late twentieth century Liberia.

Doe's corrupt government endured 16 attempted coups, but the reign of terror unleashed by members of his own Krahn tribe upon Liberia's 14 other tribal peoples told against him when multi-tribal civil war began in December 1989. This diverse, widespread detestation of Doe's regime was highlighted with the creation of a multi-ethnic militia of over 200 men, trained in Libya, titled the National Patriotic Front of Liberia (NPFL) and led by Charles Taylor. The heroic masculinity thus evidenced in Liberia was to move from that embodied in political and narrative acumen to that which celebrated the warrior and mass-murderer.

The global journeyman: Charles Taylor

A former civil servant, government quartermaster and adviser to Samuel Doe, Charles Taylor fled Liberia in 1983 accused of embezzling $900,000. Finding his way to the

Liberian diaspora in the USA, Taylor was eventually arrested by the US authorities but, despite being housed in tight security, he escaped from an American jail in unexplained circumstances and with unknown assistance while awaiting extradition. Taylor surfaced in Libya where his training of militia was financed by Colonel Gaddafi. He then moved to Burkina-Faso, plotted a coup, and recruited support from Liberia's Ghio tribe. The civil war was sparked when Taylor and his forces crossed the border from the Ivory Coast in late 1989. Doe was overthrown in September 1990 and killed, and Amos Sawyer became president of the Interim Government of National Unity. Doe's death created confusion as multiple claims to the presidency were voiced by various indigenous peoples. The era of the heroic, masculine military 'Big Man' followed, as militia leaders traded diamonds, iron ore and timber under their control for small arms and payments from South African, Dutch, British and French corporations (cf. Reno 1993).

The civil conflict ruined domestic football and killed tens of thousands of young men who would otherwise have played the game. The seven-year conflict claimed over 150,000 lives and produced one million refugees with regional resonance and global implications for the transiting population. Around ten per cent (15,000) of combatants were aged 15 or under; the victors, the NPFL led by Charles Taylor, had a Small Boys Unit with combatants as young as eight, who would later campaign for him in the 1997 democratic election. As the man who started the conflict, the electorate obviously considered Taylor the most appropriate figure to end it: he won with 74 per cent voter backing (cf. Harris 1999). In pursuit of normality, Taylor promoted games of football and awarded himself the accolade of 'Chief Patron of Sport'. The unorthodox 'all against all' Liberian civil conflict made it hard for organized sport to function. During lulls in the conflict domestic football fixtures were played, albeit the football programme was not always finished due to the proximities of war. This fact may be an indication of the intrinsic nature of football in Liberia; even as the war raged, the populace sought out the game (Armstrong 2002).

During Taylor's early reign, the regional and international communities allowed him time to implement peace and democracy, and among other policies sent football equipment for grassroots tournaments (Armstrong 2005). The success of football-for-peace rhetoric and practice is hard to evaluate. What undoubtedly continued was conflict, which never actually ended in Liberia's remote border areas (despite a nominal 'peace') but became more low-key in public debate. In 2002 a civil conflict resumed when the forces known as Liberian United for the Restoration of Democracy (LURD) attacked from the north and eventually overwhelmed Taylor's forces in Monrovia in 2003. Taylor stepped down from the Liberian presidency in August 2003 under pressure from the USA and African presidents. His safe departure from Liberia was to make way for a peace deal that brought 14 years of on–off civil war to an end but required a 15,000-strong UN force of police and military personnel to enforce. Nigeria's president Olusegun Obasanjo offered Taylor exile in a seafront mansion in the southern Nigerian town of Calabar where he lived with his retinue in considerable comfort. His presence however was unsettling to the region. Many considered his supporters in Liberia were carrying out his instructions. Eventually in 2006 under UN instructions Taylor was arrested by Liberian authorities (with the assistance of Nigeria) and extradited to Sierra Leone (and later The Hague) where at the time of writing he faced 17 counts of war crime spanning a decade.

George Weah: mundial man?

In the early years of the civil conflict, the Liberian football player George Weah discovered that sporting skills could provide an unexpected and liberating escape from the atrocities. Weah soon took on the local mantle of 'The King' and, while his playing skills were divine to his many admirers, his personality proved to be very human.[2] Born in October 1966 in Monrovia's Clara Town slums to the Kru ethnic group, which originated from Grand Kru County (one of the poorest regions in Liberia), Weah's start in life as one of nine siblings would have seen great poverty even by Liberian standards. Although his parents were alive and worked (his father in carpentry), Weah was primarily cared for by his grandmother and through her efforts was able to attend primary school before dropping out of high school. Weah began work for the Liberian Telecommunications Corporation as a switchboard technician, but his brilliant dribbling and goal scoring as a 16-year-old for the Young Survivors club led to his signature by one of Liberia's two big sides, Invincible Eleven (IE). His performances for IE were a platform for his transfer to top Cameroonian club Tonnerre Yaounde in 1987, which he propelled to the league title that year amid growing interest from European clubs. Weah was eventually to achieve what millions of aspiring African youngsters sought, both then and now – a lucrative contract with a famous European football club. AS Monaco manager Arsene Wenger bought Weah for $20,000.

Weah escaped just before he would have been caught up in the murderous chaos of the Doe years. In the global financial haven of Monaco, Weah won the French Cup in 1991, scoring 47 goals in 103 appearances in four seasons (1988–1992) and proving himself a world-class player. He was bought by a bigger club, Paris St-Germain, where he scored 32 goals in 97 appearances over three seasons, winning the French League title in 1994. Italian giants AC Milan then bought Weah at the beginning of the 1995 season. In his first season he won his most prized accolade of FIFA World Footballer of the Year (the first African-born player to do so), as well as the African Player of the Year. At the pinnacle of his career, Weah played for Milan for five years scoring 46 goals in 114 games, winning the Scudetto (Italian League) twice, the Italian Cup once and reaching the Champions League Final in 1995. Towards the end of his Milan career Weah was loaned out to English Premier League club Chelsea where he earned an FA Cup medal. He then played briefly for Manchester City before moving to France with Olympique de Marseille. From his transfer to Yaounde in 1987 to the end of his European career in 2001, Weah scored 148 goals in 368 games.

After Marseille Weah retired to live in New York but was tempted by a huge salary to play for two seasons in the United Arab Emirates with Al-Jazeera. The contract gave him a degree of freedom of residence, so Weah stayed mainly in his New York and Miami homes and flew to games via Concorde. Weah was thus the epitome of mundial man. While in UAE, Weah converted from Christianity to Islam, but reverted back to placate his furious and deeply Christian grandmother. Throughout Weah's exile, wars raged in Liberia and tens of thousands died, but the national side continued to play in World Cup qualifiers and African Nations Cup games; during fixtures, the warring factions operated a *de facto* ceasefire. It was this seductive notion that football could be instrumental in both stopping war and facilitating reconciliation and nation-building that no doubt attracted football-related peace processes. Weah became an unwitting global voice in both the hypotheses and the postulations of NGO policy-making. Credited with being the catalyst for the return of foreign-based players to Liberia to enable them to play for The Lone Star (Weah guaranteed them $5000 per match for travel and expenses), Weah was afforded a status in the eyes of world football of both global philanthropist and local statesman. Picking up on the rhetoric, Weah was to attend a variety of football tournaments established by NGOs, the international peace-keeping forces, FIFA and later UNICEF that sought peace through football. His relative inarticulacy was part of his appeal; a simple man with elementary education and brilliance in other abilities could see what the more educated and sophisticated could not – the simplicity of the game and its *joie de vivre* that brought untold happiness to all involved and was life affirming in its athleticism and levels of participation. Weah became totemic to the international community. Weah was also to become a representative of the African continent football body, the Confederation of African Football (CAF).

Saving the children? A global figure of hope

Altruism was bestowed upon Weah. He had done no wrong in his country, and was a living, walking example of the power of sport (and implicitly peace) over the practice of war and death. While tens of thousands died young and impoverished, Weah was by 2004 a multi-millionaire and aged 39 was close to the age of average life expectancy (42) in Liberia. He had chosen wisely the path of (athletic) righteousness. The Liberian people had become rightly proud of 'The King' and, in 1995, built his statue outside the HQ of the LFA on Monrovia's busiest street.[3] Weah then reportedly bankrolled the national team's away games and participation at the African Nations Tournament held in South Africa. This commendable act brought international acclaim. Weah was the philanthropist prepared to leave the riches of Europe and all its facilities to return to his impoverished national side to fund, play and even coach a nation that did not actually exist as an entity outside of 11 representatives on a football pitch. Weah was a heroic and sporting beacon of hope in a seemingly hopeless war drama. His appeal was the quintessential rags to riches football hero story, but with the added Liberian dimension that he had gained wealth without guns. Thus in using Weah and football for peace, international NGOs were building on pre-existing networks and passions that the game provided in Liberia (cf. Long and Sanderson 2001).

The growth of anti-colonial resentment in 1950s Africa came with a desire of many nations to be globally recognized, and sports such as football fitted the bill.

Consequently, the newly emerging nations joined world football's governing body FIFA (Darby 2000: 75). In the early 1970s the Brazilian João Havelange was elected FIFA's first non-European president after winning the votes of marginalized developing nations, thus setting in motion the game's greater global expansion (Darby 2003: 5).[4] Havelange increased the places available to African nations in the World Cup finals, from one in 1974 to five by 1998.

No doubt with an eye on lucrative sponsorship deals FIFA became ever more concerned in the late 1980s with the propriety of the global game. Fair Play awards were introduced from 1988 onwards, to honour teams, associations or people under its jurisdiction who manifested exemplary behaviour and sporting excellence. It was Weah's turn in 1996 to receive a FIFA award for 'his conduct and his professionalism', reflecting well his lack of histrionics during matches and his financial sacrifices to assist the Liberian national team. Weah soon became a UNESCO Football Ambassador, in recognition of his persona; standing above the factionalism and killing, he personified hope-through-sport as an attractive figure appealing to global youth. Weah was thus globally recognized for his status on and off the pitch, and became a useful figure to have onside for those in high office.

A time to make friends: FIFA and George Weah

The 1998 FIFA presidential election became a two-horse race between the Swedish president of the Union of European Football Associations (UEFA) Lennart Johansson, and the Swiss-born FIFA general secretary Sepp Blatter. The latter, a long time Havelange confidante promised a policy of continuity; the former was presented as a new beginning for the game. The CAF Executive Committee at the general assembly that met in Ouagadougou, Burkina Faso, in February 1998, endorsed Johansson's manifesto. The preceding months saw both candidates scour the globe for votes. A trump card played by Blatter was his increasing support for South Africa to host the 2006 World Cup, alongside the promise of financial assistance for football-related development (primarily via the Goal! projects)[5] in Africa. George Weah, the talisman of African football, endorsed Blatter, thereby eroding support for Johansson (Sugden and Tomlinson 1998: 243).

Referring to the amount of power Blatter acquired during his term under Havelange as FIFA's general secretary, Johansson clearly felt he was in an election campaign against two men. This mutual patronage embittered the Swede, leading him to voice his opinion that some sort of corruption was underpinning African delegates' decisions to switch their votes. Rumours circulated that delegates from developing countries had received payments of $50,000 in return for their support. Relations between Johansson's UEFA and CAF floundered at the FIFA Congress in Paris (which resulted in his ally and CAF leader Cameroonian Issa Hayatou being denigrated by various African representatives for corruption allegations against FIFA) and led to the collapse of his election campaign. Johansson polled 80 votes, Blatter 111. Once Blatter was installed as president, Weah voiced his support for the victor.[6] Somewhat unsurprisingly, Liberia was the first country to receive funds from the

Goal! Programme: $1.2 million was allocated for an artificial pitch in the Tubman stadium.

Goals, cheers and rewards

The relationship between Liberia and Blatter did not end with Weah. The president of the Liberian Football Association (LFA), Edwin Snowe, was also close to Blatter as a result of their personal introduction by Weah. Snowe, son-in-law to President Charles Taylor, was elected unopposed to his LFA post. FIFA allocated around $5 million from 1998 to 2002 to Liberia under the National Assistance Programme. Such funds were intended for technical assistance, youth development, building a football infrastructure and assisting the national team. Any inquisitor as to where such monies were spent has to search high and low for evidence in Liberia. Many people close to the higher echelons of Liberian football allege that much of the income went into Swiss bank accounts.

Despite FIFA's donations, fundamental problems of both football and national unity remained unresolved in Liberia. By the 2002 African Cup of Nations hosted by Mali, Weah and President Snowe seemed to have exhausted ways to obtain funds. The Liberian national team was subsequently in turmoil. The monies promised to the squad from the Minister for Youth and Sport never appeared at their Mali hotel. An angry Weah publicly accused Snowe of embezzlement. No doubt in recognition of the assistance Blatter had received from Snowe and Weah during his 1998 campaign another $150,000 of FIFA money went towards funding the national team, reportedly from the $250,000 annual FIFA grant due to Liberia that year.

Blatter clearly appreciated (and had required) Weah's electoral endorsement. In return, Blatter effectively employed Weah as his personal patron of African football. Unlike the Brazilian Havelange, Blatter could not relate well to the world's poorer nations by virtue of his wealthy European origins. This shrewd acknowledgement of Weah as a facilitative icon not only bolstered FIFA's acumen, but also gave the Liberian star, a humble footballer and global sporting ambassador, a grounding in political intrigue and diplomacy.

From king to president?

The adulation and patronage Weah thus received in both sporting and diplomatic milieus no doubt convinced him he could move into formal politics. Weah was assisted in his aim by the absence in Liberia – indeed Africa – of any predecessor who had combined football celebrity with political acumen. He was thus able to present himself as a new broom, a facilitator of hope, and a candidate of national unity, unencumbered by previous political baggage. He duly announced his presidential candidacy in autumn 2004 for the election scheduled for the following April but delayed until October. The establishment by Weah of a radio and TV station in Monrovia in 2003 (modestly titled 'Royal Communications' – with the insignia of a crown) was undoubtedly a gesture towards assuming the position of the Liberian presidency. In 2004, as the streets of Monrovia were patrolled by the UN police and armed forces,[7] Weah sat in his office on his wooden throne receiving visitors, who would notice the word 'King' carved above a crown that rose behind his head. With ruched curtains and a flag of the country behind him, Weah was – unconsciously or not – making a presidential-like statement. Having declared his candidacy in November 2004 and having created a new political party; the Congress for Democractic Change (CDC), Weah's campaign began.

Weah and his followers were seeking to represent themselves as the party of national unity, one that would appeal to first time voters – that is, the youth of the country, which carried no political legacy from the previous century. Questions about Weah's suitability for such a position dominated Monrovian gossip. Those in favour considered him equipped to remove the corrupt and factional regimes that epitomized Liberian governments, including the loathed interim government tenuously holding some semblance of political office. Weah's standing with both the UN and FIFA was considered in his favour. For while he might be a footballer of little formal education, his presence for over a decade in the corridors of these two world powers would have taught him the arts of *realpolitik* which he could utilize to Liberia's advantage.

In the lead up to the elections Weah singled out corruption and peace as his primary focus; on the first issue he was to state: 'We cannot move forward on any front as a nation without fighting corruption throughout our government … we will implement a "zero-tolerance" policy. We will catch, prosecute and punish anyone found guilty of corruption.' While welcome, the actualities of Weah's anti-corruption drive were not explained. The rhetoric of peace was a similar risky narrative in a society that had neither peace nor much to offer former combatants and even non-combatants. Weah's core supporters were the disfranchised young men who had fought in the conflict and lost everything in peace. They and those too young to fight but now of voting age were not easily placated by a politician's promises; trusting actions over words, they took what they wanted from households on the electoral trail, knowing that if people attempted to stop them violence would ensue. In April 2005 a rally of his supporters turned violent when the refreshments on offer were finished without reaching hundreds of people. In protest some vandalized the hustings premises; others were content to steal furniture.

The same week, the promise to flush out corruption looked doomed upon the discovery of fraudulent membership listings for Weah's party – somewhat embarrassing to a man campaigning on an anti-corruption ticket.[8] Answering accusations that he was uneducated and, therefore, incapable of the realities of world diplomacy and local complexities, Weah responded by buying a degree certificate from an obscure US educational institution. The degree certificate carried no dates of study and was awarded by 'Parkwood' University, which had its internet domain closed in 2003 on the demands of the US Federal Trade Commission.

The crown slips?

Weah's candidature needs to be considered within the context of the problems besetting contemporary Africa. The (Transparency International 2005) Corruption

Perceptions Index placed Liberia in 137th position out of 158 countries in terms of transparency in business and governmental dealings. The index defines 'corruption' as the abuse of public office for private gain, and measures the degree to which corruption is perceived to exist among a country's public officials and politicians. Out of the top ten most corrupt countries, five were African. Corruption exists at every level of African organization, from hospitals through government departments, and, many would argue, sporting establishments. Corruption is however not essentially a malevolent characteristic but in some societies a necessary one (Theobald 1990: 79).

Some of Weah's activities and motivations may have been questionable; whether or not these actions can be defended is another issue. Due to the civil war, Weah in the 1990s was trusted with the national team by both the Liberian government and its Football Association. He was to carry out directions ostensibly on their behalf. In this same period, Weah signed a sponsorship deal for the Liberian national team with sports manufacturer Diadora; the details on the contract are known only to him. Around the same time, Weah was involved in activities that brought him strong condemnation from his own people in 1997. Weah was involved in a squabble with members of the Invincible Eleven. On being transferred to Europe, Weah negotiated a position as IE's president of foreign affairs. Acting as a conduit between the Liberian-based club and Europe, Weah's role was ideally to negotiate deals in Europe for Liberian players and bring the resulting funds and football apparel to Liberia. Weah, with the agreement of the IE president, took five players to France for mid-season trials, during which time IE lost their remaining games and the Liberian championship. The fans, obviously displeased, questioned Weah's motives. He and the president faced allegations that the transfer fees for the Liberian players had not gone into the club's coffers.

A few years later, a breakdown between Weah and some of his playing compatriots came to a head in a crucial football match. In the 2001 World Cup qualifier between Liberia and Ghana, the home team, with Weah in his role of 'Technical Director' (but *de facto* team manager) lost 2-1. The Liberian line-up was under-strength as a result of Weah benching players who had fallen foul of him for a variety of reasons.[9] The defeat effectively lost Liberia a place in the 2002 World Cup Finals, jointly hosted by Japan and South Korea. For such a small and poor nation to get to the finals would have been one of the most momentous achievements in the history of football. The defeat stunned the Liberian people and resulted in Weah being vociferously denigrated by a crowd of 30,000. After the game armed personnel had to protect his home from thousands of furious Liberians, who blamed him for their nation's ignominy. Charles Taylor's offer of his own personal bodyguard was not accepted by Weah, but he left Liberia soon after. Days later, from his place of refuge, Weah vowed neither to play again nor to return to Liberia.[10]

Weah left international football in January 2002 following Liberia's defeat to Nigeria in the African Nations Cup Final in Mali. His reputation was not helped when rumours surfaced that the Liberian FA had reimbursed Weah in full for all his donations to the team, including his ostensible pre-tournament gift of 18 brand-new kits. In the eyes of many in the higher echelons of Liberian football, Weah was not quite the philanthropist others made him out to be. In his defence, Weah might well have believed that money was owed to him because of the huge revenues he had drawn into Liberia as a result of his lobbying on their behalf. It is not known whether he apportioned some of this money for his personal use; humanitarian ambassadors are reputedly not paid. The extent to which this mattered in a society where corruption was and remains endemic will never be fully known.

The president-elect?

At one time the LFA president Edwin Snowe was actually head of the LFA while residing full time in the USA, reading for a Masters level business degree that was funded by FIFA. He was also believed to be working concomitantly as a manager in a Liberian oil refinery. Eventually the LFA Executive Council issued him with an ultimatum to choose a career, so Snowe quit the LFA in 2004 and moved permanently to the oil refinery. A search through LFA accounts on Snowe's departure found around $150,000 unaccounted for. Following his departure FIFA made future funding for Liberia from their Special Development Fund (SDF) dependent on more transparent accounting. Five years after funding was awarded, the stadium's refurbishment was incomplete, the women's football league had lost two of its nine teams, and the attempt at nation-building through football saw 50 balls distributed among hinterland county teams. A couple of football scholarships were also provided as part of the money. Snowe's successor – and former deputy – Izeeta Wesley took office by virtue of a consensus of 120 representatives who approved her appointment in March 2006, as the first woman to head a national football association in Africa. A former president of Survivor FC Wesley at one time had a very good relationship with George Weah who would call her daily to discuss football. Their relationship deteriorated when in 2004, Weah insulted her in a radio interview alleging she was frequently seen drunk in nightclubs. There was more to this than moral censure. It was widely believed in Liberia in 2005 that Weah wanted the position of LFA president. His desire for such a position might have been obvious two years previously when, during a radio interview at the African Nations Cup in Mali, Weah criticized Snowe's integrity when in charge of LFA funds. He furthermore accused Charles Taylor of being a thief and using prostitutes. It was not a great surprise when Weah announced his post-Mali exile from Liberia. Weah then spent one year in the United Arab Emirates, one year in the USA, two months in Ghana (where his mother now lived) only returning to Liberia in September 2004 – shortly after Taylor's departure.

A little local issue then ensued. In 2004 a Monrovia-based football club named Bassa Defenders FC approached Weah to become president. Weah accepted stating that the position was in honour of his mother who hailed from Grand Bassa, the club's original home. However the LFA Secretary General instructed the club that Weah's presidency was not permissible because such a status was only awarded via elections by club members that were scrutinized by LFA officials. The football club in response claimed discrimination. The incident brought to a head the rhetoric surrounding football democracy. Although football statutes required transparency, the law and procedure were always negotiable in the Liberian context. Perhaps more crucial was the stipulation that club presidents had to be in office for two years before being eligible for election to the LFA presidency. To his critics, Weah wanted the latter office by circumnavigating the regulations.

An unfair contest?

Weah knew well the depths of the Liberian political process. In the late 1990s, a cousin was raped by Taylor's militia and Weah's house had been attacked by Taylor's Special Operations Unit. In response Weah had pleaded for international intervention against the Taylor regime. His presidential candidacy was in part a courageous statement in defiance of such atrocities and the personnel, still at liberty, who had perpetrated these crimes. The election, beginning in early 2005, saw Weah as the youngest of the 22 presidential candidates. His primary challenger, known as Liberia's 'Iron Lady', was Ellen Johnson-Sirleaf; a political figure since the 1970s who had suffered much more than Weah. She had twice been forced into political exile; in the 1980s, the Doe regime had jailed her on separate occasions for alleged treason and coup-plotting. She had stood against Charles Taylor in the 1997 election, finishing second. With a Harvard degree Johnson-Sirleaf had been Minister of Finance in the late 1970s and had once been African Director of the UN Development Programme. She was to campaign on a promise of installing a well in every village within two years and providing universal education and health care. A further promise was a broad-based representative government. A mother of four and grandparent of six, Johnson-Sirleaf spoke of bringing 'motherly sensitivity and emotion' to the presidency. The T-shirts of her supporters read 'All the men have failed Liberia – let's try a woman this time.'

By contrast, Weah's rallies saw him proclaimed the messiah by his predominately young male entourage, who would celebrate his lack of education, chanting 'you know no book, we vote for you'. All 22 candidates were appealing to an electorate of 1.3 million registered voters, 80 per cent of whom were unemployed. The outcome in a 74.9 per cent turn out was Weah attracting 28 per cent of the vote and Johnson-Sirleaf 20 per cent. However, under the 2003 peace deal, a second vote was stipulated if any candidate failed to poll 50 per cent of the vote plus one. A run-off between Weah and Johnson-Sirleaf took place a month later in November, with the latter pulling over 60 per cent of the vote. When the result was announced UN peacekeeping personnel had to baton-charge thousands of Weah's supporters protesting against the result. Weah publicly appealed to his followers to leave the streets of Monrovia, stating 'there is no need to cry because we have not lost the election'.[11]

Electoral analysts explain Weah's loss in terms of complacency. Two weeks before the run-off vote, Weah and his partisans ignored the intensive lobbying of his rivals, and did relatively little themselves. Weah may well have overestimated his popularity; his supporters – as is congruent with the fame he received in football –

were the youthful male population (the median age of the Liberian population is 18.06 years). Weah's life and masculine image had less relevance to the female population, something Weah overlooked. While girls in Liberia play football, the rewards on offer are negligible, and the nation has no female sports heroes. Weah suffered a cultural blindness in a society where violent attacks on women are so commonplace that AIDS campaigns run adverts imploring men not to rape women. Ellen Johnson-Sirleaf had, in Liberian women, around 50 per cent of the population, which held more reason to support her than an icon eulogized mainly by males. Liberian females voted for her both as a female and to tackle the inherent male bias that pervaded their society since its origins.

When the result was announced Weah claimed electoral fraud. This may have been expected considering his pre-election fixation on Liberian corruption. The allegation was ignored and a few weeks later Weah declared: 'I kneel down in peace to all my supporters and peace-loving people in Liberia.' Weah seemed easily silenced. Allegations that Johnson-Sirleaf was accompanied by a US secret service entourage at her inauguration and that Weah received some $3,000,000 from the Nigerian government in exchange for his retraction of the fraud accusation will fuel debates for years to come in Liberia.

Extra time needed?

Weah's football career illustrated the power football has on contemporary political processes and imagery. Revered by Nelson Mandela as an icon of 'African Pride', Weah stood as a figure of optimism for both a nation and a continent. His career illustrated what Rorty (1998) might recognize as sport's sentimental education. The collective effort the game of football requires and the resultant aesthetic implies a large measure of tolerance that prioritizes that which is shared over that which divides.

Nevertheless, Liberia challenges the notion of global idioms. The intervention of Western powers and global institutions in the past 15 years was based on the assumption that, while a presence was maintained, the carnage would cease, a democracy could evolve, and a European model of social responsibility could flourish. However, reason cannot explain much of what happens in Liberia where violent identities are not easy for an onlooker to comprehend. The tyranny of such local identities remain and the emergence of the nation-state is still provoking bloodshed (Holton 2005; Sen 2005). In all of this football is a cosmetic exercise – it is not a necessity. It is a global quasi-religion but it is not the epitome of liberal values; such values were never global idioms anyway (Appadurai 1990; Stiglitz 2006).

One might argue that Liberia is unique; it has its own circumstances and wisdom. If so, we need to beware experts who now colonize it in the name of the UN, or to watch closely those NGOs who seek to mould world opinion and to offer guidance on the way of the West. It could be argued that the absence of colonialism denied Liberia the veneer of national identity and cohesion that emerged elsewhere. Such cohesion might have provided better for a united and disciplined group of athletes who could have been a force in football. Liberia lacked not only European colonial elites, who could kick-start this process; it also lacked economic and cultural integration. Also missing were the institutions for nation-building and modernity, which might have preceded sport in encouraging a sense of national discipline. Ironically, the processes elsewhere dismissed as 'Americanization', and 'corporatization' and seen in other contexts as destructive towards national culture and identity – particularly in undermining young working-class affiliations to place, and threatening amateur involvement and standardizing world sport – might themselves at some point have had a role to play in preventing the atrocities that afflicted late twentieth century Liberia (cf. Cohen and Kennedy 2000).

In the same month that Weah had declared his presidential candidacy, Liberia played at home to Senegal in front of 50,000 supporters. The match was preceded by disputes over funding between the Liberian FA and the Minister for Youth and Sport. As a consequence, foreign-based players were not approached to represent Liberia for the fixture. Furthermore, a stipend promised for the Liberian players was not paid. Pre-match radio debates centred on public expectations were believed to be politically motivated. The game saw Liberia miss three goal chances in the first 15 minutes, incompetence perceived by many fans to be deliberate. Two late goals for Senegal provoked the crowd to throw bottles and missiles; gunshots were also fired into the air. A 30-minute stoppage period ensued before the game was completed with a Senegal victory. After the match a mob of thousands rioted along the route between the stadium and the Monrovian suburb of Sinkor. The LFA president's house was looted and people considered rich by Liberian standards were attacked and their cars stolen. Shops were ransacked. The mob was met by the joint forces of the UN police personnel alongside the national interim government's police force. The clashes produced three dead and 100 people injured. Football disappoints those who consider it an ideal vehicle for peace and reconciliation.

In 2001 Sepp Blatter stated that football's future was female. He was proven correct in Liberia. Despite being the most globally renowned African male figure after Nelson Mandela (and possibly Eusebio of Mozambique and Portugal) George Weah could not defeat his female rival in this highly patriarchal and religious society. Izeeta Wesley was to retain the position of LFA president at the time of writing. Liberia is now globally renowned for electing the first African female president. The elections for both offices were games that Weah was unable to win. For many in Liberia, a victory for Weah would have been a victory of style over substance. His own entourage were aware from the beginning of his somewhat tenuous abilities to make the leap from sublime footballer to astute statesman. Weah could entertain but was not versed in the qualities that make for nation building. For many, Weah's candidature was more attractive to Western eyes fascinated by the novelty of a footballer becoming a politician and nation-builder. The Liberian populace however were astute enough to realize that when the Western media circus left town, their reality remained and something greater than celebrity was needed to resolve their problems.

While the epitome of masculine credibility in both the African and indeed global context, Weah was not considered qualified to lead a country. Faced with a contest between Weah and an elderly female with a greater grasp of economics and world politics, the electorate chose the latter. Weah is believed to be preparing for the election of 2012. Many of the main political players will by then have left politics or, considering life expectancy in Liberia, have passed away.

Acknowledgements

The author is indebted to the scholarly advice given at the early stages of this article by Paul Kennedy. Thanks are due to Richard Giulianotti and Roland Robertson who extended the invitation to submit to this special edition. Gratitude is also extended to Ali Rogers in his capacity of journal editor and the constructive comments of the two anonymous readers. Special thanks are due to the variety of Liberian-based informants who for a variety of reasons wish to remain anonymous. A crucial role in the text was provided by Luke Kavanagh who assisted in the correspondence with Liberia and commented on earlier drafts of this article. The IT and formatting was done with typical competence by Irmani Darlington. The research was in part funded by the School of Sport and Education, Brunel University. This article is based on four recent visits to Liberia, between 1997 and 2005.

Notes

1. See Schiller (1969), Tomlinson (1991), Maguire (1991) and Robertson (2003) for elaboration on the concept of 'Americanization'.
2. The tag 'King' was originally a media creation, used to describe his football achievement. Other nicknames applied to Weah were 'Black Diamond of Africa' and 'Africa Wonder Boy'.
3. The connotation with royalty in Africa's first republic appealed to Weah, who founded a hotel called 'The King Hotel' and a 'King's bar'.
4. Once elected, Havelange strongly reduced FIFA's Eurocentrism and sought to establish good football standards and concomitant infrastructures within the developing world. Havelange committed himself to cash subsidies for the construction of stadiums, the provision of top-class coaching, and support for more club competitions throughout Africa and Asia.
5. FIFA's publicity explained the ethos: Goal! projects include the construction or renovation of association headquarters (to ensure independent football administration), training centres and artificial weatherproof turf pitches that improve the quality and quantity of football facilities both locally and nationally.
6. The first four years of Blatter's presidency saw FIFA lose £340 million as a consequence of financial mismanagement, cronyism and alleged corruption. FIFA's general secretary Michael Zen-Ruffinen accused Blatter of using FIFA funds to reward those that voted for him. Accusing Blatter of being a dictator, the 21-page report submitted by Zen-Ruffinen was read by the Executive Committee. They questioned Blatter who admitted to mistakes but dismissed the report as 'not serious'. The report specifically stated that the Goal! project was a vehicle for Blatter to buy votes. Blatter's response was that the allocation of such funds was dealt with by a committee and not just him.
7. Western Europe had sent soldiers from Sweden and the Republic of Ireland. Africa was represented by troops from Nigeria, Ghana, Ethiopia and Namibia. The rest of the world provided military personnel from the Ukraine, Jordan, Nepal, Pakistan and Bangladesh.
8. Objections were raised regarding the names of some of Weah's party candidates, which appeared on electoral literature without their consent. Other candidates listed proved to be

ineligible to vote by virtue of not being of voting age. One by the name of Paul Wiah was listed as an electoral candidate but was in fact aged ten.

9. Weah had public fall-outs with colleagues Frank Seator, Louis Crayton and Zizi Roberts.

10. Debates around the defeat amongst Liberia's football-loving public saw them manifest a global awareness in apportioning blame. There were three dominant theories: the most popular was that the Nigerian government had bribed the Liberian players to lose the game so as to qualify at the expense of Liberia. Another theory apportioned blame to the bribes of FIFA who paid off the Lone Star because they could not afford to not have so populous a country as Nigeria missing out on the World Cup finals. The third theory was that the Lone Star players were bribed to lose the game by Liberians opposed to Charles Taylor and currently in exile in the USA. These same people were considered to be friends of George Weah. According to this theory a Lone Star victory would make the people happy and sustain Charles Taylor's regime.

11. Monitors from the European Union, Carter Centre and National Democratic Institute judged the elections as credible and peaceful. Observers from the Economic Community of West African states judged the election 'fair, free and transparent'.

References

Allison, L. (ed.) (1986) *The politics of sport*, Manchester: Manchester University Press.

Allison, L. (ed.) (2002) *The global politics of sport*, London: Routledge.

Anderson, B. (1991) *Imagined communities: reflections on the origin and spread of nationalism*, London: Verso.

Andrews, D. (ed.) (2001) *Michael Jordan Inc.: corporate sports media culture, and late modern America*, Albany, NY: State University of New York Press.

Andrews, D. and S. Jackson (2001) *Sports stars: the cultural politics of sporting celebrity*, London: Routledge.

Appadurai, A. (1990) 'Disjuncture and difference in the global cultural economy', *Theory, Culture and Society*, 7, 295–310.

Aris, S. (1990) *Sportsbiz: inside the sports business*, London: Hutchinson.

Armstrong, G. (2002) 'Talking up the game: football and the reconstruction of Liberia, West Africa', *Identities*, 11, 471–94.

Armstrong, G. (2005) 'The lords of misrule: football and the rights of the child in Liberia, West Africa', *Sports and Society*, 7, 472–501.

Armstrong, G. and R. Giulianotti (2004) 'Drama, fields and metaphors: an introduction to football in Africa', in R. Giulianotti and G. Armstrong (eds) *Football in Africa: conflict, conciliation and community*, Basingstoke: Palgrave/Macmillan, 1–25.

Bale, J. and J. Maguire (1994) *The global sports arena: athlete talent migration in an independent world*, London: Frank Cass.

Budd, A. and R. Levermore (eds) (2004) *Sport and international relations*, London: Routledge.

Cashmore, E. and A. Parker (2003) 'One David Beckham? Celebrity, masculinity and the soccerati', *Sociology of Sport Journal*, 20, 214–31.

Clapham, C. (1989) 'Liberia', in C. O'Brien (ed.) *Contemporary West African states*, Cambridge: Cambridge University Press.

Cohen, R. and P. Kennedy (2000) *Global sociology*, Basingstoke: Palgrave.

Crawford, G. (2004) *Consuming sport: fans, sport and culture*, London: Routledge.

Darby, P. (2000) 'Football, colonial doctrine and indigenous resistance: mapping the political persona of FIFA's African constituency', *Culture, Sport, Society*, 3, 61–87.

Darby, P. (2003) 'Africa, the FIFA presidency and the governance of world football: 1974, 1998, and 2002', *Africa Today*, 50 (1), 3–24.

Forster, J. and N. Pope (2004) *The political economy of global sports organisations*, London: Routledge.

Gilchrist, P. (2005) 'Local heroes and global stars', in L. Allison (ed.) *The global politics of sport*, London: Routledge, 118–39.

Giulianotti, R. (1999) *Football: a sociology of the global game*, Cambridge: Polity.

Goldblatt, D. (2006) *The ball is round: a global history of football*, London: Viking.

Guttmann, A. (1994) *Games and empires: modern sports and cultural imperialism*, New York: Columbia University Press.

Harris, D. (1999) 'From "warlord" to "democratic" president: how Charles Taylor won the 1997 Liberian election', *Journal of Modern African Studies*, 37, 431–55.

Holton, R. (2005) *Making globalization*, Basingstoke: Palgrave.

Jarvie, G. (2005) *Sport, culture and society*, London: Routledge.

Jubwe, S. (1994) 'A social analysis of the Liberian crisis', Unpublished Paper, Dept. of Sociology and Anthropology, Monrovia: University of Liberia.

Jubwe, S. (1997) 'Hegemony and class consciousness in Liberia 1944–1989: a sociological perspective', Unpublished Paper, Dept. of Sociology and Anthropology, Monrovia: University of Liberia.

Klausen, A. M. (1999) *Olympic Games as performance and public event: the case of the XVII Winter Olympic Games in Norway*, Oxford: Berghahn Books.

Libenow, G. J. (1987) *Liberia: the quest for democracy*, Bloomington: University of Indiana.

Lines, G. (2002) 'The sports star in the media: the gendered construction and youthful consumption of sports personalities', in J. Sugden and A. Tomlinson (eds) *Power games: a critical sociology of sport*, London: Routledge, 196–215.

Long, J. and I. Sanderson (2001) 'The social benefits of sport: where's the proof?', in C. Gratton and I. Henry (eds) *Sport in the city: the role of sport in economic and social integration*, London: Routledge, 187–203.

Maguire, J. (1991) 'The media-sport complex: the emergence of American sport in European culture', *European Journal of Communications*, 6, 315–36.

Maguire, J. (1994) 'Sport, identity politics and globalization: diminishing contrasts and increasing varieties', *Sociology of Sport Journal*, 11, 398–427.

Maguire, J. (1999) *Global sport: identities, societies, civilisations*, Cambridge: Polity Press.

Maguire, J. (2005) *Power and global sport*, London: Routledge.

Marshall, P. D. (1997) *Celebrity, power and fame in contemporary culture*, Minneapolis: University of Minnesota Press.

Miller, T., G. Lawrence, J. McKay and D. Rowe (2001) *Globalization and sport*, London: Sage.

Nalapat, A. and A. Parker (2005) 'Sport, celebrity and popular culture: Sachin Tendulkar, cricket and Indian nationalism', *International Review for the Sociology of Sport*, 40, 433–46.

Reno, W. (1993) 'Foreign firms and the financing of Charles Taylor's NPFL', *Liberian Studies Journal*, 18, 175–88.

Robertson, R. (1992) *Globalization: social theory and global culture*, London: Sage.

Robertson, R. (2003) 'Globalization, an overview', in R. Robertson and K. White (eds) *Globalization, cultural concepts in sociology*, London: Routledge, 1–44.

Rorty, R. (1998) *Truth and progress*, Cambridge: Cambridge University Press.

Schiller, H. (1969) *Mass communication and American Empire*, Boston, MA: Beacon Press.

Sen, A. (2005) *The argumentative Indian*, New York: Farrar, Strauss & Giroux.

Smart, B. (2005) *The sports star: modern sport and the cultural economy of sports celebrity*, New York: Sage.

Stiglitz, J. (2006) *Making globalization work: the next steps to global justice*, Harmondsworth: Penguin Allen Lane.

Sudgen, J. and A. Tomlinson (1998) *FIFA and the contest for world football: who rules the people's game?*, Cambridge: Polity Press.

Theobald, R. (1990) *Corruption, development and underdevelopment*, Durham: Duke University Press.

Tomlinson, J. (1991) *Cultural imperialism: a critical introduction*, London: Pinter.

Transparency International (2005) *Transparency International corruption perceptions index*, Berlin: Transparency International.

Turner, G. (2004) *Understanding celebrity*, New York: Sage.

Vertinsky, P. and J. Bale (eds) (2004) *Sites of sport: space, place and experience*, London: Routledge.

Whannel, G. (2002) *Media sports stars: masculinities and moralities*, London: Routledge.

Index

AC Milan 111, 126
Adidas 115, 20, 21, 34
advertising 13, 14, 15, 19, 23, 34, 42, 90, 100; first
    modern Olympics 20
Advocaat, Dick 114
Afghanistan 94
Africa; African Nations Cup 127, 129, 131; cricket
    99; soccer 20, 48, 52, 56, 58, 63, 122–36
Ajax 110, 111, 114, 115, 116, 117
Akron Firestones 12
Al-Jazeera 126
Albertville 10, 17(fig), 49
Alex 72
All Nippon Airways 72
'All Star' shoes/sneakers 12, 13
alpine skiing 54
American football 2, 6, 20, 48, 54, 61, 80, 88
American sports 23, 49; in Japan 72
Americanization 61, 122, 123, 135
Among the Thugs 51
Ancient Greece 9
Antoinette Tubman Stadium 124, 129
Appadurai, Arjun 32, 83, 99–100, 134
Argentina 20, 55, 62, 66, 110, 116
Arlott, John 101
Arsenal 50
AS Monaco 126
AS Roma 72
Ashland Manufacturing Company 12
Asia; baseball 80, 83, 91; cricket 1, 4, 95, 98, 99,
    100, 101–5; footwear production 13; short track
    skating 53–4; soccer 20, 63; supporter
    subculture 66
association football *see* soccer
Athletic Bilbao 68
athletics 9, 14, 31, 32, 80, 84, 89, 95
audiences; fragmentation of 19; Gaelic sports 55;
    Indian cricket 102; Olympics 2, 36; receive US
    popular culture 40; television 18, 19, 36, 53, 62,
    70, 74, 82, 95, 101–2; UK 70–1
Australasia 1, 8, 33, 61, 62, 69
Australia 96, 112; cricket 8, 97, 99, 100, 102, 103,
    104; Murdoch and 37, 38; rugby league 38–9,
    96; tennis 8; world cup soccer 116
Australian Rules Football 54, 61

badminton 12
Baltic Republics 66
Bam 49

bandy 49, 54
Bangladesh 97, 102
Barcelona 10, 17(fig), 18, 65, 110, 111, 116, 118
    barras bravas 66
baseball 2, 4, 23, 49, 50, 79–91; commercialized
    80; early diffusion 83; Japan Series 90; Japanese
    compared to American 86–8; large spectator
    sport 48; MLB dominance 82; multi-ethnic
    MLB teams 91; Olympic history 81;
    professionalization 84; Spalding 'father of' 11;
    uncanny mimicry 85–6, 91; World Cup 81;
    World Series 90
basketball 11, 12–13, 23, 32, 35, 48, 83–4, 90
Basques 68
Bassa Defenders FC 132–3
Baudrillard, Jean 59
Beckham, David 23
behaviour, on field 61, 100
Beijing 2, 17(fig)
Beveren 50
Bhabha, Homi 85–6
Bird, Larry 13
Blatter, Sepp 7, 63, 103, 128–9, 135
Blue Ribbon Sports 14
Bosman case 50, 96
Bradman, Don 98
brands 6, 7, 9; associate with performance 19,
    22–3; Dutch soccer as 115; local culture and 34;
    Olympic Games promote 10; soccer clubs as 96;
    sports goods 11–14; sportswear fashion 67;
    television promotion 16
Brazil 14, 49, 58, 62, 68, 72, 83, 85, 110
British Commonwealth 49, 50, 61, 98, 102
broadcasting 9, 23; global audience 19; MLB 82,
    83; Murdoch and 18; Olympics and World Cup
    10–11, 18, 36–7; radio 15; rights bidding 20, 38;
    rights revenue 18; satellite television 17, 69, 82,
    102, 123; soccer clubs and 70; speed skating 53
BSkyB 37, 38
Bukatsu 34

Camp, Walter 6
Canada 8, 33, 54, 97, 98, 99
capitalism 6–24, 35; deregulation of 46; grobal 39;
    grobal–glocal 35; imperial and late 32–3
celebrity(ies) 7, 23, 34; George Weah 122–36;
    promoting sports goods 12, 14, 15–16; role
    models 22; soccer players 68; tennis players 9
Chelsea 51, 96, 126

Chicago Bears 16
China 60, 83
Chirac, President Jacques 58, 75
clothing 9, 11, 12, 14, 16, 20
Coca-Cola 20, 34, 46
colonialism 123, 134; British 31–2, 98–9
commodification 33, 39
Compton, Dennis 20, 101
Confederación Sud American de Fútbol 62
Confederation of African Football (CAF) 127, 128
Congress for Democratic Change (CDC) 130
connectivity 59, 62–3, 65, 67, 70, 71, 74, 75, 76;
    Japan 72–3; media 68, 69; telecommunications
    66; transnationalism and 74
consumerism 3, 11
Converse 11, 12, 13, 14
corporatization 33, 39, 122, 135
corruption 2, 58, 103, 128, 130–2, 134
cosmopolitanism 59, 63–6; banal 64, 67, 68, 69,
    73, 74; 'thin' and 'thick' 64, 65, 67, 70, 71, 73,
    74, 75
cricket 8, 79, 94–105; 20/20 matches 101; and
    British imperialism 31–2, 49; in Canada and
    USA 99; Champions Trophy 98; 'chucking'
    104, 105; compared to baseball 80; in India 32;
    indiginized 99; one-day internationals (ODIs)
    95, 97–8, 104; post-Westernization 95; tension
    between two versions 97–102; Test Matches 98,
    104; in West Indies 31–2; World Cup 49, 98,
    104
Cricket: more than a game 104
Cruyff, Johan 107, 110, 111, 114, 115, 116
Cuba 80, 81, 82, 83, 84

Dalmiya, Jagmohan 103–4
Davis Cup 8
Davis, Dwight 8
De Coubertin, Baron 9–10
Dempsey, Jack 15
deterritorialization 108, 118
disconnectivity 63, 69, 74, 75
Doe, Samuel K. 124–5
Dominican Republic 80, 91
dress code 9, 95
duality of glocality 61, 66, 71, 74, 75
Dubai 94, 95, 102
Dunlop Rubber Company Ltd. 11–12

economic liberalism 15
England 11, 50, 68; cricket in 101
England and Wales Cricket Board (ECB) 97
EU 96, 108, 109
European Cup/Champions League 63, 96, 110
evolution 46–7, 48, 50–1

fans 66–73 *see also* spectators; 'casual' style 67;
    Dutch 109–19; diasporic formations 68;
    Japanese culture 73; Manchester United sale
    40–1
Federation Internationale de Basketball 32
Federation Internationale de Football Association 8,
    32

Feyenoord 110, 114
FIFA; concern for propriety 128; conflict with
    Africa and Asia 63; developing nations join
    127–8; and George Weah 128–32; marketing
    partners 20; membership 10; sponsorship 7, 19,
    20; supranational governance 80; universalism
    123
Finney, Tom 20
First Higher School Baseball Club 88–9
footwear 12–14
Fortuyn, Pim 108
Foster, Joseph 12
Freud, Sigmund 85

Gaelic Athletic Association (GAA) 54, 55
Gaelic football 54–6, 61
Gebruder Dassler 11, 13
Glasgow; transnational supporter networks 69–70
Glazer, Malcolm 40
global–local 29, 41
globaloney 42
glocalization 29–30, 32, 34, 36, 37, 56, 59, 64, 65,
    66, 67, 71, 75, 79, 85, 86, 88; definition 60–1
Goal! programme 128–9
governing bodies 7–8, 10, 32, 33, 48, 62, 75, 94,
    98, 123
Grange, 'Red' 15, 16, 20
grid-iron football 15, 23 *see also* American
    football
grobalization 28–42, 56

Havelange, João 20, 58, 63, 75, 128, 129
Hawaii 83, 84
Hayatou, Issa 128
heterogeneity 60, 61
heterogenization 29, 61, 66, 69, 71, 72, 74, 75
hinchas 66
homogeneity 60, 61
homogenization 29, 36, 61, 66, 67, 69, 71, 72, 74,
    75
hooliganism 51, 66
hurling 54–6
Hutton, Sir Leonard 101

ice hockey 10, 23, 48, 49, 85
imagined communities 107–19
immigration 84, 108, 117
imperialism 31, 49, 55
India; cricket 32, 49, 85, 97, 98, 99–102, 103–4;
    cricket superpower 99; Davis Cup 8; football
    secondary status 61; globalization winner 95
indigenization 79, 100, 123
International Amateur Athletic Association (IAAF)
    8, 80
International Association of Athletics Federations
    32; world championships 35
International Baseball Federation (IBAF) 81, 82, 90
International Cricket Council (ICC) 32, 94, 97, 98,
    102–3, 104, 105; calendar 103; move to Dubai
    95, 102
International Football Association Board 8
International Lawn Tennis Challenge Trophy 8

International Lawn Tennis Federation 8
International Management Group (IMG) 16
International Olympic Committee (IOC) 22; anti-
   American politics 91; broadcast revenue
   beneficiary 17–18; compared to UN 2; corporate
   sponsorship 22; embrace of private enterprise
   10; founding 9, 32; games schedule changed 10
International Rugby Football Board 8, 32
International Sport and Leisure (ISL) 14, 22
internet 7, 17, 18, 67, 69
Invincible Eleven (IE) 126, 131
Ireland 54–6, 61

James, C. L. R. 31–2, 50
Japan; baseball 80, 81, 82, 83, 84, 85, 86–91;
   football 71–5; Nike campaign 34–5; origin of
   glocalization 60; World Cup spending 18
jet travel 9
J-League 72, 73
Johansson, Lennart 128
Johnson-Sirleaf, Ellen 133–4
journalists 66, 70–1, 74
J. W. Foster & Sons 11, 12

Khan, Imran 98
'Kolpak' countries 96
Kolpak, Maros 96
Korea 60, 73, 81, 83, 112, 116

lacrosse 84
Latin America 48, 49, 58, 66
Lawn Tennis Association of Australasia 8
leagues; baseball 80, 82, 86; corporatization 33;
   emergence of 32; News Corporation investment
   38–9; television coverage 67
Lenglen, Suzanne 9
Le Pen, Jean-Marie 50
Liberia 4, 122–36
Liberian Football Association (LFA) 129
Liberian United for the Restoration of Democracy
   (LURD) 125
Little League World Series 82
logos, sponsors' 14, 23–4

magazines 11, 15, 19, 67, 70
Major League Baseball (MLB) 4, 80, 81–3, 90–1
Manchester United 40–1, 51, 65, 96, 111
Mandela, Nelson 6, 134, 135
Mani, Ehsan 105
marketing; broadcasting and 19; Coca-Cola 46;
   FIFA 20, 22; ISL 14, 22; J-League 72; local
   culture in 34; MLB 82, 90; Olympics 10, 36;
   sports goods 12; sports stars 15, 16
match-fixing 103, 105
MCC 102
McCormack, Mark 16
McDonalds 34
McDonaldization 2
media; amount of coverage 48, 53; club channels
   and websites 70, consultants 23; cricket power
   shift 101–2; disproportionate attention to football
   52; Dutch soccer greatness 110–11, 116–17; and

football 70–1; golden triangle 7; growing
   interest in sport 10–11, 16–19; Japan 72, 86;
   multinational corporations 18; Murdoch 37–8;
   rights bidding 80; transnational 51
mediatization 3, 62, 67
Mexico 49, 68, 69
Microsoft 46
mobile phones 17, 18, 67
Monrovia 124, 125, 126, 127, 129, 132–3, 135
Murdoch, Rupert 18, 37, 38
myth-making 108–9, 113, 115, 117, 118, 119

national identity 95–6; corporate loyalty and 14;
   Dutch 109, 112–19
National Football League (NFL) 33, 37, 72, 90;
   Super Bowl 35
National Patriotic Front of Liberia (NPFL) 124, 125
National Rugby League 38
Negro Leagues 80, 82
Netherlands 4, 49, 53, 98, 107–19
New York 64, 82, 126
New Zealand 8, 49, 102, 103; cricket World Cup
   97
Newport RI 8
News Corporation 18, 37, 38, 39
newspapers 15, 48, 52, 53, 54, 74, 89
NGOs 75, 127, 134
nihonjinron 72
Nike 6, 12, 13, 14, 34, 35
Nippon Professional Baseball (NPB) 81, 91
Nissan FC 72
Norway 49, 50, 52–3
nothingness 39, 41
Nottingham Forest 19

Olympic Committees, National 2, 10
Olympic Partner Programme (TOP) 22
Olympic Games; Albertville (1992) 49; Amsterdam
   (1928) 13, 20; Antwerp (1920) 10; Athens
   (1896) 9, 10, 20; Athens (2004) 2, 10, 17(fig),
   18, 36; Barcelona (1992) 10, 17(fig), 18, 118;
   baseball in 81, 91; Beijing (2008) 2, 17(fig);
   Berlin (1936) 13, 81; Chamonix (1924) 10, 62;
   first televised 17; football at 62; global
   dimensions 2; and globalization 9–11;
   Lillehammer (1994) 10; marketing and television
   rights 14; Montreal (1976) 14; nationalist
   sentiment 96; opening ceremonies 36; Partner
   Programme (TOP) 22; pre-eminent tournament
   95; sponsorship 19–22; television coverage 17,
   18, 36; unite world populace 35; winter 10, 49
orange craze/myth 107–19
orienteering 52, 54

Packer, Kerry 38, 100
particularity 30, 34, 35, 37, 74, 118
pay-per-view 17, 38
politics 24, 49, 68, 82, 91, 123–36
postmodernism 42
postmodernity 59
post-nationalism 96
post–Westernization 4, 94–105

Professional Golf Association Match Play
    Championship 19
player mobility 96
professionalism 8, 9, 23
Puma 11, 14

Reebok 11, 12, 14, 34
Rijkaard, Frank 112, 116
rugby 8, 31, 32, 38–9
Ruth, 'Babe' 15–16, 50

Samaranch, Juan 103
sameness 29, 60
samurai baseball 86–90
schools 80, 88–9
Scotland 8, 66, 68, 69
short track skating 53–4
skiing 53, 54
Sky Sport 51
slavery 123
Slazenger 11, 12
sneakers 12–13
Snowe, Edwin 129, 132
soccer; aggression 61; *catenaccio*-style 116;
    compared to baseball 80; dominance 48; early
    diffusion 83; global game 32; growth in
    televised games 64; *Hollandse* school 107; in
    Ireland 54; origins of players 50; player
    migration 70; 'total' 107, 108, 111, 114, 115;
    transnational character 50; working class
    demeanour 31
Societe Monegasque de Promotion Internationale
    (SMPI) 20
sociocultural compression 62
Sons and Daughters of Zimbabwe 97
South Africa 8, 69, 95, 96, 97, 102, 128
South America 2, 62, 64, 68, 72, 73, 123
South Sydney Rabbitohs 38–9
Spain 20, 50, 67, 68, 71, 116
Spalding, Albert G. 11, 79, 80, 82, 83, 84, 85, 90
spectacularization 33, 39
spectators 7, 10, 15, 22, 23, 48, 53–4, 73, 98
spectatorship 7, 15, 32, 80, 81, 82, 86
speed skating 52–4, 55–6
Sphairistike 11
spikes 12, 13
sponsorship, corporate 7, 9, 10, 11–15, 24, 80, 128;
    cricket 103; disproportionate attention to football
    52; global market growth 19; growth with
    television 20; Olympics 22
sports agents 16, 23
sport studies 1
sporting hero 122–3, 124, 127
sports goods 7, 11–15
sports reporting 15
Sri Lanka 97, 102
streaming video 18
students 88–9
Super 14 competition 34
supporter subcultures 65–75
supporters' clubs 69

Taliban 94–5
Tartan Army 66–7, 68
Taylor, Charles 124–6, 131, 132, 133; Chief Patron
    of Sport 125
tennis 7, 8–9, 10, 48; no world championship 95
    players' global ranking 52; professional tour 16;
    racket manufacturing 11, 12; shoes 13
The globalization of nothing 56
Tilden, Bill 9, 15
tipping-points 47
Tobita, Suishu 89
Toronto 64, 69
trade 23–4, 31, 62
transfer market 50, 54
transnationalism 59, 61–2, 63, 65, 70, 74

Ul-Haq, Inzamam 105
Ulster 55
ultras 66, 67
UNESCO 128
UNICEF 127
Union des Societes Francaises des Sportes
    Athletique 9
Union of European Football Associations (UEFA)
    128
United Arab Emirates 73, 103, 126, 132
United Nations 2, 6, 10
unity-in-difference 36
universalism 29, 35–6, 58, 75
Uruguay 62, 66
utility maximization 33

van Basten, Marco 107, 110, 114, 115, 116
Van Gaal, Louis 112, 116
van Hanegem, Willem 108, 115
van 't Schip, John 107, 111, 114

wages 11
We were the best 111, 115
Weah, George 4, 122–37; mundial man 126–7;
    presidential candidacy 129–34
Wesley, Izeeta 132, 135
West Indies 31–2, 95, 103
Wilson Sporting Goods Company 11, 12
Wimbledon 8, 9, 11
Women's Baseball World Cup 81
working hours 11
World Athletics Championships 14
World Baseball Classic (WBC) 81, 90
World Cup, FIFA; African teams 56, 63; global
    10; Japan and 73; nationalist sentiment 110,
    112; rights to 14; sponsorship 19–22; television
    and 17, 18, 19, 49, 62; universal 6, 35
World Series Cricket 100
Woods, Tiger 23, 98

Yokohama 72, 88

Zico 72
Zidane, Zinedine 50
Zimbabwe 49, 96, 97